The Soviet Volunteers

The Soviet Volunteers:
Modernization and Bureaucracy
in a Public Mass Organization
By William E. Odom

Princeton University Press – Princeton, New Jersey

Copyright © 1973 by Princeton University Press
L.C. Card: 72-6517
ISBN: 0-691-08718-0
This book has been composed in Linotype Primer
Printed in the United States of America
by Princeton University Press
Princeton, New Jersey

to Anne

Table of Contents

List of Charts

Preface

This book is about politics in a large voluntary organization. It was written not only for the specialist in Soviet affairs but also for any student of government. It may seem rather specialized, but it is related, nonetheless, to the central concepts and questions in the study of political life. A narrow research focus should not limit the broader relevance of a study if it helps us tie concrete experience to the general vocabulary of politics. Only thus can we improve the analytical value of that vocabulary. Such a viewpoint has guided my analysis.

The entire volume need not be read in order to appreciate single portions. The Introduction presents the analytical perspectives. Part One can be read alone as a policy study or simply as history. Parts Two and Three describe the voluntary organization. Part Four is about organizational politics, but it requires at least some scanning of the preceding parts in order to be understood properly. The same is true of the Conclusion.

Selecting those persons whom I should thank for assisting me in the preparation of this book is not unlike the social scientist's task in identifying "causes" of human events. The more the social scientist reviews the evidence, the more causes he is likely to find. In some respect he must be arbitrary if he is to limit them. So it is also for me in choosing persons who have influenced this book. I choose, therefore, to be arbitrarily restrictive—even if unjustly—in proclaiming my debts.

Brigadier Generals George A. Lincoln and Amos A. Jordan, Jr., professors of the Department of Social Sciences at West Point, allowed me time to begin the study while I was teaching in their department.

Professor John Hazard supervised an earlier version of the study from its inception to its completion as a doctoral dissertation at Columbia University. During this period Professor Joseph A. Rothschild also read and criticized the manuscript.

Professor Zbigniew K. Brzezinski, Director of the Research Institute on Communist Affairs at Columbia University, provided me support and encouragement in carrying the study to completion. The resources of the Institute and its intellectual environment greatly facilitated my work.

Harvey A. Garn, a friend and mentor, will find his critical influence reflected here and there in the text. And my wife, Anne, lent assistance at every stage of the manuscript's preparation as critic, editor, and typist.

In proclaiming my debts I am not distributing responsibility for weaknesses and faults in the book. I alone must answer for them.

Glossary

aktiv	Those voluntary members of Osoaviakhim who were especially active in programs and were therefore recognized as distinct from the rank and file.
Aviakhim	Society of Friends of Aviation-Chemical Construction.
Chusosnabarm	Extraordinary Deputy Council of Labor and Defense for Supply of the Army. Existed only until 1921.
Corner	A propaganda and literature display.
Dobrokhim	Society for the Friends of Chemistry.
GTO	"Prepared for Labor and Defense"; a status awarded for passing certain military and physical fitness tests.
khozraschet	Cost accounting. A system used in the Soviet economy to enforce financial and material accountability.
KVZ	"Circle for Military Knowledge"; a small study or training group.
kustarnichestvo	Amateurish work; used particularly to describe local initiative in Osoaviakhim that did not conform to standard patterns.
MTS	Machine and Tractor Station.

NARKOMFIN	People's Commissariat of Finance.
NKVD	People's Commissariat of Internal Affairs.
ODVF	Society for the Friends of the Air Fleet.
OSO	Society for Assistance to Defense.
Osoaviakhim	Society of Friends of Defense and Aviation-Chemical Construction.
otchet	Production reporting; a term used to describe reports of all Osoaviakhim activity to higher authorities.
Practical organization	Any organization, installation, or other structure used in Osoaviakhim programs and training activities.
Pre-inductee	A young male of draft age engaged in elementary military training required for all youths before being inducted into the regular military forces. Not all pre-inductees were called up, usually only about one in every six.
Revvoensovet	Revolutionary Military Council.
Section	A staff section on an Osoaviakhim council staff.
Sector	A functional line of Osoaviakhim work or training; also used in place of "section" as the label for a staff section or group of staff sections.
subbotniki	Days of labor freely given to the state on holidays.
Training points	Small Osoaviakhim training installations located in factories, schools, villages, and collective farms.
vnevoiskovik	A person fulfilling his military training obligation not in the regular forces but in the militia and through

periodic attendance at summer training assemblies.

VNO   Military Scientific Society.

VNOS   Air Observation, Notification, and Communication Point; part of the passive air defense scheme.

voenkomat   Military commissariat; part of the military department's regional structure under the military districts. It handled a variety of measures among the most important being the annual call up for the Red armed forces and local plans for wartime mobilization.

vseobuch   Universal training; this acronym gained currency in connection with the decree in 1918 that all members of the toiling classes were obligated to receive elementary military training even though they might not actually serve in the Red Army. The bureaucracy created to administer *vseobuch* also went by that name but was abolished in 1921. Later the term was connected with pre-inductee training, which was universally mandatory from 1925 on.

uchet   Production accounting; a term used to describe all techniques for measuring the results of Osoaviakhim programs and activities. *Otchet*, production reporting, was based on data from *uchet*.

The Soviet Volunteers

Introduction

Founded in 1927, the Society of Friends of Defense and Aviation-Chemical Construction[1]–or "Osoaviakhim," the acronym by which it was known–became the largest mass voluntary association in the Soviet Union before World War II. This study of Osoaviakhim in its first decade is not simply a discursive historical essay. It is a study of the politics of a mass organization in a modernizing society. It is an inquiry into the realities beneath the rhetoric of slogans and public assertions about the purposes and practices of Soviet mass voluntary societies. It is inspired by several questions. Are such organizations simply a lot of public sound and fury? Or do they have substantive programs? How are programs materially supported? How do their activities fit into the scheme of the political system? Are they truly unique or do they have counterparts in several political systems?

Answers to these questions require that we have a strategy for selecting relevant comparative concepts before launching into the records and evidence bearing on the case. Our basic analytical approach is to look for middle range generalizations about politics and organization, choosing those that are appropriate for the available evidence and that promise insights. For greater methodolog-

[1] *Obshchestva druzei oborony i aviatsionno-khimicheskogo stroitel'stva* is the Russian name. It was broken up in 1948, but three successor organizations were united in 1952 to form DOSAAF, a voluntary society similar to Osoviakhim.

ical specificity, Osoaviakhim is treated as an organization, a social structure, a set of individuals concerting actions for particular goals. The literature on organization theory, therefore, is relevant as a source of conceptual tools. The mass voluntary society is also viewed as an instrumentality for the authoritative allocation of Bolshevik political values. In this connection, Osoaviakhim's general political environment is one of rapid modernization of a traditional society. The literature on political development and modernization, accordingly, provides the second major source of comparative concepts. Although this study treats only a single organization, it is comparative in the sense that it brings general concepts to a particular case. Where they seem to fit the evidence, a comparative perspective is achieved insofar as the concepts have been derived from empirical studies of one or more organizations elsewhere. Where the concepts do not fit the evidence, we have identified either uniqueness or a limitation in a concept's heuristic value.

The study is divided into four parts. Part One examines the context in which the policy decision to establish Osoaviakhim was made and the political process leading to the founding of the organization. The purpose of this part is to discover the organizational goals in all their complexity and ambiguity and to reveal as far as possible the objective and subjective factors from which the political leadership derived the criteria that Osoaviakhim was believed to fulfill. This starting point has not been chosen arbitrarily. Talcott Parsons suggests that, "as a formal reference point, *primacy of orientation to the attainment of a specific goal* is used as the defining characteristic of an organization which distinguishes it from other types of social systems."[2] Basing his conclusions upon this postulate, he contends that "the main point of reference for analyzing the structure of any social system is its value

[2] "Suggestions for a Sociological Approach to the Theory of Organization," *Complex Organizations*, ed. Amitai Etzioni (New York: Holt, Rinehart and Winston, 1961), p. 33. Italics are in the original.

pattern." Although "value pattern" is not an easy concept to make operational, surely in the case of a formal organization, it must include first of all the organizational goals. To make sense of the Osoaviakhim structure, Osoaviakhim's goals, expectations, and the policy makers' perceptions of their environment must be illuminated.

Part Two is a descriptive study of Osoaviakhim's structure. Its purpose is to elucidate the formal relations of the organizational parts, to explain the organization's special vocabulary, and to trace important linkages between Osoaviakhim and other public institutions. The reasons for this are perhaps self-evident. Such a description provides a graphic understanding of the complex structure and supplies much of the empirical data on which later analysis is based.

Part Three deals with the formal organizational process. It offers a view of Osoaviakhim as an economy, following Phillip Selznick's suggestion that any organization can be looked at from that standpoint as distinct from considering it as an adaptive social structure.[3] Inputs of resources are distinguished by type and source. The system of planning, assigning tasks, and checking outputs is examined to show how the organization functioned and to discover as much as possible about the analytical rigor characterizing planning and decision-making in Osoaviakhim. Thereby something may be learned of the potential efficiency of the organization in attaining its ends.

Part Four deals with the dynamic dimensions of the organization. Technical, material, and cultural factors that constrained the organization's growth and adaptive behavior are searched out and interrelated. Then the problem of human behavior and exercise of individual choice within Osoaviakhim is addressed. In this connection, the dynamic characteristics are explained as the consequence of organizational politics, the struggle for influence and power within the structure. It will be argued that power was diffused significantly throughout Osoaviakhim and

[3] "The Foundations of the Theory of Organization," *Complex Organizations*, p. 20.

that an understanding of organizational change can be gained only to the extent that the available evidence permits us to discover the rationale with which groups and individuals exercised choice and discretion for their own ends.

General Characteristics of Mass Voluntary Societies

Placing a study of Osoaviakhim in a comparative context requires that we clarify what we mean by the terminology "mass voluntary society." Some general characteristics are suggested here as a definition. They may be thought of as defining a subtypology of voluntary associations, but if they are not entirely persuasive in that respect, they still can provide points from which to view such organizations analytically. In other words, they present propositions and concepts used in this study and are perhaps also useful in examining mass voluntary associations in other political systems, particularly in states where modernization is only beginning or not long under way.

a. *Mass membership.* That mass membership is an essential feature of such organizations is evident from the name, but it should not be taken to imply indiscriminate recruiting. In democratic political systems, the discriminator is often thought to be a common interest.[4] There are other criteria, however. An organization may seek to deny affiliation to certain subgroups of a society. Organizational goals will most often inherently lead to selective recruiting, sometimes in a permanent way, ruling against ethnic identity for example. Or they may rule against changeable characteristics such as affiliation with other organizations, social status, lack of a certain skill, or particular attitudinal orientations. In these cases, it may be part of the organization's strategy to draw people away

[4] Arthur Bentley, *The Process of Government* (Chicago: The University of Chicago Press, 1908), p. 211. "There is no group without its interest."

from other affiliations, to entice them to accept new attitudes or to acquire new skills.

The question may also arise, how many make a "mass"? For comparative purposes it seems wiser to answer that it is not the number of members but the recruiting aims of the organization that distinguish it as a mass organization. To qualify, it must aspire to recruit great numbers, to increase its size if it is small, to involve large numbers of people in its activities. The qualification can be made more restrictive by insisting that the organizational goals must require large numbers of volunteers as a necessary resource for goal attainment.

To the extent that discriminating criteria for recruitment are restrictive, they obviously work against achievement of mass membership. Friedrich and Brzezinski have pointed out this ambivalent feature in the recruitment practices of totalitarian political parties. The mass membership may dilute the elite quality of the party. The reverse is also true; emphasis on elitism tends to undercut the mass character. Hence a series of expansions and contractions may be observed in the history of such parties.[5] Not all mass voluntary organizations necessarily experience the trauma related to this ambivalence, unless the leadership chooses to pursue one criterion more vigorously than another. The ambivalence can assume a mild form, one criterion being invoked occasionally, but not with excessive fervor, to check the dominance of the other recruitment criterion.

b. *Voluntary membership.* The organization must avow that membership is voluntary although practice may be quite at odds with the avowal. The affirmation of voluntarism is wrapped up in the problem of acquiring power

[5] *Totalitarian Dictatorship and Autocracy* (New York: Frederick A. Praeger, 1956), pp. 27-39. It should be noted that communist parties, technically speaking, do not consider themselves as "mass" organizations. Our point remains valid in any case.

for pursuing organizational goals. If "mass" is an index of strength, voluntarism can be equally important as an element of power even in highly authoritarian political systems. The political, economic, and social strength of large numbers is amplified considerably when the members voluntarily share like-mindedness about ends. This amplification of potential organizational power is so important that the formality of voluntarism is believed worth maintaining when it is quite far from reality. The appearance of voluntary membership can give the leadership advantages in dealing with other persons and groups outside the organization. This leverage may be used for various kinds of bargaining, not the least of which is further recruitment on a more genuine voluntary basis. The mass voluntary image can serve to persuade potential recruits to accept the institution in a voluntary way, to accept its values and aims, to commit their personal resources to its purposes.

If the values of a mass voluntary organization were already in widespread acceptance, questions might be raised about the need to give them organizational expression. When an organization does arise to express them, it is generally intended to defend them from encroachment or to spread them even more broadly. It is the avowal of voluntarism, the image of voluntary membership, then, that is truly important as a distinctive feature. The leadership seeks to gain support for values and goals by exploiting man's gregarious and conforming nature. Initially, the organization may be able to gain a start because a small number of persons do share common values and aims. At first it may genuinely embrace voluntary membership, but a frequent purpose for giving an already existing consensus organizational expression is to generate broader support and to make potential bargaining power real. An organization is not to be excluded from this typology, therefore, if it uses tactics in recruiting that are hardly consistent with the ostensible voluntary nature of membership. The only limitation in this respect is the point where such tactics effectively prevent recruitment by inspiring successful evasion on the part of potential members.[6]

This limit will vary according to the political system in which the organization exists. In an open society where a single party does not monopolize the means of mass communications, coercive tactics must be more subtle; but in an authoritarian system, the possibilities to restrict evasion are much greater, and the limit on coercive measures for recruitment in mass voluntary organizations is less extensive.

c. *Public societies.* For the definition of voluntary associations developed here, private associations are not included. Drawing this line may seem somewhat arbitrary, but a case can be made for such a distinction, particularly in connection with (a) the hierarchical and anti-democratic tendencies in voluntary societies, and (b) their emergence as instruments of public policy in states where modernization has only recently begun. If a typology is developed to include both public and private societies, it can become so general that it serves little purpose in revealing distinctiveness in structure and activity. If only private voluntary associations are chosen, the typology has no comparative utility for the study of organizations in communist political systems. For example, a study by Sherwood D. Fox, which classifies over 5,000 voluntary associa-

---

[6] James G. March and Herbert A. Simon, *Organizations* (New York: John Wiley and Son, 1958), pp. 83-93. Coercion may be an inducement factor in the March and Simon model of organization equilibrium for participation. Coercion simply shifts the "zero point," that point where inducements and distractions tend to be equal in the member's mind, leaving him indifferent to the question of quitting or remaining associated. See Amitai Etzioni, *A Comparative Analysis of Complex Organizations* (New York: The Free Press, 1961), pp. 4-16, for a relevant discussion of coercive, remunerative, and normative power for organizational control.

tions in the United States, rules out public- or government-sponsored societies.[7] On the other hand, public voluntary associations do persist in both pluralistic or democratic systems and communist systems.[8] What is more, a typology of public societies is useful as a comparative category especially because it can be used across the analytical boundary that has come to surround communist political systems.[9] Selznick has indentified the conceptual basis on which such a typology can be developed:[10]

[7] "Voluntary Associations and Social Structure," Harvard Ph.D. Dissertation, 1952, p. 8.

[8] For examples of government-sponsored voluntary associations in the United States, see Philip Selznick, *TVA and the Grass Roots* (Berkeley: The University of California Press, 1953), pp. 219-20. The TVA and the Agricultural Extension Service have sponsored voluntary associations. Fox, *op. cit.*, lists the 4-H Club and the Future Farmers of America as private organizations, which, technically speaking, they are, but they receive professional leadership and installation facilities from several federal and state agencies.

[9] For a discussion of the need to perforate if not remove this boundary, see a series of articles in the *Slavic Review*, 26 (March, 1967), 1-28. Especially appropriate are John A. Armstrong's remarks on the advisability of beginning with sub-systems and middle-range theory already elaborated for non-communist systems. Organization theory may prove to be the most fruitful means for breaking the isolation of the study of communist political systems. Herbert A. Simon declares that "today the Communist bureaucracies provide most valuable objects for comparison with Western public—and private—bureaucracies." See his "The Changing Theory and Changing Practice of Public Administration," *Contemporary Political Science*, ed. Ithiel de Sola Pool (New York: McGraw-Hill, 1967), pp. 86-120. T. H. Rigby, "Crypto-Politics," *Survey*, No. 50 (1964), 192, suggests that analogous problems may be identified in Soviet and Western bureaucratic behavior and used for guiding study. In developing comparative concepts, Fritz Morstein Marx, "Control and Responsibility in Administration: Comparative Aspects," *Papers in Comparative Public Administration*, eds. Ferrel Heady and Sybil L. Stokes (Ann Arbor: University of Michigan, 1962), pp. 145-71, includes

It is useful to think of the cooptation of citizens into an administrative apparatus as a general response made by governments to what has been called "the fundamental democratization" of society. The rise of mass man, or at least the increasing need for governments to take into account and attempt to manipulate the sentiments of the common man, has resulted in the development of new methods of control. These new methods center about attempts to organize the mass, to change an undifferentiated and unreliable citizenry into a structured, readily accessible public. Accessibility for administrative purposes seems to lead rather easily to control for the same or broader pur-

---

Soviet administration with cogency. Of course, two basic works on management in Soviet industry are Joseph S. Berliner, *Factory and Manager in the USSR* (Cambridge: Harvard University Press, 1957), and David Granick, *Management of the Industrial Firm in the USSR* (New York: Columbia University Press, 1954). For an interesting comparative study in the context of organizational management, see John A. Armstrong, "Sources of Administrative Behavior: Some Soviet and Western European Comparisons," *The American Political Science Review*, 59 (September, 1965), 643-55. For some comparative concepts see Merle Fainsod, "The Structure of Development Administration," *Development Administration*, ed. Irving Swerdlow (Syracuse University Press, 1963), pp. 1-26. At a very high level of generalization Alfred G. Meyer explains the Soviet political system using the modern Western industrial corporation as a paradigm in *The Soviet Political System: An Interpretation* (New York: Random House, 1965). Jerry Hough, *The Soviet Prefects: Local Party Organs in Industrial Decision-Making* (Cambridge: Harvard University Press, 1969), provides an important study of local administration and offers suggestions about comparative concepts. For musings on methodology, see Frederic J. Fleron, Jr. (ed.), *Communist Studies and the Social Sciences: Essays on Methodology and Empirical Theory* (Chicago: Rand McNally, 1969), and H. Gordon Skilling and Franklyn Griffiths (eds.), *Interest Groups in Soviet Politics* (Princeton, N.J.: Princeton University Press, 1971).

10 *TVA and the Grass Roots*, pp. 219-20.

poses. Consequently, there seems to be a continuum between the voluntary associations set up by the democratic (mass) state—such as committees to boost or control agricultural production—and citizens' associations in the totalitarian (mass) state.

It may be objected, of course, that this formulation implies a cynical reluctance to acknowledge the more humane character of democratic systems in the West, or that it is a retreat to Robert Michels' "iron law of oligarchy."[11] The problem here, however, is not one of deciding which system is preferable but rather of finding common empirical properties of organizations with electoral systems which can become the basis for taxonomies and comparative analysis.[12] But if a typology for voluntary associations is restricted to public, government-sponsored organizations, the entangled debates about democratic initiative and oligarchy can be largely avoided. Political parties, interest groups, unions, churches, and the plethora of private associations are excluded from theoretical consideration. The included associations are by definition in the hands of ruling oligarchies, and they are dedicated to the pursuit

[11] *Political Parties* (New York: The Free Press, 1968).

[12] The issues raised by Michels, Mosca, and others on the incompatibility of democracy and hierarchy are quite real. Kenneth Arrow's formal proof in *Social Choice and Individual Value* (New York: John Wiley and Son, 1951) of the impossibility of starting with individual values and deriving a community preference without an element of dictatorial imposition puts the matter beyond dispute. How to manage that element and minimize it has been the concern of continuing endeavors to state an empirical theory of democracy. Mancur Olson, Jr., in *The Logic of Collective Action* (New York: Schocken Books, 1968), offers a pertinent formal treatment of the problems of public goods and collective action. For some review pieces on bureaucracy and individual freedom, see Otto Kirchheimer, "Private Man and Society," *Political Science Quarterly*, 81 (March, 1966), 1-25; Alvin Gouldner, "Metaphysical Pathos and the Theory of Bureaucracy," *Complex Organizations*, pp. 71-82.

of goals selected by the ruling elites. The problem of democracy within organizations does not arise in a way that can render the typology inconsistent. Rather democratic doctrines and participation techniques become features more or less successfully used by both the governmental elites and the membership in deriving a preferred allocation of values.

Another reason for classifying public voluntary societies in a separate category is found in the nature of the modernization process. It has been observed frequently that private voluntary associations are most numerous in Western democratic countries. Tocqueville and James Bryce are commonly credited with noticing this phenomenon, and others have insisted that it is the most characteristic distinction between primitive and modern societies.[13] Many of the stabilizing features of traditional societies— limited communications and mobility, kinship and religious groups, cultural factors, and the low degree of urbanization—seem to impede the proliferation of voluntary associations.[14] The government, among all other institutions in such societies, is in the best position to initiate voluntary associations. When these associations arise in developing states, therefore, it is likely that the initiative will most often come from the government and that they will be used to implement government programs. In these cases, the manipulative advantages of avowed voluntarism can be extremely important to modernizing elites which believe they need all the power they can accumulate for carrying out programs.

d. *The nature of goals and programs.* There are few if any categorical limitations on the goals public voluntary societies may seek, but there are considerations that may

[13] Fox, *op. cit.*, pp. 2-8, 443. Fox follows Robert M. MacIver and others on this point.

[14] For a theory of the failure of voluntary societies to develop in backward societies, see Edward Banfield, *The Moral Basis of a Backward Society* (New York: The Free Press, 1958).

guide our judgment in anticipating the kinds of programs that will most likely be chosen and can aid in explaining why certain aims and programs were selected.

First, by definition, the official aims of a public voluntary society will not be the advancement of a non-ruling faction's interest in the sense of trade union, interest group, or any other specifically private goals. Public voluntary associations may be used for limited and narrow purposes, to be sure, benefiting a special sector of the society or a particular region—The Friends of Children in the USSR and the voluntary associations sponsored by the Tennessee Valley Authority being examples. The aims of these organizations, nevertheless, were chosen by state officials, members of the ruling elite, and ostensibly they were selected with the public interest in mind as those elites perceived it. This analytical distinction does not rule out, however, the cases where factions within the ruling elite effectively control the program choices for the advantage of factional power. Almost always factional disputes lie behind goal and program choices, especially when the choice is not amenable to rigorous analytical methods, or when there is "no one best way" to select and accomplish a task.[15] The point here, the purpose of making the distinction, is to clarify the location or arena where bargaining takes place. In the case of public voluntary programs, the political processes for selecting them remain largely within the government or ruling bureaucracy, giving the ruling elites an upper hand in goal and program selection.

Another consideration for program choice has to do with the functional roles public voluntary societies can play. In other words, in what meaningful way can they be used

[15] See Michel Crozier, *The Bureaucratic Phenomenon* (Chicago: The University of Chicago Press, 1964), pp. 154-59, for a discussion of the implications of "no one best way" in policy-making and program execution. March and Simon, *op. cit.*, pp. 140-49, 156, on the same point advance a proposition about the inverse relationship between analysis and bargaining in decision-making.

in a political and social system? Sherwood Fox argues that private voluntary associations in the United States are essentially "compensatory" and "interstitial mechanisms" that aid integration of societal functions.[16] Selznick implies as much about public voluntary associations in his discussion of the need "mass" states find for voluntary associations. Looking at programs and goals from the functionalist point of view is certainly instructive, but the integrative characteristics it puts into relief are by no means the whole story. Dysfunctional programs may be chosen and sustained, even in the face of valid feedback information, because those programs are deemed to increase or secure the policy makers' power.[17] There is no reason why successful integrative programs implemented through public voluntary societies may not frequently coincide with the power interests of the ruling elites. In any case, the compensatory or interstitial character of programs is to be expected since it makes little sense to duplicate programs of non-voluntary institutions. Osoaviakhim programs, nevertheless, did duplicate and overlap in many instances the programs of non-voluntary institutions.

What are examples of public voluntary programs? Welfare services, education, political socialization, and some kinds of economic production are certainly possible. Where welfare alone is the task, the organization is likely to be little more than an apparatus for collecting a voluntary tax

[16] *Op. cit.*, p. 2.

[17] On this point Fox provides the best sort of evidence against his own thesis by recounting an episode in which he had recently investigated a voluntary association that ostensibly served educational purposes by funding grants for economists to spend time in business firms. He warned the faculty of his college that the organization was actually a front for concealed interests of twenty large business corporations. But he fails to say whether such associations truly perform an integrative function for the social system although his moral indignation leads one to infer that he believed the concealed aims to be dysfunctional for society. *Op. cit.*, pp. 92-94.

(contribution) although it may also redistribute such income by criteria that require considerable organizational complexity.[18]

In cases of education and political socialization, programs can be much more complex, requiring both the member's time and money as well as large cadres and material for training.[19]

Although all kinds of programs have economic ramifications, some may be more directly concerned with production activities. For those that are, programs requiring a low capital-labor ratio seem more probable because mass voluntary societies, if they recruit effectively, are rich in labor. If the program demands capital intensive activity, the use of membership simply as a tax base would be more sensible, as is the case with many private societies devoted to medical research.[20] Labor intensive programs certainly appeal to modernizing elites in developing states where capital is relatively scarce, and thus one would expect to find public voluntary societies with economic production goals more frequently in backward countries where a modernizing elite has consolidated power and is implementing rapid change. But the interchangeability of capital and labor has real limits as the Chinese Communist program of small backyard blast furnaces vividly revealed in the late 1950's.

As a last point, it must be noted that goals and programs are tied up with incentives for voluntary participation, especially where coercive means are limited (either due to cultural attitudes or the lack of administrative ca-

[18] Soviet organizations such as the Peasant Society for Mutual Aid, The Friends of Children, and The International Society for Aid to Revolutionaries are examples of the tax-collecting kinds of societies. Some aspects of the Social Security Program in the United States meet the criteria for this category.

[19] Osoaviakhim in the USSR and the Job Corps, the Youth Corps, and Head Start in the United States are examples.

[20] See David Sills, *The Volunteers* (Glencoe, Ill.: The Free Press, 1957), for a study of the National Foundation for Infantile Paralysis.

pacity for exercising coercion). It is tempting to suggest that the more attractive the goals appear, the more volunteers are apt to participate in programs for public interests. Mancur Olson, however, makes a strong case for the view that a rational person will not contribute to a group program aimed at achieving a collective benefit.[21] The rational individual will participate only where non-collective benefits can be attained. Voluntary associations, then, must offer some kind of non-collective benefit to the individual to the extent that they depend on volunteers. Shrewd leaders may secure participation without paying for it in every case. Richard M. Merelman suggests an analogy in learning value symbols between teaching rats to run a maze at the flash of a light and teaching political symbols to a public in order to use them in manipulating support for public policies.[22] The reward, or non-collective benefit, for running a maze, is cheese, and the reward that mass voluntary societies can grant for participation ranges from material incentives (salaries for cadres) to social approval and moral approbation. In the case of rats, after several rewarded runs, the light alone is sufficient to stimulate a run. But if occasional reinforcement learning through rewards is not practiced, the light loses its "legitimacy" as a stimulus. The promise of social acclaim can be symbolized in slogans, badges, ceremonies, and praise for individuals in the press. But if the prevalent cultural values are at odds with the symbols, either material rewards or coercion must be used. In developing states, material rewards are scarce while modern value symbols and traditional values are likely to be in serious conflict. Teaching the legitimacy of programs and goals, therefore, will require coercion. If goals can be chosen that minimize the cultural conflict, the leadership has a greater chance for securing participation for a cheap and abundant resource substitute: moral approbation expressed in badges and

[21] Op. cit., pp. 2-12.
[22] "Learning and Legitimacy," The American Political Science Review, 60 (September, 1966), pp. 548-61.

public attention. Several corollary propositions could be worked out here, but enough has been said to reveal the complex connections between programs and incentives for voluntary participation.

e. *Organizational structure.* Certain structural and administrative characteristics are commonly found in voluntary associations. They do not usually take people away from their normal place of employment and abode except perhaps for short periods. The mass membership is looked upon as a source of support, the major resource input, not a liability or a cost to the organization. Physically the organization is apt to be dispersed, spread out through the entire society, not concentrated in the sense in which a school, a cooperative, or a large enterprise is.

The permanent bureaucratic core of the organization is proportionally small yet also physically dispersed in order to maintain supervision over the areas of the society that provide the mass membership. The technology of communications and the degree of institutional discipline among the cadre become two crucial constraints in the capacity of a mass voluntary organization to pursue its aims. The cultural and skill levels of the cadre are equally important, especially in backward states.

Although there may be democratic rules for the selection of personnel to assume the cadre roles, the bureaucratic leadership does not generally look to the mass membership for guidance in value choices and policy decisions. Recruitment of leaders is by cooptation in fact if not in theory. By its nature, the organization is not governing a group at the group's behest and in terms of goals established by the mass. Rather its purpose is connected with exerting the influence of the center in order to generate resources for the center's ends, for gaining mass acceptance of the center's value allocations. The appearance and style of the hierarchical relations between the cadre center and the mass can vary greatly, but the levers of control and the authority to allocate values are not fully dependent on the mass membership. The most the mass can usually do to exert influence is to deny their resources to the organization. Such behavior may constrain the center's policy choices and thereby indirectly allow a role for the mass in policy making, but the role remains passive. Policy and program initiative is effectively a prerogative of the cadre. Because of this feature, mass voluntary organizations are apt to be more significant in polities where the leadership believes that social and economic change can be rapidly wrought through conscious political action. Passive or conservative leadership is most likely to beget apathy in mass voluntary organizations. Spontaneity on the part of the mass membership is hardly able to produce coordinated and coherent organizational programs.[23]

Where and in what kinds of societies are public mass voluntary organizations most likely to be found? Certainly not in those states that Edward Shils classifies as "traditional oligarchies" and "theocratic oligarchies,"[24] that is, not in states where the leadership is not committed to modernization and change. Where political and social mobilization is virtually nil, and not desired, the mass voluntary organizations have little appeal as instruments of public policy. Leaders in developed states may find them useful, but highly differentiated societies, as these states are, tend to have a variety and complexity in institutions that leave less room for the improvised quality of mass voluntary organizational techniques. It is where polities are in transition, where the political leadership is breaking down traditions, building new social patterns, restructuring the productive forces of the society, building new in-

---

[23] All of the points made here on structure have been noticed frequently by students of politics and organization theory. See especially Philip Selznick, *The Organizational Weapon* (Glencoe, Ill.: The Free Press, 1960), pp. 96, 114-26; James Bryce, *Modern Democracies* (New York: Macmillan, 1921), II, p. 542; Sills, *op. cit.*, pp. 1-20; David B. Truman, *The Governmental Process* (New York: Alfred A. Knopf, 1951), pp. 141ff; Michels, *op. cit.*, pp. 61-80.

[24] *Political Development in the New States* (The Hague: Mouton and Co., 1966), pp. 75-91.

stitutions, experimenting with organization, seeking to make social strides in mass education in short periods of time, and in possession of relatively abundant labor forces that mass voluntary organizations seem especially appropriate.[25]

[25] Soviet scholars have not ignored taxonomy and theory of the role of mass voluntary associations, especially their contributions to modernization or "construction of communism." See particularly Ts. A. Iampol'skaia, *Obshchestvennye organizatsii v SSSR* (Moscow: 1972). Iampol'skaia's typology shares several points with our own and identifies certain analogies between Soviet "public" organizations and "bourgeois" voluntary associations. See also the volume she edited with A. I. Shchiglik, *Voprosy i teorii obshchestvennykh organizatsii* (Moscow: 1971). She declares, however, that public voluntary organizations have only recently received scholarly attention in the USSR and that their proper legal and sociological classification still needs refinement.

Part I
The Origins of Osoaviakhim

Chapter I

The Doctrinal Heritage

By the period of the First Five Year Plan, Osoaviakhim was being openly proclaimed as the broad mobilization reserve for the Red Army, although it did not assume this role at its inception. The concept of creating military reserves in the context of a mass voluntary organization was not formulated at a single juncture in the making of Soviet military policy nor was it meant in its original form to be wholly a matter of military policy. Rather, the decision to establish the Society in 1927 was the consequence of an array of factors, many of which came to light in the debate over a proper defense posture. That debate took place in an environment of numerous resource constraints, both human and material. Its participants cast their arguments in Marxian categories and analytical concepts developed by the Social Democrats of both Europe and Russia but modified by the Bolshevik experiences during and after the seizure of power.

The course of the civil war and the first years of the New Economic Policy brought the Bolsheviks to grips with more than the realities of devastation by the war. The educational and technical backwardness of Russia, the enduring features of the traditional peasant society and its deeply rooted values, the desperate condition of the economy, and the innovations in military technology that appeared in the course of the World War, all contributed to the general realization that the preconditions for a socialist society were hardly present in Russia. (Most Russian

Marxists, certainly Lenin, had maintained no illusions on this point, but Bukharin and other left Bolsheviks in 1918 were overly sanguine for a time.) What the Russian bourgeoisie had failed to accomplish in their brief historical epoch would have to be hastily achieved under socialist leadership.

Thus the Bolsheviks found themselves in a dilemma not unlike that of the elites bent upon modernization in many of the developing states of the twentieth century.[1] They desired to possess the economic and cultural attributes of the modern industrial societies of the West; yet they perceived the West as bent upon destroying or exploiting them. The ambivalence in this perception can induce a sense of urgency, a single-mindedness of purpose, a distrust of spontaneous societal development, and, in the Bolshevik case in particular, an incredible confidence in planning and organizational techniques for finding novel institutional means which promise a short-cut to the resolution of problems. The use of mass voluntary organizations as an aspect of military policy provides one example of innovation in military organization. But it was also related to domestic military politics, the problem of integrating the armed forces with civil institutions, one that has proved difficult to solve in many developing states.[2]

The trend in European states, including Russia, since the seventeenth and eighteenth centuries has been toward specialization of the military defense function of the state.

[1] For a discussion of developing states and modernization see D. A. Rustow, *A World of Nations* (Washington, D.C.: The Brookings Institution, 1967). Rustow devotes critical attention to a great deal of the literature on political development and modernization.

[2] Samuel E. Finer, *The Man on Horseback* (New York: Frederick A. Praeger, 1962); J. J. Johnson (ed.), *The Role of the Military in Underdeveloped Countries* (Princeton, N.J.: Princeton University Press, 1962); Morris Janowitz, *The Military in the Political Development of New Nations* (Chicago: The University of Chicago Press, 1964). These volumes offer a variety of perspectives on the problem.

Feudal militias gave way to kings' standing armies. The technological advances in weaponry and transportation in the nineteenth century made differentiation of the state's military activities seem all the more imperative. Clausewitz gave this functional delineation its most eminent theoretical articulation. In order to integrate the military with other government functions, however, he tried to confine the military to a role as exclusively an instrument of foreign policy. The modern states have more or less followed his approach in defense organization.

There are serious weaknesses in Clausewitz's conceptualization. It directs primary attention to interstate relations and tends to ignore inter-institutional domestic politics. Moreover, it has proved difficult if not impossible to establish the demarcation between political and military prerogatives in policy decisions. James Harrington, the seventeenth-century English political theorist, recognized clearly the problem of the military's place in domestic politics, and in a sense anticipated the coming military-civil institutional division.[3] Harrington noticed that emerging strong central governments had mobilized large armies in their struggle with the landed aristocracies. Such armies' claims on states' resources (for Harrington this primarily meant land) caused a political imbalance and posed a severe threat to stable government. How to avoid the imbalance? Simply abolish the army and rely on a militia.[4] At the IX Party Congress in 1920, Trotsky's proposal to resort to just this solution was accepted. Trotsky pointed out the enormous economic burden a regular army would place on the state, and his case for a militia has much in common with Harrington's view.[5]

[3] *Harrington: His Writings*, ed. Charles Blitzer (New York: The Bobbs-Merrill Company, 1955), pp. 97-104, 162-64.

[4] Harrington, of course, was looking to his own image of the passing feudal political structure, "the Gothic balance," in search of a remedy. The efficacy of his solution need not concern us here but only his perception of the problem and his reaction.

[5] D. Fedotoff White, *The Growth of the Red Army* (Prince-

It was hardly possible for the Bolsheviks to resolve the problem of defense in such an easy fashion. Although a mixed militia and regular force structure was chosen, Trotsky's scheme became the subject of heated debate in the party and Red Army hierarchy.[6] As a consequence of the quarrels, the question of the domestic politics of the military establishment came under serious scrutiny and a search was begun for new ways to institutionalize the state's defense function. The first new institution of the Soviet state that received major attention and demonstrated the Bolshevik capability for effective organizational leadership had been the Red Army. At the end of the civil war, they essentially dismantled it and began anew, structuring it as best they could in coordination with the host of other institutional developments that had to be managed.

Because it was in the context of this vast undertaking of institution building that mass voluntary defense societies emerged, it is useful to review the leadership's conceptualization of the tasks it faced and the constraints it confronted.

The Bolsheviks, in designing a military policy and structuring the Soviet military institutions, claimed originality from the first. At the VII Party Congress in March 1918, ten theses were promulgated as guidance for building a new state apparatus.[7] In explicit contrast to the functional divisions in parliamentary democratic governments, the Soviets applied a principle of integration. The

---

ton, N.J.: Princeton University Press, 1944), pp. 189-91. White calls attention to the analogy with a feudal military system. See Lev D. Trotsky, *Kak vooruzhilas' revoliutsiia*, Vol. 2, Bk. 2 (3 vols.; Moscow: 1923-25), pp. 33-36, for an elaboration of his plan for a militia. Hereafter Trotsky's work will be cited as *KVR*.

[6] White, *op. cit.*, pp. 183-198. Also John Erickson, *The Soviet High Command: A Military-Political History 1918-1941* (London: Macmillan, 1962), pp. 115-38.

[7] *Sed'moi s"ezd RKP(b)*, Stenographic Record, March 6-8, 1918 (Moscow: 1923), pp. 205-07.

executive and legislative functions were to be combined as one task for the Soviet apparatus. Not only was there to be horizontal integration but vertical as well; the general population was to be drawn into the Soviet apparatus on a mass basis, linked more tightly with it than in democratic states of the West. Special attention was given to the armed forces. Following the ideological lore of Social Democracy concerning the military question, largely founded on Engels's formulations,[8] and perhaps on Lenin's essay of 1917, *State and Revolution*, Soviet military structures were not to be isolated from the mass of the populace. Structural separation in the bourgeois states had permitted the use of the military as a repressive instrument in the hands of a ruling minority. According to the lore, the upheaval of revolution would involve arming the masses. Thus the theses on Soviet power declared that "the Soviets are armed workers and peasants" and represent the first step toward a classless "armed people."

The civil war forced the Bolsheviks to mobilize and train a large army, over five million in strength, but the principles set down at the VII Party Congress were not entirely dismissed. At the VIII Party Congress in 1919, the military question once more occupied a central place on the agenda. The resolution taken on the matter was rhetorically cast as an answer to the charge that the Red Army was hardly a classless all-people's militia divorced from military camps and barracks. It provided a critique of the Social Democratic program that had prescribed an all-people's militia, the soldiers quartered in their own homes, carrying on their normal industrial production tasks, and devoting to military training enough time from their non-working hours to maintain an effective defense organization.[9] The mistake of the old program, it was argued, had been to pose the question as a choice between

[8] D. Fedotoff White, "Soviet Philosophy of War," *The Political Science Quarterly*, 51 (September, 1936), pp. 324-53; and *The Growth of the Red Army*, pp. 158-59.

[9] *Vos'moi s"ezd RKP(b)*, March 18-23, 1919, Stenographic Report (Moscow: 1933), pp. 401-11.

bourgeois barracks-type armies and an all-people's militia. "When civil war breaks out, an all-people's militia loses its meaning."[10] Because the toiling classes had seized power in Russia, it was possible to use the state apparatus, particularly a newly recruited proletarian "class army," to defend the power of the revolution. The civil war left no choice but to build a new army of the barracks type for defense of the working class interests. The resolution carefully maintained, nevertheless, that the party had not abandoned the concept of an all-people's militia. It admitted that in an atmosphere of "healthy industry" the best possible army could be built "on the basis of obligatory training of workers and toiling peasants *in conditions near their everyday labor.*"[11] But the present class war, it was asserted, is a transitional phenomenon requiring a barracks-type class army and mass mobilization. After the transition, when a militia would become appropriate, it had to involve more than limited individual training. Units up to division in size would be organized and exercised. At the next party congress, in 1920, the Bolsheviks made it clear that they had indeed not forgotten the militia scheme and would try to implement it in the aftermath of the civil war.

Three organizing principles emerge from the resolution of the VIII Party Congress, which find repetition at later congresses and in much of the published record of views in the party hierarchy on military force structure. The first is "universal military training" (the Russian acronym is *vseobuch*). It expressed the notion that every citizen should receive military training of an elementary sort but not necessarily by serving in a full-time military unit. It amounted to the continuation under Soviet power of what had been the practice of the Red Guard training conducted under the guidance of the Bolshevik Military Organization in 1917.[12]

[10] *Ibid.*, p. 401.

[11] *Ibid.*, p. 403. Italics in the original.

[12] *KPSS o vooruzhennykh silakh Sovetskogo Soiuza, sbornik dokumentov 1917-1958* (Moscow: 1958), pp. 11-13. An All-

The second principle is the concept of providing military training without taking the recipient away from his home and place of labor. The expected advantage, of course, was that military manpower requirements would not essentially compete with or deny manpower to the industrial production process. Industrial labor's organization, work discipline, technical skills, and population density had already created conditions not dissimilar to barracks life. The concept of extra-barracks military training allowed the regime to take advantage of these conditions and to avoid both the costs of additional resource outlays and the disruption of the worker's productive activity that regular army service would entail. The terms "outside of barracks" and "outside of forces" are part of this concept and are frequently used in Soviet literature in discussing force structure. The term *vnevoiskovik* is a neologism deriving from the concept and referring to a person who receives his military training without a long term of full-time military service.

A third principle, the class nature of the army, is also worth underscoring because of its wide use in the discussion of military policy. It is generally recognized that the Bolsheviks made much of class identity as an index of objective political reliability, and one might be tempted to dismiss it as misleading metaphysical nonsense. Certainly its ambiguity has allowed incredible elasticity in its use. In fact the new Red Commanders of the Red Army adeptly invoked the class criterion to justify a large regular army for carrying the revolution beyond Soviet borders.[13] Nor

---

Russian Conference of Bolshevik Military Organizations allegedly convened in Petrograd on June 29, 1917 (old style), and took a resolution on *vseobuch* which explained that with the victory of the revolution, military training would be universal but would not require two or three years; rather a month or two would suffice. The decree of the All-Russian Central Executive Committee of April 22, 1918, basically adhered to this formulation.

[13] White, *The Growth of the Red Army*, pp. 158-82; Erickson, *op. cit.*, pp. 113-43.

have Soviet historians made lucidity a virtue in their discussions of the class nature of the Red Army and in the deductive syllogisms about a so-called "army of a new type."[14] But a rationale may be gleaned from the way the standard was used in practice during the demobilization after the civil war and throughout the 1920's. Implicitly the class criterion came to identify soldiers who were literate or had become so during service, who had become somewhat "modernized" through military service (modernized in the sense that Lucian Pye has used the term in discussing armies in underdeveloped countries).[15] That is, military skills and experience had modernized the soldier with respect to the village traditional society from which he came. Trotsky displayed a keen awareness of this modernizing effect on peasants in articulating his program for militarizing labor, using armies for organizing and supervising portions of the economy's labor force.[16] After the civil war it became policy to treat the ex-Red Army soldier as a source of cadre for soviet work in the villages and among the national minorities.[17] In effect the class criterion meant two things: first political loyalty; second, possession of skills and knowledge useful for overcoming Russian industrial backwardness.

All three of these principles concerned the integration of the military with civil society. It is not the intention here to ascribe a causal role to the ideological baggage that the Bolsheviks brought to the modernization process in Russia; rather it is necessary to clarify how they related their ideological parlance to that process. In one respect their

[14] N. I. Shatagin, *Sovetskaia Armiia—armiia novogo tipa* (Moscow: 1957).

[15] "Armies in the Process of Political Modernization," *The Role of the Military in Underdeveloped Countries*, ed. J. J. Johnson, pp. 69-90.

[16] *KVR*, Vol. 2, Bk. 2, pp. 33-79.

[17] See a circular letter from the Bolshevik Central Committee, dated March 17, 1924, for an example of instructions on pursuing this policy. *KPSS o vooruzhennykh silakh Sovetskogo Soiuza*, p. 261.

perspectives were more advanced than contemporary views in the West. They focused sharply on the old problem James Harrington had identified with the emerging king's armies: what are the implications for domestic politics?

As mentioned earlier, the Clausewitzian description of the military function in a state, combined with the increasing requirements for role differentiation as new technology was adapted to military use, had not encouraged significant theoretical attention to new ways to integrate the growing military institutions in the political, economic, and social systems of the state. Engels, therefore, was somewhat unique in trying to conceptualize this integration process in the mid-nineteenth century.[18] He insisted, perhaps quite rightly, that armies are a reflection of political and social systems, not something apart; but he rested his analysis on the assumption that the material and technological conditions of the society are the lone determinants of the structural integration. The essential and useful point is attention to the domestic politics of the military.

It was natural for this point to remain central in the ideology of European Social Democracy. Revolutionaries calculating the overthrow (or merely predicting this outcome) of domestic regimes had to reckon with the armies of those regimes. They knew, too, that the problem of the military did not necessarily vanish with the demise of the old regime, and they constantly warned against the danger of Bonapartism.

The Party Program (1919) formally committed the Bolsheviks to deny the military a separate existence and to insure its political and institutional integration in the Soviet order. Not only was a major section of the program devoted to the military question, but the section also included fairly specific operational guidance on the policy of integration. Point (4), for example, prescribed that:[19]

[18] See a discussion of this point by David C. Rapoport in *Changing Patterns of Military Politics*, ed. S. P. Huntington (New York: The Free Press of Glencoe, 1962), pp. 90ff.

[19] Translated in *Soviet Communism: Programs and Rules*,

> As a counter-balance to the older order of things in the army, the following changes are necessary: shorter periods of barracks training, barracks to be nearer to the type of military and military-political schools, closer connection between military formations and mills, factories, trade unions and organizations of the poorest peasantry.

The experience of the civil war, the failure of revolution to materialize in Western Europe, Bolshevik perceptions of a hostile external environment, and domestic events such as the Kronstadt and Tambov revolts were among the factors that led the Bolsheviks to decide to retain a certain level of regular forces in the 1920's. They did not, nevertheless, dismiss entirely the guidance of the party resolutions and the new party program. Trotsky's plan for demobilization was followed in spite of the "military opposition." Frunze, among Trotsky's opponents and his successor as head of the Red Army, did not essentially modify the territorial militia program but rather became its vigorous proponent. The implementation initially followed both the class principle and the concept of organizing militia formations to conform with the location of industry. Moscow, Petrograd, and the Urals, where industry and industrial population were relatively dense, were the areas first to receive militia formations.[20]

But the militia scheme proved temporary and was completely abandoned in the 1930's. If the ideological preconceptions had been sufficient to call Bolshevik attention to the problem of integrating a modern military establishment into the society, they were hardly adequate in establishing the structural designs of organization which could provide a solution. Mass voluntary societies were part of the innovation in civil-military linking that the Bolsheviks devised to give practical content to verbalized abstractions.

---

ed. Jan Triska (San Francisco: Chandler Publishing Company, 1961), p. 139.

[20] Trotsky, *KVR*, Vol. 3, Bk. 1, p. 12.

Chapter II

Bolshevik Perceptions of

Cultural Backwardness

The problem of "backwardness" vis-à-vis Western Europe has been a central theme in all Russian political, economic, and cultural history at least since the seventeenth century. Recent Western political science concepts such as modernization, political development, and underdeveloped countries take as their reference the comparative change that has occurred in Western European states since the Reformation. Other regions are modern or backward, developed or underdeveloped, by comparison with what has happened in the West. Precisely what categories should be used in making comparisons is a matter of dispute,[1] but one characteristic of the late-comers to the modernization process has been emphasized by Cyril Black and is implicit if not explicit in most of the literature on the topic.[2] The experience of the early modernizers is unique in that they had no examples to follow. Their political leaders could not look to the experience of other states to gain a perspective on what they might hope to achieve in their own states. The late modernizers, in contrast, are beset by the experience of the leaders in the process and frequently respond to the knowledge of being behind by attempts to expedite their own development. They are less likely, if they want to modernize, to be satisfied with allow-

[1] Gabriel Almond—level of secularization; Shils and Apter—degree of democratic diffusion of power; Rustow—achievement of identity, authority, and equality.

[2] *The Dynamics of Modernization* (New York: Harper and Row, 1966), pp. 96-99.

ing social and economic development to take its course, unpressed by anxious political leaders who believe they know how the future society ought to look.

The Classical Liberal doctrines of the early modernizers, England and France, combine macro-determinism, e.g., Adam Smith's invisible hand in the market place, with micro-voluntarism, e.g., political freedoms, responsibility before the law. The late-comers, in conspicuous cases such as Germany, Japan, Turkey, and Russia, have reversed this relationship. They have combined macro-voluntarism with micro-determinism. The modernizing elites of these states have believed they could consciously carry through vast change in their societies according to patterns they have purposely chosen to follow. The individual in those societies who has not wanted to conform to the regimes' programs has been reminded of inexorable historical laws, divine guidance, and race myths as inconsonant with such individuality. In other words, at the state level, there is a tendency to have faith in almost unlimited possibilities for conscious use of political power to effect change, to foresee the consequences of voluntarily selected policies. The chaos of uncoordinated and spontaneous individual decisions in a society, likely to disrupt the realization of proclaimed goals, not unnaturally becomes an anathema to these super-voluntarists. They do not have the patience to wait for "invisible hands" and to accept the outcome of conscious political choices made by a multitude of leaders and individuals throughout the society.

It is more than mere chance or quirk of character that brought Lenin and his careful disciple Stalin to transform a macro-determinist theory of modernization, Marxism, into a macro-voluntarist dogma justifying denial of individual freedoms. It fits precisely the need to give legitimacy to policies restricting individual choice and to increase the scope of choice for the leadership, needs peculiar to late modernizers who are in a great hurry.[3]

[3] See Adam Ulam, *The Unfinished Revolution* (New York: Vintage Books, 1964), for an argument that Marxism is a "natural ideology" for a modernizing state. Karl deSchweinitz,

It is necessary to draw out and underscore this paradox, which is found in an extreme form in Soviet politics because it is the fundamental characteristic of the politics of a mass voluntary society. Such an organization is an instrumentality for limiting individual choice, for persuading the individual to make a choice in the use of his time and resources in accordance with criteria established by the central leadership.

The specific Bolshevik values, which became the criteria for choosing Osoaviakhim goals, arise from the leaders' perception of the Soviet peoples' cultural backwardness, especially as it pertains to the modern instrumentalities of war. This special meaning of cultural backwardness, however, was not seen as primarily relating to the military establishment. The context was broader. It included literacy and all of the elementary technical skills required in industrial production and ancillary services. Beyond that it connoted an attitude, an acceptance of modernity, a rejection of traditional agrarian values, and a sense of personal discipline and frugality quite similar to characteristics embodied in Max Weber's idea of the "Protestant ethic."

Trotsky set the pace as head of the Red Army in pointing out the cultural backwardness of the Red Army personnel. After the civil war, he used his lofty office as Commissar of War to castigate, cajole, and humor the Red Army Commanders into paying "attention to details" in military organization and training.[4] His speech to a con-

---

Jr., "Growth, Development and Political Modernization," *World Politics*, 22 (July, 1970), 518-40, also develops the thesis that the more developed states can tolerate more voluntarism from below. Alec Nove, *Economic Rationality and Soviet Politics* (New York: Frederick A. Praeger, 1964), p. 33, observes of the Bolsheviks, "they cannot be satisfied with the pace of a tortoise." For an insightful and well-known treatment of the role of ideology in the Soviet political system, see Z. K. Brzezinski, *Ideology and Power in Soviet Politics* (New York: Frederick A. Praeger, 1962).

[4] *KVR*, Vol. 3, Bk. 1, pp. 27-34.

gress of military commanders and party workers, in the fall of 1921, is a treatise on the care of boots, uniforms, and weapons, and a cry against the low standards of hygiene and performance of elemental duties in the army. It creates a vivid image of the sloven and devious, mistrustful, and illiterate peasant who appears everywhere in nineteenth-century works of fiction. Only now, after the revolution, this peasant is found in the hands of a political leadership determined to bathe him, to trim his beard, to teach him to care for a rifle, work by a schedule, refrain from drunken debauches, be honest in dealing with superiors, and be interested in world affairs—in other words, to abandon his traditional cultural patterns overnight in exchange for those of a modern industrial society. According to Trotsky, the cultural gap was often no less acute in the new Red Army command staff, swollen as it was with persons of peasant and working-class origin.[5]

Trotsky's quarrel over strategy and doctrine with the military proponents of an innovative proletarian version[6] led him to describe the problem of cultural backwardness in a caustic and incisive fashion as being neglected by the Red Commanders, while undue attention was devoted to formulating grand strategy. Rather than dabble with doctrine, a word "tainted with metaphysics," the Red Army should "learn the ABC's," and this required taking much from the bourgeoisie in the West.[7] In 1923, when Trotsky spoke to a meeting celebrating the founding of the "Society of the Friends of the Air Fleet" (ODVF), he drew a sharp picture of the problems of mass cultural backwardness.[8] The British, he declared, created panic on a wide scale by flying an airplane over Soviet troops in the North during the intervention by the allies. The population had to learn that the airplane is not a "mystical thing." Even a harmless

[5] *Ibid.*

[6] White, *The Growth of the Red Army*, pp. 158-82; Erickson, *op. cit.*, pp. 113-43.

[7] White, *The Growth of the Red Army*, pp. 163-64.

[8] *Pravda*, May 30, 1923.

Ford automobile could create chaos in a village by frightening horses pulling carts and wagons, whereas in London and Moscow a horse did not "twitch an ear" in the midst of motor traffic. Apparently the need for mass familiarization with modernity, in Trotsky's view, involved horses as well as the *homo sapiens!* More seriously, Trotsky seemed to have in mind in this case, and in others when he addressed the topic for the Red Army, the immediate tasks facing the leadership that were very elemental, absolutely unexciting, but they had to be faced with candor and could not be long concealed by ideological obfuscation.

Reporting to the XI Party Congress in 1922 on the reorganization in the Red Army, Trotsky complained that the Soviet youth were of a poor sort and that all branches of the Soviet work force were competing for the small number of capable ones. To develop a reservoir of desirable youth, he said, "The army is that school where the party can instill its moral hardness, self-sacrifice, and its discipline in our worker-peasant youth." In a polemical aside to the "esteemed Comrade Pokrovskii," Commissar of Education, who had complained that army service interferred with educating engineers, Trotsky argued that in the Russian cultural milieu engineers needed the background of military service and would be "worth twice as much" as a result, even if it delayed their completion of higher education. In the more general question of elementary education, "communist pedagogy" would not, he insisted, "break the peasant from this environment" and make him politically reliable. Better first make the peasant a soldier, then a communist.[9]

Frunze, Trotsky's successor as head of the Red Army and his erstwhile opponent and leader of the group of senior commanders that disagreed with Trotsky on military doctrine, was equally sensitive to limitations that cultural backwardness placed on Soviet military potential. Even in his theoretical treatise, "A Unified Military Doctrine" of 1921,[10] which drew Trotsky's biting ridicule, Frunze gave

[9] *KVR*, Vol. 3, Bk. 1, pp. 123-24.
[10] *Izbrannye proizvedeniia* (Moscow: 1934), pp. 9-25.

the cultural gap serious attention. He cited Bismarck's re-
minder that the Prussian victories against France had been
in great part due to the village school teachers' good work
for decades beforehand. The lesson for the Soviet regime
was to expedite a program for achieving mass literacy.
This had become even more essential with the advent
of new military technology. The event of war, if it occurred
in the near future, would bring the Red Army into battle
against superior Western technology. Although Frunze,
like his colleague Tukhachevskii, insisted that the social
composition of a workers' army offered an advantage that
could more than compensate for inferior armament, he
did not seem eager to test the proposition by an aggressive
foreign policy.

After Trotsky's departure from the office of Commissar
of War, Frunze's didactic addresses and articles, even if
they did not recapture Trotsky's verbal eloquence, began
to repeat Trotsky's frequent plea for "attention to details."[11]
At an all-union conference of the Komsomol in June 1925,
Frunze expressed serious concern about the poor standards
of discipline in the Red Navy as well as in the Red Army.
In the Baltic Fleet during 1924, 61 percent of all disciplinary cases involved Komsomol members. The figure
was 44 percent for the Caspian Fleet. One rifle division
in the Red Army had reported that 32.9 percent of its
cases of disciplinary action were against Komsomol members. He concluded that the political education of the
Komsomol youth was not really above the average for
the masses.[12] The implication in Frunze's reproach to
the communist youth is very near to Trotsky's assertion of
the priority of instilling basic military virtues over "communist pedagogy."

But Trotsky's opponents, who gave their group corporate
expression in the Military Scientific Society, never disputed
the cultural gap. In a statement of its position on military
policy for the fifth anniversary of the Red Army, the Society declared that overcoming this gap rapidly was im-

[11] *Ibid.*, pp. 464-67.
[12] *O molodezhi* (Moscow: 1937), pp. 89-90.

perative, but that it was ". . . a mistake to reach panicky conclusions . . ." from the fact that Western states had a cultural and technical lead.[13] The enduring issue remained what to do about backwardness.

[13] 5 *let Krasnoi Armii (1918-1923); Sbornik statei* (Moscow: 1923), p. i.

Chapter III

Implications of Technological Backwardness

There was general recognition among the Bolsheviks that new technology, applied to military use, especially during the World War, brought with it significant implications for military organization and doctrine. The more spectacular cases, aviation and chemical warfare, soon gained a wide currency in debate and acquired a symbolic character for the entire range of dimly perceived changes that technological innovations might bring in future wars. At the same time it was realized that the problem of new technology could not be treated purely as a military problem. In at least three ways it linked the military with the remainder of society. First, production of new weapons and equipment required new and expanded industrial capacity. Second, scientific research and development had to proceed apace if the Soviet state hoped to catch up to the West. Third, the broad population from which the Red Army drew its personnel had to possess an educational level that allowed it to be easily trained for more complex military duties.

At the root of party debate on the military question and especially the quarrel between Trotsky and the military proponents of a proletarian military doctrine lay the matter of priority and causal direction. Frunze, Tukhachevskii, Svechin, Verkhovskii, Voroshilov, and others tended to place priority on building an effective military capability. Changes in the remainder of the society were necessary not least of all, and sometimes first of all, because they were essential to the modernization of Soviet forces. The proper sequence in Soviet development, they argued, began with military and defense requirements. Desirable social development would follow implicitly or secondarily. Trotsky, on the other hand, treated the military requirements as secondary, requirements that would inevitably be met or that could be properly dealt with only after broad social changes and economic transformation had been wrought. If the military could be made to serve the development of the whole society, then it should be, but not vice versa in time of peace.

A book of essays on military doctrine, published by the Military Scientific Society on the fifth anniversary of the Red Army, presented a consensus of the views of those officers who generally opposed Trotsky's military policies. It declared that the Military Scientific Society could not restrict itself to "memoirs and historical sketches" (which Trotsky had called for in 1920) while bourgeois armies expanded and the Red Army demobilized. The Society found itself compelled to turn to the concrete tasks of identifying "those forces which are the exclusive property of the army of the revolution." Three propositions were advanced as guides for accomplishing these tasks:[1]

> 1. . . . History teaches that technology, which survives the classes that originated it, may be used against those classes.
> 2. At the same time it is mistaken and inadmissible to neglect the implications and experience of the World War. The Red Army must strengthen its technology and master it in order to comprehend the weaponry of possible enemies.
> 3. Organization, strategy, and tactics of the Red Army cannot be derived from examples of capitalist armies. The Red Army has its own weaponry for which its organization may be adjusted to the general economic and political situation of the Soviet Republic.

[1] 5 *let Krasnoi Armii (1918-1923)*, p. i.

The key to understanding these impious declarations is the Red Commanders' uneasiness about demobilization. They were concerned about their decreasing importance to the regime as the period of reconstruction began. They wanted to continue to share greatly in whatever industrial production the Soviet state could enjoy. By donning the cloak of a "new science," they hoped to serve the image of their own importance and justify their access to resources. At the same time, they were placing a claim on industrial development that could provide the kinds of new technology that were appearing in Western armies. That one could borrow Western technology without also adopting some of the organizational and tactical doctrine developed for its use by the West was an article of faith—surprising for students of Marx and Engels. But, as one student of politics has declared, "political philosophies justify preferences";[2] the same is equally true of military doctrine and strategic dogma.

Frunze's particular view, while it shared much with the general position of the Military Scientific Society, was somewhat more coherently framed. He began his analysis by establishing three groups of assumptions, or "moments" as he called them: (a) the character of future war; (b) the enemy's means; (c) one's own means. Depending on how one perceived the nature of future war and the enemy's forces, a variety of conclusions could be reached on what force structure the Soviet state ought to have. Frunze had been emphatic, in his "Unified Military Doctrine" of 1921, that technological innovations in the capitalist countries would give war a new character.[3] The implications for the Soviet state included not only acquiring new technology as rapidly as possible but finding alternative means for its employment in order to offset the capitalists' lead. Two other important ramifications flowed from Frunze's

[2] Harold D. Lasswell, *Politics: Who Gets What, When, and How?* (New York: Meridian Books, 1958), p. 1.

[3] *Izbrannye proizvedeniia*, p. 22.

analysis. First, the nature of the most spectacular of the technological innovations, aviation and chemical weapons, had made it possible to attack deep in the rear of an opponent, to bring the mass of the civilian population under attack. The old notion of solid "fronts" as the confined area of conflict no longer would be the case. "Front" and "rear" would cease to be a satisfactory way to divide the battlefield. The second ramification concerned the preparation of the rear. The population as a whole had to be propagandized, made aware of the new technology, and organized in a fashion that might minimize the destruction and disorder arising from aerial attacks on the industrial and population centers of the rear.[4]

Frunze's conceptualization of the problems of defense made technology the primary determinant. Because the enemy physically possessed the new weaponry, one could not dismiss Frunze's assumptions out of hand. If one accepted them, his conclusions were not without cogency. He told a conference of workers in the army's political apparatus in 1924 that, as the confusion from reorganization and demobilization was brought under control, the crucial question was becoming technology.[5] Furthermore, when it came to expressing a preference between acquisition of new technology or maintenance of a large regular army, Frunze, at least by the time he was the de facto head of the Red Army, preferred technology. He told another conference of the military political apparatus in 1925 that to have kept a large army at the end of the civil war would have broken the economy.[6] But Frunze's vision of future war had taken him beyond mere choices between capital-intensive and labor-intensive military organization. "From the technical character of future wars flows the necessity . . . to train in advance not only those youth obligated to military service but also the wide mass of the population."[7] In practical terms this meant that the military ". . . must conquer the village with the militia system."[8]

[4] Ibid., pp. 17-22.   [5] Ibid., p. 190.   [6] Ibid., p. 378.
[7] Ibid., p. 375.   [8] Ibid.

"The entire population must realize the Soviet Republic is a besieged fortress."[9] Implicitly Frunze was insisting that military factors were the determining variables in Soviet development. He quoted Lenin to the effect that war was inevitable and a final victory of the revolution in one country was impossible.[10]

If the technological considerations for future war dictated "militarization" of the entire populace,[11] they also had implications for industrial development. In the first instance, priority in industrial production should lie with expanding the capacity for producing new equipment and weapons and next with expanding the production of the weaponry itself. During the period of industrial expansion Frunze was anxious that industry maintained mobilization plans. "The state character of Soviet industry eases this mobilization problem and provides a significant advantage over capitalist governments."[12] He showed concern, however, that central planners were not sufficiently sensitive to the military factors as he perceived them. The military, he acknowledged, could not take full control of the state planning apparatus, ". . . but the army must influence the character of production from the point of view of defense requirements."[13] Furthermore, organizational forms existed

[9] *Ibid.*, pp. 18-19.   [10] *Ibid.*, p. 339.
[11] *Ibid.*, p. 180. By "militarization" Frunze meant preparation of the population for efficient military utilization. Insofar as the process involved inculcating new values and attitudes, they were communist or highly compatible with communist values and attitudes. It is necessary to make this point because of a rather widely accepted view in the West that the two are contradictory and incompatible. See Roman Kolkowicz, *The Soviet Military and the Communist Party* (Princeton, N.J.: Princeton University Press, 1967), pp. 21-22, for an example. It is, we believe, misleading to present soldierly virtues and communist virtues as mutually exclusive or fundamentally different where they concern individual participation in a hierarchical organization.
[12] *Izbrannye proizvedeniia*, p. 199.
[13] *Ibid.*

for this military influence, the defense voluntary organs being examples.

In 1925, speaking to a conference of factory directors, Frunze candidly revealed that there were difficulties between the military and the industrial departments. Basically they were of two sorts. The military wanted more response to its demands for research and development. Also, the problem of quality control in production had caused serious quarrels. Expressing sympathy with the directors' financial plight, Frunze still pressed the military's priority.[14] Later he was prepared to suggest that the industrial leadership might learn something from the Red Army experience in reorganization, although he denied his own competence to rule on industrial matters. Relations between the military and industry, according to his own report to the Military Scientific Society in 1925, were still not congenial. Although both departments were in part to blame, Frunze emphasized that the army could not be related to military industry simply as a buyer to a seller.[15] Referring to industry's reluctance to pay serious attention to mobilization planning, he declared that, "understandably, it cannot be demanded of all our economic leaders . . . such knowledge of military affairs which would automatically lead to certain fulfillment of these requirements. Help in this respect is first of all a task for the military department. The military department is obligated . . . to influence the character and direction of work of economic institutions."[16]

Frunze's analysis had led him away from the group of military proponents of a regular army that resisted the militia system (he openly rebuked them on several occasions in 1925), but it had not divested him of his partisan military perspective. Rather, his assumptions about the implications of new technology supported a case for extending the tentacles of the military establishment into a wide variety of state, economic, and educational in-

[14] *Ibid.*, pp. 464-69.   [15] *Ibid.*, pp. 470-71.
[16] *Ibid.*, p. 198.

stitutions. Military constraints were to confine and dictate institutional and social change. This was a bold and aggressive claim bound to meet objection among Bolsheviks who conceived programs for Soviet political development from other than a military point of view. It was also a vague realization that modernization not only requires differentiation and specialization both in skills and in institutions, but it requires institutional integration of the new roles and functions.

Trotsky initially seems to have treated the problem of anticipating the implications of new technology for military organization and doctrine as a matter of secondary importance, one that was not yet appropriate for serious theoretical speculation. Undoubtedly his attitude was influenced by finding that several of the senior Red Army commanders were devoting extensive time to the study of the doctrinal implications of technology while the day-to-day administrative life of the Red Army, especially during the demobilization at the very end of the civil war, was chaotic, almost catastrophic. Yet it would be misleading to charge him with neglect of the problem or with a lack of understanding.

Trotsky has taken specific issue with the military theorists on the view that the Red Army could defeat the modern armies of the West without first acquiring something like an equal technological level. He did not believe acquisition and organizational integration of new military technology could be achieved in a short period of time by using improvised planning and production methods.[17] Trotsky's conceptualization of the impact of modern technology was broader than that of any of the military theorists, including Frunze and Tukhachevskii. Trotsky, unlike Frunze, did not take military requirements as the dominant constraints for his analysis. He began by asking what had to be accomplished across the whole of society. As he put it, "The army is a copy of society," not vice versa.[18]

[17] *KVR*, Vol. 3, Bk. 1, pp. 143-44.
[18] *Ibid.*, Bk. 2, p. xi.

He was prepared to acknowledge a specialized military role in society, but the exigencies of military technology were not to be the horses hitched to the cart of Soviet political and economic planning.

In fact, when considered in this context, most of Trotsky's policies as Commissar of War, beginning with demobilization and including the territorial militia system and the employment of military formations as an organized and centrally controlled labor force, appear as measures designed to make the military serve not only in a defense role but also in a domestic modernizing role. The military was to be the servant of domestic construction, not the master.

Trotsky's imagination proved as fertile as Frunze's in speculating on the implications of aviation and chemistry for Soviet development. "A special characteristic of our age is . . . that support-types of weaponry rapidly move into the first line. This is primarily relevant to chemistry and aviation. . . . Aviation must occupy first place in our concern about technology. . . . It has an enormous economic cultural significance."[19] He believed that aviation offered certain shortcuts in developing and overcoming the vast Soviet spaces. A network of airlines, not requiring the capital outlay for a vast road net, could more cheaply and quickly insure communication with remote provinces and the rural population. Newspapers and regular mail service to the village would facilitate Bolshevik control in economic and cultural development.[20]

Trotsky accepted Frunze's assertion that aviation and chemistry had altered the character of war. The "front" in its traditional sense had lost its meaning, and the populated and industrial regions of the rear could expect aerial attacks.[21] But the implications in Trotsky's estimate were different. "It is completely obvious that the business of technology is most difficult for us. We are impoverished

[19] *Ibid.*, Bk. 1, p. 149.   [20] *Ibid.*, Bk. 2, pp. 196-97.
[21] *Ibid.*, p. xi.

in aviation . . . in armored forces . . . in transportation. . . .
Our enemies know this. . . ."[22] But to gain technological
equality with the enemy, he continued, required an industrial base. "It is essential that the state industry provide
the army . . . the maximum it can. But sacrifices cannot
be demanded from the economy . . . which threaten to
disrupt the development of industry. . . . To define the
boundary for economic sacrifices to defense . . . is one of
the most important problems of our general state plan."[23]

In contrast to Frunze, Trotsky emphasized the non-military applications of military technology. Aviation, he declared, had "significance independent of the military, something one could not say of howitzers and poison gases."
Moreover, it would be ". . . incorrect to press civil aviation
into the framework of military models and diagrams . . ."
even if it was necessary ". . . to secure a junction between
them."[24] A practical aspect of realizing this "junction" was
to seek "standardization" in airplane design, that is, to
choose models that could perform both military and civil
tasks.

"Standardization" (*odnotipnost'*)[25] as a planning concept appealed to Trotsky because it seemed to illustrate the
advantages both of central planning and of borrowing
technology that accrues to the late-comers in modernization. As a principle it can apply both to organization design and to equipment design. Turning armies into labor
forces and schools for political socialization are examples
of striving for multiple service from a single organizational
form. Standardizing equipment for military and civil use
illustrates the possibility for gaining broader service for
a given instrument in technology. Trotsky seems to be
among the first of the Bolsheviks to understand this possi-

[22] *Ibid.*, Bk. 1, p. 146.   [23] *Ibid.*
[24] *Ibid.*, p. 149.
[25] *Odnotipnost'* means the same thing as "commonality," the
term made popular by the U.S. Department of Defense in connection with multi-purpose equipment and weapons, for example, the TFX swing-wing aircraft.

bility, but it gained an enduring currency that is readily visible in the present-day armed forces.[26] It was applied in many ways in Osoaviakhim. It has already been argued that a distinctive feature of mass voluntary organizations is the attempt to exploit labor and minimize capital outlays for securing a particular service or product. In underdeveloped countries where capital is always relatively scarce and labor plentiful, finding ways to substitute labor for capital is highly desirable. David Granick, in his study of the Soviet metal-fabricating industry,[27] concludes that Soviet managers were quite successful in doing this. Although standardization, or *odnotipnost'*, as a criterion for either equipment or organizational structure, does not ensure the selection of the most labor intensive solutions to allocation problems, it can possibly reduce the capital outlays for engaging in a certain mix of activities simply by reducing the varieties of capital equipment that must be available for those activities. The overall effect may be a reduction in the actual capital-labor ratio. It is of some interest, then, that "standardization" as a criterion for making allocation choices that conserve capital is to be found in the earliest discussion of the problems of defense resource allocations.

For the most part, the Bolshevik military leadership tended to emphasize the opportunities presented by new technology for military-civil relations, and Trotsky had cut to the root of the issue by underscoring the problem of deciding on a limit for economic sacrifices to the maintenance of military forces of the most modern type. The problem involved not only allocations for military equipment but also the general education of the entire population. Tanks and airplanes that peasant soldiers could not drive and fly would provide no defense.

[26] W. E. Odom, "Soviet Training Economies," *Military Review*, 47 (September, 1967), pp. 81-85.
[27] *Soviet Metal-Fabricating and Economic Development* (Madison, Wis.: The University of Wisconsin Press, 1967), pp. 171-206.

Chapter IV

The Red Army as an Instrument of Social Transformation

As the control over the military establishment shifted from one faction of the party leadership to another in the 1920's, a common attitude developed among the incumbents regarding the contribution the Red Army could make in helping to narrow the cultural gap and in imparting new political and social values. Even Stalin was explicit in his opinion of the army's possibilities in this role. "I look upon the Red Army as a rally point for workers and peasants . . . ," he said in April 1923.[1] In his view, it mixed together citizens from all regions and cultural backgrounds and formed an organizational apparatus that tied them together. The army apparatus provided "strong transmission belts" for policies of social transformation.

The first and most ambitious undertaking in this respect, Trotsky's plan to shift military units from the tasks of war directly to labor functions in the economy, was short lived and met stubborn resistence both within the military and without.[2] His defense of the program, nevertheless, clearly revealed his appreciation of the cultural values common to military life and the milieu of industrial labor.

This understanding was the basis for a program in 1921 and 1922 for eliminating illiteracy in the army. An order went out in February 1922, which outlined an expansion of the literacy program in coordination with the Commis-

[1] *Pravda*, April 19, 1923.

[2] *KVR*, Vol. 2, Bk. 2, pp. 33-88. His initial presentation of the plan and later statements in defense of it as it was put into practice are included in this citation.

sariat of Education.[3] It called for improvisations such as five-man study groups, self-study, and employment of the most recently trained literates to teach the beginners. Praise, encouragement, and rebuke for the Red Army program followed throughout 1922 and 1923.[4]

The program did not diminish when Trotsky left the military department. Frunze told the III Congress of Soviets in 1925 that about 20 percent of the recruits taken into the Red Army in 1924 and 1925 were illiterate and that the policy was to allow none of these to depart the army without a modicum of literacy.[5] As a result, 144,342 soldiers had been removed from the illiterate category in those two years. The Red Army's organization for this work included 4,500 self-study circles, and the number of books in army libraries increased from six to ten million.

The beneficiaries of this program were the party and the Soviet apparatus no less than the military. In 1928 Voroshilov boasted to a group of French communists that "the Red Army has become a unique university." Because 77 percent of the army was from the peasantry, an opportunity presented itself to detach this element from backward cultural values and to make of it a source of politically conscious and culturally advanced cadre for public work in the villages. The Leningrad district alone had prepared 10,000 lads for such work. In Kursk Province, for example, 51 percent of the village soviet chairmen were ex-Red Army men, as were 78 percent of the *volost* soviet executive committee chairmen. In the whole of the RSFSR, the analogous figures were 49 percent for the village soviets, and 66.7 percent for the *volost* executive committees.[6]

Perhaps these figures were presented to create an overly sanguine impression of the Red Army as an institution for communist political socialization, but the impression was not entirely without basis. Samuel Harper, an American

[3] *Ibid.*, Vol. 3, Bk. 1, pp. 171-72.

[4] *Ibid.*, pp. 179, 186, 195.

[5] *Izbrannye proizvedeniia*, p. 438.

[6] K. E. Voroshilov, *Stat'i i rechi* (Moscow: 1937), pp. 170-71.

scholar personally familiar with pre-1917 Russia, observed, after returning from a visit in 1926 to study Soviet "civic training," that compared to other institutions sponsoring political education, such training was "particularly well organized" in the Red Army.[7] He was impressed also by the possibility of taking peasants from the village and exposing them to two years of life in or near urban centers, an experience he felt would go far in breaking the cultural patterns of the agrarian society.[8]

If the efficacy of the military was so great in the political and social transformation of the peasant society, one is bound to ask why it was not used on a greater scale. Ideological preconceptions and the shadows of the French Revolution might be cited in response. Certainly there was a basis for concern about a drift of political initiative to the military leadership, but Voroshilov's simple answer to his French comrades, who raised precisely this question, should not be dismissed lightly. He declared that the costs were prohibitive for the Soviet Union to maintain an army that could induct and train every youth who reached the age for military service. No matter where one began, with ideology, strategy, or economic development doctrines, all schemes led inexorably to the budget and resource constraints.

[7] *Civic Training in Soviet Russia* (Chicago: University of Chicago Press, 1929), p. 289.

[8] *Ibid.*, p. 296.

Chapter V

Resource Constraints and
the State Budget

Views on military doctrine and the implications of technology for military and economic policy could only be consequential to the degree that their proponents were able to command resources and to control the budgetary outlays. Normally, control of the state budget gives an institution, faction, or party a strong if not determining say in what views will provide the basis for resource allocations. Both institutional and monetary chaos resulting from the revolution and the civil war kept matters from being so unambiguous in the early years of the Soviet regime.

The period of War Communism was characterized by considerable institutional improvisation aimed to insure the Red Army's place as the preferred consumer. Organizational control, not money, was fundamental at this time in commanding resources. With the advent of the New Economic Policy, institutional control was greatly relaxed by the center, but retention of a loose system of state industrial trusts prevented the full play of market forces.[1] In the resulting economic and institutional environment, the military's access to resources could not be fully dictated simply by budgetary measures, at least not until some regularity had been introduced into state administration and economic organization.[2]

[1] Maurice Dobb, *Soviet Economic Development Since 1917*, rev. ed. (New York: International Publishers, 1966), pp. 125-76.

[2] For a history of this struggle, see Robert W. Davies, *The*

Manpower, of course, appeared to be effectively controlled by the party. The decision to demobilize and implement a militia system was not something the military could avoid, but it did delay on the matter. The official state budget also could be controlled, but the size of the military budget and the kind of military inputs remained a matter for dispute. Guidelines of a general and vague sort were drawn by the XI Party Congress in 1922. The Red Army leaders were said to have acknowledged that the Soviet Republic had to have peaceful relations with capitalist states for economic reasons. To insure restraint in military consumption, a "definite force size" and a "firm budget" were deemed essential, a budget that would correspond to the required force size and technical needs of the army.[3] In the published records, the first mention of the actual size of the military budget concerned the fiscal year 1923/24.[4] By 1924 Frunze seemed interested in adhering to the prescribed monetary outlays and told a conference of the army's political apparatus that "we must adapt all our plans and proposals to the confines prescribed by this budget." Nonetheless, the following year he admitted that two budget increases had been necessary to make funds sufficient for programs.[5]

Frunze's good intentions should not be taken for granted because several of the army's schemes and plans were reaching into both labor and capital in a way that the budget hardly reflected. Effective restraint on military consumption depended less on budgetary control than on the manner in which the new bureaucratic state was organized. The process of regularizing organizational patterns and links in the state economic apparatus presented an opportunity for the military to reap a bigger harvest by

Development of the Soviet Budgetary System (Cambridge: At the University Press, 1958).

[3] *KPSS o vooruzhennykh silakh Sovetskogo Soiuza* (Moscow: 1958), p. 234.

[4] I. B. Berkhin, *Voennaia reforma v SSSR (1924-1926)* (Moscow: 1958), p. 450.

[5] *Izbrannye proizvedeniia*, pp. 175, 361.

securing administrative access and thereby influence over economic planning and production in the state bureaucracy. It is beyond the scope of our study here to trace the politics of this economic institution-building process, but some general observations are essential in order to understand the complex aims that went into the establishment of the initial voluntary defense mass organizations. The defense societies were in part a military gambit for a larger share of resources. At the same time they were part of the party's scheme for control over both resources and the military. To be sure, they were not the only scheme for military aggrandizement.

The militia system, combined with the renewed decree for universal obligatory military training, actually gave the military access to a larger labor force, one it did not have to house and feed the year round. Frunze understood this and was vigorous about putting the militia in proper order even though it had been the creation of his critic, Trotsky.

Frunze also worked regularly to compel all industrial organizations and the Supreme Economic Council (VSNKh) to comply with planning for the event of a mobilization. Mobilization planning offered potential authority over industry as a whole. He was not pleased with his achievements in this respect,[6] and it was not until later that his successor, Voroshilov, could announce to the XV Party Congress that "at last a special apparatus has been created in the bowels . . . of Gosplan" to coordinate mobilization work.[7]

Another access to resources for the military depended on the kind of consumer relationship the military department could achieve with the so-called military industries, industries that sold most of their output to the military and that, owing to the nature of their products, had little civilian market. During the civil war, this consumer relationship had been an administrative one in which the military could not only dictate its desires to the producers but

[6] *Ibid.*, p. 199.   [7] *Stat'i i rechi*, p. 196.

had extraordinary authority to arrest and try personnel in those industries that failed to meet the military's demands. Particularly this power was vested in the Extraordinary Deputy Council of Labor and Defense for Supply of the Army (*Chusosnabarm*), an apparatus for Red Army logistical support headed by Rykov.[8] This powerful body existed for only two years, being disbanded in August 1921. Already in April of that year the Military Industrial Council (SVP) was established for receivership of a small part of the control that had been *Chusosnabarm*'s. The SVP became subordinate to, not superior to the Supreme Economic Council (VSNKh) as *Chusosnabarm* had been. In fact the SVP amounted simply to a trust controlling sixty factories.[9] Like all other government trusts in the NEP period, it regulated its consumer relations with other institutions on a money exchange basis. Frunze thought poorly of this market association with military industries. His remarks to the directors of military industrial firms in 1925 included references to a "new system" of finance that he believed would improve hitherto difficult relations.[10] The military never favored the NEP supply arrangements and was quite pleased when the SVP was abolished in 1926. Control of the industries passed to a department of the VSNKh, the Military Industrial Administration (VPU), and the market feature of supply disappeared.[11]

Finally, Frunze was interested in securing military guidance over research and development, a function that would require increasing resource outlays. He made this point clear to the Military Scientific Society in 1925, when he declared that it should take the leadership and initiative in research. He urged the Society to extend its member-

[8] A. Vol'pe, "Voennaia promyshlennost' v grazhdanskoi voine," *Grazhdanskaia voina (1918-1921)*, eds. A. S. Bubnov, *et al.* (Moscow: 1928), p. 377.

[9] *Ibid.*, p. 393.

[10] *Izbrannye proizvedeniia*, p. 471.

[11] Vol'pe, *op. cit.* Vol'pe says the SVP proved most unsatisfactory.

ship in industrial firms and to press home the military point of view on new designs.[12]

Taken together, these dimensions of organizational linkage between the economy and the military provided the army a pervasive influence on resource allocations, one that could have serious implications for both the structure and rate of industrial growth.[13]

[12] Frunze, *op. cit.*, p. 455.

[13] See Erickson, *op. cit.*, p. 292. In Erickson's judgment this development did not reach a ". . . degree disproportionate with that in many other countries." He does not suggest which other countries, but examples in which the military was such a privileged consumer are difficult to cite. The civil-military linkages were certainly under party control, but they remained extensive.

Chapter VI

Osoaviakhim's Predecessors

Our excursion thus far has revealed something of the psychological and social situation in which the Bolsheviks searched for alternative ways to organize and allocate for modernization programs. In particular it has shown why mass voluntary organizations appealed to them as instruments that could be used for several purposes simultaneously. In principle, however, there was something paradoxical about mass "militarization"—as Frunze described the scheme for making the populace and the economy administratively accessible for elementary military training and potential mobilization—within voluntary societies based on electoral systems. A historical exploration of the founding of the three voluntary societies that were united to form Osoaviakhim discloses the implications of the paradox. If the military was ambivalent toward the new form of organization for military purposes, some civil leaders feared that Red Army participation in such organizational innovation would subvert the societies and turn them into military hierarchies. The formation of Osoaviakhim merely reinforced the paradox. Military activity gained new emphasis, but the voluntary and electoral structure was strengthened against military encroachment.

In this chapter, by examining the history of the three predecessor societies and their amalgamation, we are moving from the abstract level of policy debate—treated in previous chapters—to the practical level of organizing activity. In the end, two things will be accomplished.

First, we shall complete the tracing out of a "means-end" analysis, that is, the policy process of moving from general political goals to specific programs that were presumed to serve those goals. The debate over the ways and means for modernizing Russia was decades old among those in favor of "westernization," and the Bolshevik program of 1919 was merely one more in a long series of attempts to proceed beyond talk to meaningful action. Yet it was incomplete. When we narrowed our focus to the military question, we found the Bolsheviks far from settled on precise organizational structure and programs. If it was agreed that a strong military posture and industrialization were essential "means" for achieving the "ends" of Soviet development, there was less agreement on the means for achieving the instrumental ends of industrialization and defense. The history of the three mass voluntary organizations and their unification is the record of the continuation of the means-end analysis in one narrow sector of the Bolshevik overall program. Taken in all its aspects, it is the record of the conscious linking of general concepts of modernization to action programs.

Second, we shall gain a fuller knowledge of Osoaviakhim's goals. Elucidation of goals is an undertaking frought with ambiguity. We have already noticed the intrusion of personal and factional preferences into the policy process and the resultant intertwining of private and organizational goals. Thus we cannot be satisfied with the formal statement of goals in the Osoaviakhim statutes although it must be given due scrutiny. Clues about how to proceed can be found in our typology of a "public mass voluntary society." This typology treats the organization as an instrument for administrative mobilization and direction of the masses for purposes chosen by the elites. The organization is a political arena in which the elite coerce and persuade the membership to accept a particular allocation of values. The formal goals, from this point of view, can be seen as tactics worked out by the leadership to cause their own interests to prevail. The formal goals, when backed by and entangled with the leaders' goals, become the "value pattern," to use Parsons' diction, and "the main point of reference" for analyzing the organization. The value pattern for Osoaviakhim, however, was not worked out synchronically but rather over a period of years. That is yet another reason why we must turn to the history of the Society of Friends of the Air Fleet (ODVF), the Society of Friends of Chemistry (Dobrokhim), and the Military Scientific Society (VNO).

Formally speaking, Osoaviakhim added nothing to the purposes of these societies as they stood in 1927. The official statutes stated that Osoaviakhim's purpose was to provide a general plan for all the work of the three societies. We shall approach our subjects, therefore, looking for the public statements of goals, aims, and ends. At the same time, we shall infer as much as possible about what the central leadership intended as purposes but did not announce explicitly. Furthermore, we can take what we already know of factional goals and infer more about intended outcomes that were not unanimously desired by the leadership. In other words, the search is for consciously motivated ends.

ODVF

On February 15, 1923, *Pravda* published a small column announcing that within the year the matter of aviation had to be brought to the attention of the entire population in order to elicit both public understanding of the importance of aviation and mass support in building an air fleet. It noted also that because aviation had a civil as well as a military service to perform, mass support should be more readily forthcoming. On March 6, a lengthy editorial by Trotsky, "The Air Fleet—The Order of the Day," graced the front page of *Pravda*, providing a manifold analysis of the aviation problem. Three days later *Pravda* reported that the first session of ODVF had been held on March 8 and had included representatives from the supreme military staff, the air fleet, the trade unions, the Industrial Bank, and the state administration. A presidium had been elected, rules adopted, dues approved, and a technical and agitational apparatus established.

Both *Pravda* and *Izvestiia* began daily coverage of the progress of ODVF. Membership and donations surged, reaching a high point during the "Week of Aviation" in late June. Monetary donations were collected for the purchase of aircraft, even of entire aviation detachments and squadrons bearing agitational names such as "Lenin" and "Ultimatum" (after Curzon's ultimatum to the Soviet government in May).[1] After two years, ODVF embraced about 2,000,000 members, had contributed more than 5,000,000 rubles to the air fleet, part of which had been used to purchase 159 aircraft, and had devoted considerable effort to mass propaganda on elementary knowledge about aviation.[2]

The purpose of the ODVF, to draw the masses into the development of aviation, was sweeping and ambiguous and yet embodied a revolutionary determination to overcome Soviet cultural and industrial backwardness. Everyone agreed that an air fleet was needed. To obtain one, however, involved an enormous undertaking. Only a modest, inchoate aviation industry had been inherited from the old order. There existed no system of airfields and the associated administrative infrastructure for weather reporting, communications, supply, and training of qualified personnel. While a few engineers and designers could be found among the ruins of the old order, an adequate structure for research and development could not. Aviation was also new in the industrial states of the West, but conditions were far more favorable for its growth there than in the Soviet Union. The Society for the Friends of the Air Fleet, therefore, had the broad task of assisting in many sectors of a crash campaign to develop all the necessary ancillary organizations and functions for Soviet aviation. Diverse as they were, the tasks of ODVF involved

[1] See Louis Fischer, *The Soviets in World Affairs* (Princeton, N.J.: Princeton University Press, 1951), I, pp. 433-35, for background on the British note.

[2] Berkhin, *op. cit.*, pp. 453-54; *Pravda*, April 8, 1925.

two aspects: economic and educational. Through mass propaganda it was hoped that both elementary knowledge of aviation for the whole populace and varieties of specialist skills for a reservoir of aviation-associated workers could be imparted in a short while. Through agitation the Society aimed to stimulate voluntary contributions of labor and money for the development of an aviation infrastructure.

From the point of view of the revolution's ideological lore, the decision to use a mass voluntary society for developing aviation can be described as an attempt to tap the energies and creativity of the masses. If one takes an economic point of view, the ODVF can be seen as a means for mobilizing free labor and for accumulating capital through voluntary donations. These resources could then be put into the aviation industry, construction of aviation facilities, research and development, and training of skilled cadres for the entire spectrum of aviation activities. From the military viewpoint, the ODVF appears as a tangible response to demands for a rapid improvement in the technology and weaponry available to the Red Army. From the leadership's perspective, aviation had a novel and exciting character that promised to engender popular curiosity and enthusiasm. Furthermore, the individual could be given the laudable object of defense of the state as a reason why he should join the mass endeavor. Potentially it provided him a means of participating in a spectacular venture, one that might assuage traditional inferior feelings toward Western cultural superiority. But it also had the danger of generating popular resistance when it involved economic sacrifice. Grand designs for overtaking the West were likely to compete poorly with individual interests in finding a stable and adequate standard of living in the aftermath of the war with Germany and the civil war.

All of these desired outcomes, however harmoniously they seemed to blend into ODVF goals, depended on an effective organizational structure. When one considers the

disorder in Soviet institutions in general, the tenuous nature of the Soviet apparatus in the villages and the republics, the chaos in the military, the mere beginnings in industrial reconstruction, and the disorder in the monetary
system, the prospects of an organization for coordinating
the ancillary services to aviation were not encouraging.
There was also the possibility of conflict of interests among
those elite groups that sought gains from ODVF. After all,
who would control this organization? Would its leadership
have the authority to resolve the inevitable disputes when
it tried to perform the linking and integrating tasks envisaged for it?

Several articles and speeches by Trotsky at the time of
the founding of ODVF reveal the outline this conflict of
interest was already taking. According to him, the plan
to expedite the development of aviation had been worked
out during 1922. On February 4, 1923, the Military Revolutionary Council approved an earlier decision to "turn
all organs of the Soviet state, the entire public opinion . . .
on to the question of creating in the country a wide movement behind aviation. . . ." In mid-February the decision
was taken to organize ODVF. Trotsky said the initiative
by the military in this matter was "natural."[3] When his
remarks are placed in the context of NEP and the new Red
Commanders' views on military doctrine, Trotsky's mixed
feelings become apparent.

During the civil war, the existing aviation industry was
under the control of *Chusosnabarm* (the powerful logistical apparatus that supported the Red Army).[4] With the
advent of NEP in 1921, aviation was lumped in the con-
glomerate trust of military industries. That it should receive no special emphasis obviously did not please the military proponents of new doctrines of war such as Frunze,
Tukhachevskii, and the coterie that had suffered Trotsky's
strictures about the metaphysical nature of their policies.
Trotsky, himself, had no reason to resist a policy of giving

[3] *KVR*, Vol. 3, Bk. 2, pp. 186-87.
[4] A. Vol'pe, *op. cit.*, p. 382.

aviation priority. As he pointed out, a network of air lines could greatly improve the regime's communications with the provinces and republics, and it could do so without the investments required for rapid expansion of the highway system. As he put it, "Aviation is an aid for overcoming the evil qualities of our vast spaces. Without doubt, in this area we are on the right path for achieving significant success in a short time with the least difficulties."[5] He was prepared to argue that ". . . aviation industry must have first place. . . . Shock branches of industry are necessary during NEP. . . ."[6] But he was not completely lowering the bar to military demands. ". . . The state cannot devote more resources to military industries than it now does."[7]

In less than two months after the formal establishment of ODVF, Trotsky stated directly that the organization was not to be a Trojan horse for military access to the economy. It would be wrong to submit aviation to ". . . a dictatorship of interests of the military department and the Red Army. . . ." If the military took a longer term view, it would realize that ". . . it is only possible to develop a base for our military industry . . . by applying aviation to the economic and cultural life of the entire country . . ." and thereby to widen the market for aviation.[8] By seeking the maximum commonality in types of motors and models of aircraft between military and civilian users, an optimum satisfaction could be achieved. "Military aviation must be planned in connection with the aviation industry, and the aviation industry must plan for civil aviation as well. . . . It must be planned from the beginning so that our civil . . . transport aviation is a powerful reserve, a tactical base for our military aviation."[9] Trotsky insisted that a coordinated program embodying this broader perspective had to be "negotiated" between the Red Army and ODVF.

Trotsky's annoyance at the military's attempt to use ODVF for access to the economy can be inferred from his

[5] *KVR*, Vol. 3, Bk. 2, p. 186.   [6] *Pravda*, March 6, 1923.
[7] *Ibid.*   [8] *KVR*, Vol. 3, Bk. 2, p. 188.
[9] *Ibid.*

caveats concerning the state budget allocations for aviation:[10]

> If the state cannot provide aviation with more funds directly from the state budget, that does not mean that it can provide funds obliquely through firms which feed on the budget's account. . . . To demand that trusts give the Red Army aircraft is wrong. Trusts are organs of the state vested with certain rights for the administration of state industrial enterprises in the conditions of a market. The rights of a trust do not include the right to correct the state budget according to its own view. . . . I dare say that one day before long the managers of trusts will be brought to answer for "donations" . . . as squandering state property.

It was legitimate, Trotsky declared, to find alternative means to the budget for increasing the resources of the aviation industry. ODVF could provide access to such alternative means through its fund-raising campaigns, but Trotsky feared abuse of this source unless it was handled properly. Many institutions and firms were using funds from their budgets to make block contributions for individual employees.[11] Industrial firms could "buy an airplane" for the air fleet in response to ODVF pressure.[12] The purpose of ODVF, as Trotsky saw it, was not to tap industrial finances; rather ODVF was meant to induce the individual citizen to forego consumption by sacrificing some of his personal income to aviation.

Trotsky did not mean to deny trusts, syndicates, and banks a role in helping aviation. "On the contrary, in a purely economic way they can do a hundred times more than doubtful philanthropy. One can only praise the great initiative . . . of the Russian Commercial-Industrial Bank

[10] *Pravda*, March 6, 1923. Also *KVR*, Vol. 3, Bk. 2, p. 182.

[11] *Pravda*, April 26, 27, 1923.

[12] *Pravda*, April 26, 1923. The price for one airplane was set at 12,000 gold rubles. Presumably this was the price for importing an aircraft.

which convened a conference of trusts and syndicates for discussing questions about aid to the air fleet." The allusion here was to the Voluntary Air Fleet (Dobrolet), which was formed a few days after the beginning of ODVF.[13]

Dobrolet's ostensible task was to develop "a thick network of air communications among all the centers of heavy industry . . . at no burden to the state budget."[14] In effect it was to be a commercial airline syndicate controlling affiliates in the Ukraine, the Caucasus, and Central Asia. Dobrolet depended for its capitalization on selling stock and was authorized an initial issue of one million shares to be sold at one gold ruble each. Any organization or firm that purchased 25,000 shares had the right to acquire and use one of its airplanes.[15] ODVF was apparently directed to assist in the sale of Dobrolet stock, in the construction of airports and weather stations, and in elementary training of workers to man these facilities.[16] In sum, the civil aspect of Soviet aviation was given independent organizational expression in step with the spring and summer campaign to make ODVF a union-wide reality.

Perhaps a factor in the decision to establish Dobrolet was the rapprochement with Germany at Rapallo. A German airline established a flight from Koenigsberg to Moscow in 1923.[17] If the Soviet Union was planning to do commercial business with Germany, it was convenient to have a civil airlines firm on the Soviet side. Whatever the case, Trotsky apparently hoped Dobrolet would also

[13] *Pravda*, March 22, 1923.   [14] *Pravda*, March 30, 1923.

[15] *Pravda*, March 22, 1923. Krasnoshchekov of Prombank, Malkin of the Transport Commissariat, and Seniushkin of the Trade Union Central Committee formed the bureau that established Dobrolet.

[16] *Pravda*, April 7; May 8; June 6 and 14; September 12, 1923. Throughout 1923 *Pravda* and *Izvestiia* carried short reports on Dobrolet activities. The exact nature of the relation with ODVF is never made entirely clear, but there is evidence for the inference that ODVF activities were directed to meet Dobrolet's needs in many instances.

[17] *Pravda*, June 10, 1923.

serve as a civil counterbalance for the aggressive military interest in aviation.

If ODVF was to integrate the broad masses with military and civil aviation both in production and utilization sectors, it would need a source of technical knowledge and guidance. For this reason, the society was connected with the Central Aero-Hydrodynamic Institute (TsAGI). Presumably assistance was to be a two-way affair, information and advice on technical matters in exchange for monetary and labor contributions to the research programs of the institute.[18] What the leaders of TsAGI thought of being tied to a mass voluntary organization is not clear, but it seems likely that they appreciated the sense of priority they were receiving from their expertise being made the object of public attention. There was not much chance for them to play an active policy-making role. The institute was inherited from the old regime along with its founder, N. E. Zhukovskii (who died in 1921). Scientists who worked there had been educated under the old regime and were certainly not in a position to become involved in organizational politics. Professor Chaplygin, an eminent aerodynamics engineer, did speak to the presidium of ODVF about coordinating mutual activities.[19] The literature published by ODVF and Osoaviakhim later on, especially the journal, *Samolet*, which began in the fall of 1923,[20] indicates that the engineers were perhaps overly successful in placing technical articles before the public, articles far too complex to be either interesting or comprehensible to a peasant or a worker who had probably never seen an airplane.

The spring of 1923 was a time when Trotsky was very much at loggerheads with the party apparatus, with Stalin in particular. It was also a time when he was asked by Lenin to carry the fight against Stalin's pervasive role in the party bureaucracy and in particular Stalin's handling of the Georgian nationality problem.[21] Trotsky turned

[18] *Pravda*, April 7, 1923.   [19] *Pravda*, April 7, 1923.
[20] *Pravda*, October 5, 1923.
[21] R. V. Daniels, *The Conscience of the Revolution* (Cam-

down Lenin's request that he take a deputy chairman's post on the Council of People's Commissars in order to check the growth of bureaucratism in the state apparatus. The work of deputy chairmen such as Kamenev and Rykov did not please Lenin.[22] He also failed to induce Trotsky to lead an open fight at the XII Party Congress against Stalin's control of the party apparatus. At this mysterious juncture in his career, Trotsky failed to enter the intra-party political fray with all the weapons Lenin had recently provided. Rather he restricted his public remarks to inveighings against poor economic planning, bureaucratic pathologies in both the state and party apparatuses, and the need to overcome these difficulties through increased intra-party democracy, good-will, and the panacea of scientific planning. Because he was particularly concerned with economic policy—the pressing need to build a broad industrial base in Russia—he conveyed his views in a letter to the Central Committee a month before the XII Party Congress. "In the last analysis the working class can maintain and strengthen its guiding position not through the apparatus of government, not through the army, but through industry, which reproduces the proletariat itself. . . . Industry which lives off the budget, i.e., off agriculture, cannot create a firm and lasting support for the proletarian dictatorship."[23] Certainly this perspective is implicit in his discussion of the aviation industry and ODVF.

Not only did Trotsky see ODVF as an instrument for military influence in deciding allocations for industrial development, but he also viewed it as another manifestation of hastily conceived bureaucratic schemes that added to

bridge: Harvard University Press, 1960), pp. 180-87; Isaac Deutscher, *The Prophet Unarmed: Trotsky, 1921-1929* (London: Oxford University Press, 1959), pp. 65-74.

[22] Daniels, *op. cit.*, pp. 188-89.

[23] "Theses on Industry," March 6, 1923, as translated and quoted by R. V. Daniels (ed.), *A Documentary History of Communism* (New York: Vintage, 1962), I, p. 235.

an already insufferable level of red tape. He warned that ODVF faced the danger of amounting to no more than empty verbiage.[24] The objective of giving the entire population an elementary understanding of aviation was admirable, but "agitation, swamped in repetition, unavoidably turns out to be a straw fire. . . ."[25] Agitation was not enough. Meaningful information and genuine education were needed in order to inflame the masses' imagination with the importance of aviation. The trade unions and the Commissariat of Education had to be included in ODVF. They had to provide assistance and vitality if ODVF was to become more than a great deal of sound and fury. Mass enthusiasm alone, however, would not solve the aviation problem. "Planning as well as enthusiasm is essential to direct sacrifices of the masses into the proper organizational channel. ODVF must work side by side with Dobrolet and the military department—a trio."[26]

No other major political figure at the time published his views on ODVF as Trotsky did. His real purpose is difficult to discern, especially in the light of the contradictions and inconsistencies they embrace. ODVF was undesirable because it allowed the military to violate the budget. Yet ODVF was virtuous because it would tap the energy of the masses. It could serve as a rationalizer in the planning and supervision of the many ancillary activities connected with aviation; yet it was too bureaucratic, a "straw fire," producing agitational fury but no viable coordinated program. This ambivalence suggests that Trotsky accepted ODVF somewhat reluctantly. Corroboration for this view is to be found by examining the central leadership of ODVF.

An "initiative group" of forty-three persons had formally started ODVF in March.[27] Rykov was elected chairman of the first presidium of ODVF. Antonov-Ovseenko and

---

[24] *Pravda*, March 6, 1923.   [25] *Ibid.*
[26] *Pravda*, May 30, 1923. Also *KVR*, Vol. 3, Bk. 2, p. 194.
[27] *Pravda*, September 18, 1923.

Podvoiskii were in charge of ODVF agitation from the first.[28] Both of them had had quarrels with Trotsky in the civil war, but Antonov-Ovseenko had later become Trotsky's supporter in the military political apparatus. Trotsky's opinion of Rykov's performance as deputy chairman of the SOVNARKOM probably coincided with Lenin's, not a pleasant thought for Rykov. The presidium of ODVF's Central Council, elected in September 1923,[29] included not a few of the military figures opposed to Trotsky's leadership: Voroshilov, S. S. Kamenev, Frunze, Uborevich, Baranov, and Petrovskii. The military-political apparatus had its representation: Mekhonoshin and Lashevich. The latter was an ally of Zinoviev. Ordzhonikidze, Stalin's dependable ally, was also a member.

Among the presidium members, only Muralov of the Red Army and Antonov-Ovseenko of the military-political apparatus were clearly allied with Trotsky.[30] The hand of the party secretariat in making assignments for party control in the ODVF hierarchy was visibly at work against Trotsky. At the same time, the organizational style, building a mass voluntary society to assist in the integration of military, industrial, and educational functions, bespoke Stalin's technique of entangling traditionally discrete institutions in interlocking bureaucratic webs. ODVF was the kind of structure that party workers knew best how to manage. Both military and industrial leaders were being drawn into a new game where the party bureaucrat possessed the upper hand. John Erickson has traced this phenomenon in the perspective of the Red Army Commanders' successful struggle to win control of the Red Army. In the process they moved into the arena of party politics. The military-political apparatus broke into factions and fell firmly into Stalin's grip.[31] The establishment of mass voluntary societies appears to be one aspect of this development.

[28] *Pravda*, April 7, 1923.
[29] *Pravda*, September 20, 1923.
[30] Erickson, *op. cit.*, p. 171.   [31] *Ibid.*, pp. 205-06.

Dobrokhim

The first public sign that ODVF's twin organization for chemistry, Dobrokhim, would be established appeared in *Pravda* on March 7, 1924, one year after the formation of ODVF. Given a front-page position, the piece had an agitational quality in that it described developments of chemical weaponry in the West, especially in the United States, as proceeding at a feverish pace. Moreover, it declared that a chemical attack would touch most of the civilian population in a future war. These alleged realities and assumptions left the Soviet population with only one choice: "the entire populace must be prepared for chemical warfare." How was this to be accomplished? The United States, France, and Italy[32] had already provided examples of mass voluntary organizations that taught the population about chemistry in general and defense against chemical attack.

About two months later, in May 1924, Academician Ipat'ev explained in an interview why Dobrokhim had been formed and what its basic objectives were.[33] Preparation for chemical war in the West made Dobrokhim imperative. Its purpose was to assist the army by providing civil defense for communications in the rear. The whole population had to be taught basic elements of chemical defense, and mass support for chemical industries as well as chemical research was necessary to achieve this aim.

An organizing assembly founded Dobrokhim in May,[34] and the first working session of the Central Council convened in June under Trotsky's chairmanship.[35] The Central Council leaders defined the society's relationship to ODVF as one of mutual support. Functional subsections

[32] Conspicuously absent from these accusations of producing inhuman chemical weapons were the Germans with whom the USSR was negotiating a plan for military liaison and manufacture of aircraft and chemicals. Erickson, *op. cit.*, pp. 247ff.

[33] *Pravda*, May 18, 1924.   [34] *Pravda*, May 20, 1924.

[35] *Pravda*, June 7, 1924.

were formed in the council to lead the various specialty activities of the society.[36] At the same time a few industrial enterprises and several institutes of higher education took the cue from the center and founded local Dobrokhim organizations. By August the membership exceeded 100,-000,[37] but in comparison with ODVF membership, this remained a modest figure. The life of Dobrokhim was short, only one year before it was amalgamated with ODVF to form Aviakhim in May 1926.[38]

Most of the reasons advanced in favor of ODVF were repeated to justify Dobrokhim. The West was busily preparing for a new war guided by a vicious and inhuman innovative capacity in the realm of new technology. The USSR had to catch up, and it would have to do so by mass voluntary labor inputs for both the production and educational processes. Dobrokhim was to provide organizational coherence and coordination for the manifold subordinate programs necessary to the overall objective. From Frunze's conceptual view of the priorities in Soviet economic and political development, Dobrokhim made perfect sense.

He greeted Dobrokhim as essential. The Soviet Union was already living in an age when "chemical warfare" was a reality that treaties and conventions could not revoke. Yet the Soviet capacity to engage in this form of war was non-existent. Unless preparations were made in advance, such a condition meant the country was ". . . inevitably doomed to defeat."[39] Dobrokhim could do three things to help overcome this perilous situation. First, it must stir up mass enthusiasm for solving the problem. Second, the society needed to link itself closely with the Red Army for defense plans. Last, the society could compel civil organizations, especially industrial firms, to take the question seriously.[40] Moreover, Frunze called on the Military Scientific Society of the Red Army to take the initiative in aiding

[36] Ibid.   [37] Berkhin, op. cit., p. 453.
[38] Ibid., p. 454.
[39] O molodezhi (Moscow: 1937), p. 35.
[40] Ibid., pp. 35-38.

the expansion of Dobrokhim. The impression is unavoidable that he considered the society a concession to his own ideas of the strategic imperatives for the USSR.

Not surprisingly, Trotsky approached the hasty foundation of another organization with mixed feelings. He said he feared the outcry it might bring in the Western press, particularly in view of the wave of pacifism in England and France.[41] There would also be accusations of German help for the Soviet chemical industry and military preparedness.[42] Upon fuller consideration, Trotsky declared he had abandoned these reservations. There was little choice but to go ahead with the development of chemistry.

Trotsky's address to the organizing assembly for Dobrokhim is conspicuous for its differences with Frunze's. Trotsky insisted that Dobrokhim was an organization of a different type from ODVF. Fears that it would simply compete with ODVF, fears that he admitted had a sound basis at first sight, Trotsky dispensed with by means of a fallacious analogy: Dobrokhim needs ODVF as chemical weapons need aviation for delivery. Frunze not only ignored the possible uniqueness of Dobrokhim but emphasized that in almost every respect they were analogous societies.[43]

Frunze was primarily concerned with Dobrokhim's

[41] *Pravda*, May 20, 1924.

[42] Trotsky added that he would "gladly acknowledge this accusation if it were only true." Such disingenuous assertions perhaps cast doubt on the validity of Trotsky's entire statement as an accurate reflection of his views. Some of the points he raises, however, such as sensitivity for Western opinion, do appear highly plausible in this period when the USSR was struggling to put its formal diplomatic relations with the West on a regular and traditional basis. See Hans W. Gatzke, "Russo-German Military Collaboration During the Weimar Republic," *The American Historical Review*, 63 (1958), 565-97, for an account of Trotsky's personal role in the secret negotiations with the Reichwehr at this time.

[43] *O molodezhi*, pp. 33-34.

military role. One more voluntary society supporting defense programs created an additive effect, not a competitive effect. Although he was not so explicit, his remarks suggest this inference. Trotsky, of course, embellished the non-military advantages of developing chemistry in addition to acknowledging the military arguments. The chemical industry would serve numerous ancillary functions for other sectors of the economy, first of all for agriculture by way of fertilizers and insecticides. To his own rhetorical question, can the Soviet state begin straight away to build every variety of chemical industrial capacity as opposed to concentration on a few specialties, he answered that the whole range of chemical production should be started at once.

In structure, Dobrokhim seems to have been a mirror image of ODVF. The Central Council, elected by a congress and containing a presidium, was not outwardly different from ODVF.[44] Agitation, fund raising, membership recruitment and elementary training made up the central work in the beginning just as they did for ODVF. Especially in the drive to expand the membership, there was bound to be competition, but in one respect an effort was made to mitigate it. Dobrokhim sought its initial membership among student groups and persons connected in some way to chemical industry activity.[45] Such a temporary division of the public, nevertheless, was no panacea. Bukharin, speaking to the XIII Party Congress in May 1924—the same time that Dobrokhim was being formed—described the chaos existing in institutions of higher learning in connection with student organizations. In some cases, over one hundred organizations existed, most of them doing parallel work and taking up more time than study itself! The pioneers of Dobrokhim were nevertheless being dispatched into this environment with programs that could only add to the disorder.

In fact, Dobrokhim never acquired a vast membership.

[44] *Pravda*, May 18, 1924.
[45] Ipat'ev, *Pravda*, May 18, 1924.

In 1925, when it was combined with ODVF, Dobrokhim added less than a million members to the total of about three million in Aviakhim.[46] Nor was Dobrokhim given the kind of press coverage that the ODVF enjoyed. Perhaps this was partly in deference to the pacifist and disarmament mood prevailing in the West. In any event, *Pravda* and *Izvestiia* gave ODVF almost daily attention throughout 1923 and 1924. Sound and fury about funds for buying aircraft abounded, but similar attention to chemistry cannot be found in the pages of these papers. A single modest exception was publicity for campaigns Dobrokhim organized in the Ukraine and in the North Caucasus against insects,[47] but airplanes, gliders, and the air fleet held an unrivaled first place in the major newspapers.

The Military Scientific Society

In November 1920, the first of the Military Scientific Societies (VNO) was formed in the military academy of the Red Army general staff in Moscow.[48] Although Soviet historians attribute the initiative for its inception to the communist party, Frunze is acknowledged as its leader in the first years of its existence.[49] VNO circles were set up in several other military academies and garrisons of the Red Army and gradually multiplied so that, by 1925, societies were active in most Red Army units down to the regimental level.

The purpose of the VNO was twofold.[50] First it was

[46] Berkhin, *op. cit.*, pp. 453-55. No precise figures for Dobrokhim's peak membership have been found, but extrapolations from Berkhin's figures permit the estimate that it never exceeded a few hundred thousand.

[47] *Pravda*, June 5, 1924.

[48] F. N. Kuz'min, *Na strazhe mirovogo truda* (1921-1940 gg) (Moscow: 1959), p. 70.

[49] *Ibid.*; Berkhin, *op. cit.*, pp. 5-6; *Spravochnik aktivista Osoaviakhim* (Moscow: 1931), p. 15. Hereafter cited as *Spravochnik aktivista*.

[50] Frunze, *Izbrannye proizvedeniia*, p. 450.

committed to study the World War and the Russian civil war in a "scientific" fashion, distilling the new insights that would aid the Soviet state in securing victory in the inevitable future conflicts with the capitalist West. Developing new doctrine, working it out in maneuvers, and testing it in other ways, this kind of activity, too, was part of the VNO "research" work. Second, the VNO was to conduct officer education, a serious matter for the new Red Commanders who, in many cases, had almost no formal education.

For the most part, the visible work of the VNO emerged in journals and other publications.[51] Pouring out accounts of war experiences was one way for the Red Commanders to compensate for their own feelings of professional inadequacy. The military specialists and ex-tsarist officers seemed to be no less eager to place their views in the official journals of the new regime.

The VNO was apparently first asked to extend its work beyond the confines of the military department in 1924. Frunze said that it should take the initiative in assisting the expansion of the new mass voluntary organization, Dobrokhim. It did not accept this gentle suggestion gladly. In May 1925, Frunze, the chairman of the central organ of the VNO, convened the first all-union conference of the member societies for the express purpose of changing the basic direction of the VNO's work. The new policy met considerable resistance but was pressed on the VNO. Frunze told the conference that the time had come to abandon the parochial intra-army character of the VNO and to transform it into a mass voluntary organization including civilians as well as military members.[52] The first all-union congress took place in March 1926, and, in July 1926, the name was changed to Society for Assistance to

[51] Namely, *Voennaia nauka i revoliutsiia, Voennyi vestnik, Voennaia mysl', Krasnaia zvezda,* and *Voina i revoliutsiia. Voina i revoliutsiia,* published first in 1925, was the VNO official journal and became an Osoaviakhim journal in 1927.

[52] Frunze, *op. cit.,* p. 457.

Defense (OSO).[53] The begrudging spirit with which OSO accepted its new character is evident in the membership it brought to the union of all the defense societies, Osoaviakhim, in January 1927—about 85,000, less than either Dobrokhim or ODVF.[54]

The VNO's lack of enthusiasm for becoming a mass voluntary society stems from its unique origins. It was founded by some of those military leaders who were resisting Trotsky's program for demobilization in the last months of the civil war. Trotsky's feelings toward the VNO may be inferred from one of his orders as Commissar of War. The XI Petrograd Rifle Division, he declared to the editors of the division's military-scientific journal in October 1921, might do something more useful than produce a journal of pretentious erudition that the personnel of the Red Army could not comprehend.[55] In the spring of 1922, he raised the question of the appropriateness of the term "military science," by bluntly asserting there was no such thing. Military matters are a question of art, not science.[56] At a VNO meeting in November 1921, Trotsky had lectured the proponents of a proletarian military doctrine, chided them, and rejected their views as outright nonsense.[57]

If the VNO housed the military opposition to Trotsky, it had not been a single-minded faction. In explaining the new direction for VNO work to the congress in May 1925, Frunze described the VNO's past as marked by a continuing quarrel between the ex-tsarist officers and the new Red Commanders. The military specialists from the old regime had underestimated the importance of the civil war experience, he said, while the latter group had erred in the opposite direction. Yet Frunze insisted that "we can say that objective truth in the final count is on the side

[53] *Spravochnik aktivista*, p. 16.

[54] *Pravda*, January 20, 1927. Rykov reported OSO membership as 85,000. Unshlikht reported it as 300,000.

[55] *KVR*, Vol. 3, Bk. 1, p. 167.

[56] *Ibid.*, p. 174.   [57] Erickson, *op. cit.*, pp. 128-29.

of the second group."[58] Now in the period after Frunze's group had captured the top of the military apparatus, large numbers of the military specialists were being moved out and the Red Commanders were trying to secure their new predominance.[59] The former unofficial function of the VNO, articulating new views on strategy that clashed with Trotsky's perceptions, was no longer needed by Frunze, and he appeared anxious to deny the military specialists the same forum for agitating against his own strategic concepts. Re-directing the VNO objectives from the realm of theory to practical work in propaganda and mass agitation was entirely logical from the point of view of Frunze's apparent preferences.

As he told the VNO conference in May 1925, "in some respects our work is finished, for example, identifying and working out the basic aspects of force structures." He had in mind primarily the important "moments" of future war, the assumptions on which he rested all his arguments concerning strategy and force size. "Such finishing work

[58] *Op. cit.*, p. 451.

[59] Erickson, *op. cit.*, pp. 138-43, 168-72; White, *The Growth of the Red Army*, pp. 207-10. The open campaign by Stalin, Kamenev, and Zinoviev to destroy Trotsky's position as Commissar of War began in June 1923, when the Central Control Commission launched an investigation of the military department. The recommendations for rectifying the alleged inefficiency it discovered in the military department were drawn up by Frunze and presented in January 1924. In March Frunze took Sklianskii's post as Trotsky's deputy and effectively became head of the Red Army. In turning Frunze's group loose to undercut Trotsky within the army, Stalin's triumvirate had provoked the military-political apparatus to support Trotsky and to fight to secure a limit to the party's central control over the lower levels of the military-political administration. Thus Frunze's emergence as the head of the Red Army marks the beginning of two bureaucratic struggles. Erickson characterizes them as a "period of sustained and purposeful purge, which played a dual role, firstly to bring the Soviet armed forces back under the strictest control of the ruling group and secondly, to open the way for the Red Command. . . ." p. 143.

does not need the entire VNO. Therefore the center of gravity must shift from theory to daily practice. . . ."[60] Questions of strategy, he went on, worked out by VNO circles, must be relevant for the size of the unit in which the circle exists, not higher. Frunze did not intend to leave the VNO free to play the kind of oppositional role he had exploited it for earlier. He set about to break up its old structure, to dilute its intensity of interest in strategic concepts by swelling its ranks as a mass voluntary society.

Frunze had not only the ex-tsarist officers to contend with, but the political apparatus as well, insofar as it had shown genuine support for Trotsky or had sought more local party authority to question the center's policies.[61] Certainly Frunze's scheme for coping with the political apparatus, for instituting unity of command in the Red Army at the political commissar's expense, exceeded the limits of the question of VNO policy, but the new role of the VNO seems to have been part of his scheme. At a conference of political-military workers in February 1925, Frunze explained his views on reforming the military department, on force structure, and on strategic concepts. The implications in practical work for military-political workers, he insisted, included military programs among the masses. The political apparatus should lead the expansion of the VNO from its formerly restricted role to that of a mass defense society. Beyond that, they should insure coordination with other societies, in particular, ODVF and Dobrokhim.[62]

The impetus for transforming the VNO obviously did not come from Frunze alone, however sympathetic he seemed to be to the policy. *Voina i revoliutsiia*, a journal appearing first in January 1925, and dedicated to providing theoretical and practical guidance for the VNO, carried several articles in its first year encouraging an enthu-

[60] Frunze, *op. cit.*, p. 459.

[61] See Erickson's discussion of the famous Circular No. 200, *op. cit.*, p. 142.

[62] Frunze, *op. cit.*, p. 387.

siastic participation in the transition to a mass organization.[63] After Frunze's death in October 1925, the campaign for expanding the VNO picked up momentum. In January 1926, I. Klochko mentioned in an article the imminent convention of the first VNO all-union congress.[64] He raised the old notion of "an armed people" as the socialist approach to defense, still desirable, but possible only through the territorial militia structure combined with an elementary but thorough military education of the entire populace. V. Levichev added to this discussion of the militia system by praising it as the "best" possible force structure given the objective conditions in the USSR.[65] The question of the militia, both authors said, would be taken up at the VNO congress. Apparently the force structure issue was not entirely resolved as Frunze had insisted the year before.

More important for the actual development of the VNO in an organizational sense is the insight provided by K. Podgoretskii[66] in a discussion of the hesitancy with which VNO circles were opening their doors to the "wide mass of toilers." Some regimental commanders had closed down VNO organizations where the council had included more civilians than soldiers. No one openly protested the new rules, Podgoretskii reported, but they widely resisted them by passive means. Where the expansion had occurred, many officers reportedly took a condescending attitude and

[63] See especially I. M. Podshivalov, "Litsom k soiuzy," 3 (May, 1925), 123-28; and N. Sh., "VNO v derevne," 5 (August-September, 1925), 154-57.

[64] "Problemy voenno-nauchnoi raboty," *Voina i revoliutsiia*, 1-2 (1926), 4-10.

[65] "K postanovke voprosa o militsionno-territorial'nom stroitel'stve na s"ezde VNO," *Voina i revoliutsiia*, 1-2 (1926), 11-24. Levichev even insisted that because the cadre units of the RKKA were busy building barracks, the militia was actually receiving more training, making it a more battle-ready formation than the regular RKKA units.

[66] "Novaia bolezn' rosta," *Voina i revoliutsiia*, 1-2 (1926), 29-35.

treated the civilian element as not seriously interested in VNO activities. The Central Council of the VNO set a minimum requirement of 25 percent civilian membership for local councils of VNO in order to overcome this "conservatism in the forces." The consequence of the military's fear of civilian dominance had been to prevent the development of the infrastructure of cells and activities essential to the enormous task of mass military education.

When a VNO all-union congress convened in March 1926, Tukhchevskii and Svechin clashed openly on the question of military doctrine. Debate also raged over who properly should prepare the whole population for war. It was reported that few of the staff sections of the VNO were prepared for mass work. How was the new role of the VNO to affect the present internal structure of the society? Should the old VNO type of work within the army be discontinued or reduced? These questions were also addressed. The congress was induced, apparently grudgingly, to approve the policy for eventual unification of all mass voluntary defense work in one organization, and the membership was warned that there should be no vacillation on the matter henceforth.[67] Perhaps indicative of the broad resistance within the Red Army to the new VNO policies was the failure of the congress to change the name of the VNO to Society for Assistance to Defense (OSO). The name had appeared in *Voina i revoliutsiia* in 1925.[68] Yet not until July 1926 was the name officially proclaimed and the old one eliminated.

If Frunze's analysis of the implications of technology for future war had led him to declare that the entire populations of belligerents would be struck by air and gas attacks and that the industrial capacity and sophistication of a country were of crucial importance, it also served to justify his demand for the military readiness of the entire populace and economy. The changed role of the VNO

[67] S. M. Belitskii, "K itogam vsesoiuznogo s"ezda VNO," *Voina i revoliutsiia*, 3 (1926), 3-9.

[68] Podshivalov, *op. cit.*

had been defended by Frunze with the same reasoning invoked for the creation of ODVF and Dobrokhim. All three societies could, in Frunze's view, contribute to this imperative mass preparedness. The degree to which Frunze actually believed the societies could serve this goal is disputable, but it seems fair to guess from the evidence available that the VNO congress delegates both in 1925 and 1926 had serious doubts about the real direction of influence: would the RKKA and the VNO administratively coopt the civilian elements? Or would the new OSO concept lead to increased civilian influence over the military? At least some of the VNO leadership had initially been sanguine about the possibilities for extending the military's control through the society. An anonymous piece appearing in 1925 provided an extensive description of how VNO cells could be active in all reaches of the state and economic organizations, advancing the military point of view, coordinating the overall direction of research and industrial development through liaison between cells and through the VNO center.[69] Such a conceptualization was certainly compatible with Frunze's thinking, but the game of who controlled whom was definitely shifting against the military as more than a few of the leaders in the VNO must have realized.

Osoaviakhim: Unification of the Defense Societies

Although some of the factors that brought about the unification of all the defense societies are fairly clear, others can only be surmised. At the level of factional politics within the elite of the party, there is little direct evidence available. The matter did not arise in debate at the

[69] G. G., "Zadachi nauchno-issledovatel'skoi deiatel'nosti tsentral'nykh sektsii VNO i metody ee organizatsii," *Voina i revoliutsiia*, 3 (1925), 103-09. This ambitious article includes diagrams of possible organizational schemes for insuring the military's grip on all research and development activity in the country.

XIV Party Congress; nor is there mention to be found in the party press. At the level of administration and bureaucratic management, much more was said openly. Combining the defense societies must have been considered as early as 1924. In February 1925, Frunze told a conference of military-political workers that "maybe the time is not yet ripe to speak of merging all these cells [of various societies], but it is essential to speak of establishing liaison among them."[70] In uttering this admonishment, he was perhaps mindful of a resolution taken by the XIII Party Congress on the need to improve the coordination among voluntary societies.[71] In any event, the implementation of a new policy of unification was under way in the spring.

In May 1925, without great public ceremony, Dobrokhim and ODVF were combined to form Aviakhim. No record of a formal meeting of the central council or presidium of either organization to approve the amalgamation appeared in the press, unlike all other cases of major organizational changes. One is therefore encouraged to conclude that it was done by administrative fiat. But it was more likely a concession to resistance from below than a demonstration of the center's arbitrary power. Unshlikht admitted at the First All-Union Congress of Osoaviakhim that the re-registration of members had caused a "colossal strain" and the loss of 22 percent of the membership.[72] He also recounted that growth in both organizations had virtually stopped because the trade unions had issued directives opposing the payment of dues to more than one voluntary society.[73] Finances, therefore, had become a serious problem. Forming Aviakhim seems to have been a response to this difficulty, an attempt to reduce the administrative "parallelism" and to overcome the resistance in the trade unions.

Voroshilov declared that the decision for the Osoaviakhim unification had been taken in March 1926,[74] that is,

---

[70] *Izbrannye proizvedeniia*, p. 387.

[71] *Pravda*, June 3, 1924.   [72] *Pravda*, January 19, 1927.

[73] *Ibid.*   [74] *Pravda*, January 27, 1927.

probably at the first VNO all-union congress that convened in that month. An article appeared in *Voina i revoliutsiia* in April 1926[75] that outlined an organizational structure suggestive of Osoaviakhim's future form. In view of the distaste in the VNO for "leaving the bounds of the Red Army," it is doubtful that the article represented the general mood of the VNO leadership. The arbitrary nature of the center's decision for the Osoaviakhim union is also reflected in Voroshilov's admission that "many say it is not useful" to unify.[76] He warned against the opinion that the policy had not been thought through at the top and had originated outside the ranks of the societies involved. Speeches by Rykov and Unshlikht at the unification congress in January 1927 also reveal the impatience and momentum for unification that the central leadership had generated within itself over the past two years.[77] It called for full acceptance of the policy and for no reduction in organizational work during the transition.

No dearth of cogent reasons could be invoked to justify the Osoaviakhim union. The multiplicity of voluntary defense organizations had generated several undesirable circumstances. First, in gaining mass interest, they met competition from several non-defense voluntary societies: The Peasant Society for Mutual Aid, The International Organization for Aid to Revolutionaries, The Friends of Children, Society to Aid the Victims of the Intervention, Society for Invalids, and others. All of these carried out fund drives similar to those of the defense societies. The latter competed among themselves for members and funds as well. The result, as *Pravda* put it,[78] had been to overburden the individual financially and to ask for time he simply did not have. Not surprisingly, much voluntary public work in this environment proved to be no more than "paper falsification."

[75] K. Kalin, "Voennaia rabota sredi naseleniia," 4 (1926), 120-30.

[76] *Pravda*, January 27, 1927.

[77] *Pravda*, January 18 and 25, 1927.

[78] November 1, 1925.

The second source of difficulty lay in parallelism in both organizational programs and bureaucratic structure. Frunze indicated in 1925 that the apparatuses for the defense societies were composed largely of the same persons, suggesting that the actual number of personnel was, if anything, too small.[79] At the First All-Union Congress of Osoaviakhim, complaints arose about the excessive size of the apparatuses.[80] In turn, the size of the paid staff of the societies, it was argued, encouraged little dependence on the voluntary membership in program execution; that is, the apparatus "substituted itself for the mass." The unification presumably would permit a reduction in the number of *apparatchiki*, especially at the center.

Localism also had developed in OSO and Aviakhim. Through unification, it was hoped to reduce or eliminate this phenomenon. Finally, organizational chaos at the lower levels had "cooled" the attitude of the local soviets, trade unions, and party committees toward contributing resources for the societies' work.[81] Rykov, Voroshilov, and Unshlikht were unanimous in presenting Osoaviakhim as a panacea for all these difficulties.

It is uncertain to what degree party leadership at the center had pursued a preconceived tactic, but from the perspective of 1927, the regular pace of launching new voluntary societies seems to have had the rationale of embracing as wide a variety of activities and membership as possible, more than a single new organization could have achieved. The spring became a habitual time for forming new societies and for reorganizations: ODVF in the spring of 1923; Dobrokhim in the spring of 1924; VNO reorganization and the Aviakhim merger in the spring of 1925; the spring of 1926 saw the VNO make its last attempt to avoid the new label, OSO. Once the expansion slackened and the ill effects of rapid growth began to appear in epidemic proportions, a policy of consolidation was

[79] *Op. cit.*, p. 387.
[80] *Pravda*, January 20, 1927.
[81] *Pravda*, January 27, 1927.

advanced, first in 1925, beginning with Aviakhim, and culminating in 1927.

With the Osoaviakhim unification, a new accent in organizational goals appeared, a stress on the military training activities. Rykov revealed this change obliquely at the unification congress when he stressed the commonality between the kinds of endeavors that contribute to military defense and those primarily concerned with peaceful socialist construction.[82] This did not mean, he promised, that Osoaviakhim would take on a military organizational character. Quite the contrary. "The voluntary democratic nature" of the Society was to be scrupulously preserved.[83]

If there were fears, as Rykov's assurances seem to imply, that "the military would swallow Aviakhim," they were not entirely groundless. Frunze's programs for the military department had as their conceptual basis his assumption that future war with the capitalist West was the alpha and omega for guiding social and economic transformation of Soviet society. The call for militarization of the whole population found currency in almost every speech and article he wrote. His point of view apparently did not vanish with his death.

In the fall of 1926, a program for establishing VNO cells in key points in every state and public institution was put forth and approved in part by the VNO Central Council.[84] Its author, B. Bukin, asked for an elaborate network of mutually coordinated cells and listed several organizations where they already functioned, including the People's Commissariats of Education, Labor, Transportation, Trade, Finance, such economic institutions as Gosplan, VSNKh SSR, and the VSNKh UkrSSR, and a row of research institutions. He insisted that the OSO had to stimulate a proper attitude toward the needs of defense in all realms of public life, not least in the economic and

---

[82] *Pravda*, January 25, 1927.   [83] *Ibid.*

[84] B. Bukin, "Rabota i blizhaishchie zadachi sektsii podgotovki strany k oborone," *Voina i revoliutsiia*, 9 (September, 1926), 70-82.

research institutions where an apolitical attitude was the prevailing outlook. If some of the VNO membership had accepted the new role of the Society with reluctance and passive resistance, others, especially at the center, saw in it opportunities for insinuating military preferences into political and economic policy at the top levels. Neither party nor state bureaucrats were disposed to defer gladly to this scheme.

The continual organizational change, ending with an amalgamation of civil and military elements, must have had the effect of preventing the leaders of any one of the voluntary societies from forming a self-interested faction, able to structure a reliable constituency and to press its demands on the party secretariat and orgburo. With respect to the military, then, the party leadership in the defense societies provided Stalin with additional means for re-securing control over the military and military-political administration, control that had suffered relaxation for the purpose of bringing Frunze's faction of the Red Commanders into action to break Trotsky's position in the Commissariat of War.[85] Voroshilov, whose literacy and military competence had been openly challenged by the Red Commanders, became Commissar of War and the object of Stalin's ventriloquy in matters of defense policy, including Osoaviakhim activities.

Another factor, which must have played a role in the decision to form Osoaviakhim, was Stalin's First Five Year Plan. The defense societies, as their leaders had emphasized, played a part in guiding and pressing forward certain branches of industry, branches that would not on their own power, in the NEP period, have developed rapidly. With the elimination of NEP, this method of "shock branches," as Trotsky called it, was not needed. The shock approach was to be applied to the entire economy, and the meddling of voluntary societies might prove a nuisance

[85] See Erickson, op. cit., pp. 199-207, for a detailed study of Stalin's moves to capture the military apparatus after Frunze had taken charge.

rather than a help in institutionalizing a command system of central planning. The tasks of mass education and military training, as well as collecting funds, were desirable to retain. To these activities, Osoaviakhim, therefore, was directed. As far as it could successfully pursue them, it could make large masses of the populace administratively accessible, capable of being mobilized for numerous and changing purposes dictated by the Bolshevik elite.

This chapter can be brought properly to a close by sifting out in summary form the broad aims of Osoaviakhim as they stood in 1927. From the many statements about purpose and from the experience in the predecessor societies, four general and enduring goals intended by the leadership can be gleaned.

First, to tap resources otherwise unavailable—financial, material, and labor—and allocate them to the aviation and chemical industries, to agriculture, and to defense.

Second, to train the membership in basic military skills and to increase their knowledge of aviation, chemical, and military technology without taking them away from their place of work in the economy.

Third, to bring about a metamorphosis in organizational participatory patterns and attitudes among the membership.

Fourth, to raise the entire population's awareness of new technology and the likely character of future war through agitation and propaganda by the membership.

Two additional goals were factional in nature. First, we have noticed that the military was clearly attempting to make both the population and certain industries administratively accessible for its own purposes. Second, Stalin's faction intended to use the organization to diffuse and restrict the military's authority over resources. Perhaps there were other factional goals, but none rival these two for potential impact on the organization's development and objective role.

Summary

In Part One the aim has been to present the general context in which the founding of Osoaviakhim took place, to throw light on the cultural, technical, and administrative constraints besetting the ruling elites, and to understand as much as possible about the elites' beliefs and perceptions as they impinged on the decision to establish voluntary defense societies. Additionally, the politics of administrative departmentalization surrounding Osoaviakhim's origin have been examined. This background should provide at least two general perspectives. First, it gives a broad understanding of Osoaviakhim's somewhat complex goals and their intended relation to the economy, the society, and the armed forces. Second, it reveals some of the diverse and implicit factional interests that played a role in the decision to establish the Society. This latter perspective allows us to see the organization as a bureaucratic mechanism used to enhance the power of Stalin's clique at the center. The former perspective suggests the sense in which Osoaviakhim was intended to be functional for the political system as a whole, a structure for integrating a great number of activities and for closing gaps created by rapid modernization. Before these themes can be carried further, it is necessary to examine the formal organization of the Society.

Part II
Formal Structure

Chapter VII

General Terminology and Concepts

Descriptions of the formal bodies of the organization can be grouped into two categories. The first group includes those formal structures that perform representation, delegating, executive, and control functions for the organization as a whole. The second group, officially referred to as the "practical organizations," includes a wide variety of structures involved directly and primarily with Osoaviakhim's productive activities: recruiting, propaganda, military training, fund raising, and various kinds of assistance to industry and agriculture. Most of the first group are shown on Chart I in their hierarchical relationships, but some commentary on each body can clarify those relationships more fully.

The Representative Organs

Just as in the structure of Soviet government, the appearance of popular participation and representation was maintained in the ruling and rule-making of Osoaviakhim. At the cell level, every member had the right to participate and vote in the "general meeting." The general meeting elected delegates for the raion or volost congresses, the representative body at the raion level. In turn, indirect representation is found in a formal sense at every higher level ending with the congress of the Union of Societies of Osoaviakhim, USSR. Congresses were too large to administer the Society, and therefore chose from their midst smaller bodies for that purpose—councils and buros.

CHART I

The Union of Societies of OSOAVIAKHIM USSR, 1928

Source: *Ustavnoi sbornik.*

All-Union Congress of OSOAVIAKHIM	→	Central Council	→	Chairman / Presidium	→	General Secretary / Secretariat
Congress of Union Republic	→	Council	→	Chairman / Presidium	→	Secretary / Secretariat
Congress of Krai, Oblast, or Republic	→	Council	→	Chairman / Presidium	→	Secretary / Secretariat
Congress of Okrug	→	Council	→	Chairman / Presidium	→	Secretary / Secretariat
Congress of Raion or Volost	→	Council	→	Chairman / Presidium	→	Secretary / Instructors
General Meeting of the Cell	→	Buro	→	Chairman and Treasurer		

Note: Revision commissions, not shown, were elected by the congress at each level and by the cell general meeting.

The Councils

Presumably the councils looked after the executive and administrative matters. They also could make binding decisions when the congresses were not in session. Generally, however, a council was too large for this task. At the Union level, plenums of the Central Council took place in practice only once a year, although the rules called for more frequent sessions. Council membership always included persons from the military, the party, trade unions, and the Komsomol. At the higher levels representatives from the People's Commissariats, the soviets, industry, educational institutes, and research institutes were always present. This mix of other institutional representation gave formal expression to the linking of military, industrial, and educational activities that Osoaviakhim purported to achieve. A hundred or more was not an unusual number to find on the Union Central Council.[1]

The Presidiums

The council size made it imperative to elect a smaller body that could meet more frequently and exercise the council's authority. Still it maintained the wide institutional representation of the council and tended to become rather large at the higher levels.[2] Most of the presidium members also worked on the staff of the council, in the "sections" specializing in particular aspects of the society's work such as aviation, chemistry, propaganda, and so on. The cells, and sometimes the raion council, did not have presidiums.

[1] *Pravda*, February 15, 1930, reported 167 members elected to the Central Council. Also see *Pravda*, January 28, 1927. The first Central Council had 300 members. The RSFSR Council had 257.

[2] *Pravda*, January 25, 1927. The first presidium of the Central Council had 31 members; *Khimiia i oborona*, 7 (1932), 20; the III Plenum of the Central Council elected 51 persons to the presidium.

The Chairman

The presidium elected a chairman from its midst to preside over its meetings as well as those of the congress and the council. Ostensibly he was the senior official of the Society, its chief. In the beginning (1927) this post appeared at the Union level to be more decorative than substantive. Rykov held it until 1931. Because he was also Chairman of the Council of People's Commissars, it is likely that the executive matters of the Union of Societies probably received little of his time. On the other hand R. P. Eideman, who held the post from 1932 to 1937 and was a senior commander in the Red Army, seems to have devoted most of his energies to Osoaviakhim. At the lowest level, the cell, the secretary performed the crucial leadership. He had a treasurer to assist him and, if the cell was a large one, a buro of seven or more persons. At the intermediate levels and at the top, the executive and administrative functions fell largely to the secretary and the secretarial staff.

Secretary and the Secretariat

At the Union level, the presidium selected a full-time general secretary. He and his secretariat staff sat at the top of a full-time salaried apparatus. The Osoaviakhim rules are not at all enlightening on the shape or size of the apparatus. There are reasons for this other than the Soviet proclivity to treat such organizational features as state secrets. First of all, the secretariat's non-voluntary nature stood in undesirable contrast to the professed voluntary character of the Society. Second, it tended to change frequently and showed a propensity to expand. This phenomenon will be discussed later in detail, but it is worth remarking here that it extended down to the raion level in theory if not always in practice in the early years, 1927-1930. Where raion secretaries did exist, they were usually reserve commanders of the Red Army.[3] As a rule, all

[3] *Krasnaia zvezda*, September 21, 1929.

members employed in the apparatus were party members. Rykov, however, told the First All-Union Congress of Osoaviakhim that the apparatus should include a few non-party persons among its rank and file workers.[4]

Snabosoaviakhim

A major problem for the apparatus was supply of material for Osoaviakhim activities that could not be produced or procured locally. Snabosoaviakhim, the supply system, was directly under the control of the Union but was granted the status of a legal corporation (*iuridicheskoe litso*) and was required to operate on the financial accounting basis of *khozraschet*. In practice it sold supplies to lower organizations. It did not provide them on a free administrative basis. Technically speaking, Snabosoaviakhim was a staff department of the Central Council's secretariat. It was not run by volunteer personnel and therefore was part of the apparatus at all levels. (See Chart II.)

Sections, Sectors and Commissions

These were the staff elements found in the councils at every level. They reflect the management's efforts to make departmental divisions based on functional lines. Especially in the early years these divisions were periodically changed and shifted in search of more effective staff arrangements. To be sure, the more than twenty kinds of distinct activities carried on by Osoaviakhim made departmentalization a complex affair.[5] Another way to underscore the complexity is to remember that Osoaviakhim had

[4] *Pravda*, January 25 and 30, 1927.
[5] L. Borisov, "Oborono-massnovaia rabota Osoaviakhim (1927-1941)," *Voenno-istoricheskii zhurnal*, 8 (1967), 40. Borisov reports that this great number of activities became a brake on the Society and was therefore reduced in the mid-1930's. Although hardly the whole story to the narrowing of the span of activities in 1935 and 1936, this was apparently one of the genuine reasons for the reforms.

CHART II

General Administrative Structure of Osoaviakhim's
System of Supply

Source: *Ustavnoi sbornik*, pp. 160-65.

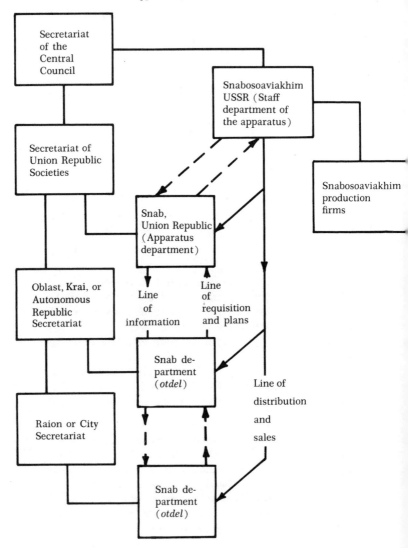

united three major spheres of activity: military, aviation, and chemistry. In each of these spheres it was insisted that an overlap across the military-civil boundary should exist, linking military and civil activities, exploiting commonalities in skills, equipment, and organization. In addition, the administration, self-maintenance, and expansion of the Society added extra staff and operational requirements. A list of the sections on the Central Council (the Union level) as they were in 1928 can give some idea of the departmental boundaries:[6]

1. Agitation and Propaganda
2. Military Training
3. Marksmanship
4. Aviation-chemical Defense
5. Military Scientific Research
6. Naval
7. Defense Training for Toiling Women
8. Cavalry Affairs (raising and training horse stock)
9. Aviation
10. Aviation Law
11. Chemical-scientific-industrial
12. Assistance to Invention Work
13. Transportation
14. Dog Training and Carrier Pigeon Work
15. Finance
16. Snabosoaviakhim (supply)

The sections alone do not present the full picture because most of them had several subsections or commissions. Commissions could also be set up by the council to deal with temporary problems and projects.

The republic, oblast, okrug, raion, and other local societies were required to follow the pattern of departmentalization for all the types of work they engaged in. Naturally very few of the member societies had the full array found

[6] *Ustavnoi sbornik soiuza Osoaviakhima SSSR* (Moscow: 1929), p. 41. Hereafter cited as *Ustavnoi sbornik.*

at the Central Council. At the lower levels, too, a limit of nine was placed on the number of personnel per section.

While the sections ostensibly accomplished a great deal of planning and coordination, they were not allowed to deal directly with subordinate organizations. The Osoaviakhim rules were explicit in requiring that instructions and communications of a directive nature be passed down the command line of the secretariat apparatus. Such a restriction of the flow of commands downward through the hierarchy certainly put control in the hands of the *apparatchiki* and indicated the reluctance to rely on the volunteer members on matters of leadership and direction of the voluntary society.

The Revision Commissions (See Chart III.)

Every representative body from the cell's general meeting to the Union congress elected a revision commission to check the scope, nature, and legality of the activities of all Osoaviakhim organizations and personnel. The members of the commission could not at the same time be members of the councils or other bodies of the organization. The revision commissions had a free hand to investigate and observe any meeting or activity at their particular level and lower. If a revision commission fell into dispute with its own council, the next higher revision commission resolved the dispute. Reports were rendered upward through revision commission channels on a periodic basis but were appropriate on any other occasion when a revision commission believed it had a matter worthy of investigation. Reports of irregularities alone were not sufficient. Proposals for remedies also were expected as an appendix to reports of investigations. To encourage and facilitate revision work, the commission's members had extensive rights to attend meetings of its own society's executive organs and, of course, of all the organs, both revision and executive, at subordinate levels of the organization. Revision work, nevertheless, was not spectacular for its success because there were always pressures

rganization of Revision Commissions Below
ie Union Level

Source: *Pervoe vsesoiuznoe soveshchanie revizionnykh*
komissii soiuza Osoaviakhim SSSR (Moscow:
1931). pp. 58-59.

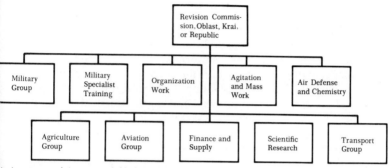

iis nine or ten group design was prescribed for large and well
veloped societies at the oblast, krai, and autonomous republic
el.

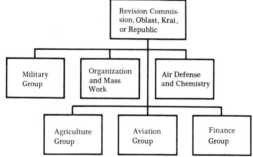

s five or six group design was the alternative for lesser
ast and krai societies and for raions in Moscow, Leningrad,
I Kharkov.

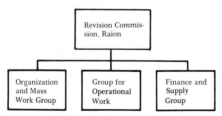

s three group design, primarily for the raion organization,
ld be used at higher levels where personnel available for
ision work were in short supply.

against individuals who tried to take the disinterested revision role in the spirit formally intended.

The Practical Organizations

The "practical organizations" may be viewed as the production units of Osoaviakhim. In them the organizational
inputs of equipment, materials, training facilities and
space, cadre, and rank and file membership came together
to permit the accomplishment of training, recruitment,
and assistance to industry and agriculture, that is, the
broad range of goals Osoaviakhim was meant to achieve.
In practice, especially before the mid-1930's, the names,
structure, and functions of these organizations varied considerably from place to place. Sometimes Society-wide
reorganizations simply changed names without a significant
change following in the organizations. Furthermore, the
region, if it was entirely industrial, had its own particular mix of practical organizations.

The management of the practical organizations fell
directly to the councils and secretaries at each level in
the Osoaviakhim hierarchy, or to the buro at the cell level.
(See Chart IV.) The staff work, the planning, and the
general coordination for any council's practical organizations were ostensibly the tasks of the sections of the council. For the sections to deal with practical work at a lower
council's level, they had to work entirely through the
secretariat, a control feature that made it necessary, especially at the higher levels, for the secretariat to have
staff "departments" analogous to the sections of the council
with respect to functional interests.[7]

Before describing the typical practical organizations,
some general observations are helpful in understanding
their distribution throughout the hierarchy. First, the cells
were expected to have numerous practical organizations.

[7] *Ibid.*, pp. 19, 33. The rules for the RSFSR, as well as for
the Union, make it clear that "Sections and commissions . . .
effect communications with the local organizations only
through the secretariat."

rganization of the Council and Secretariat Staffs

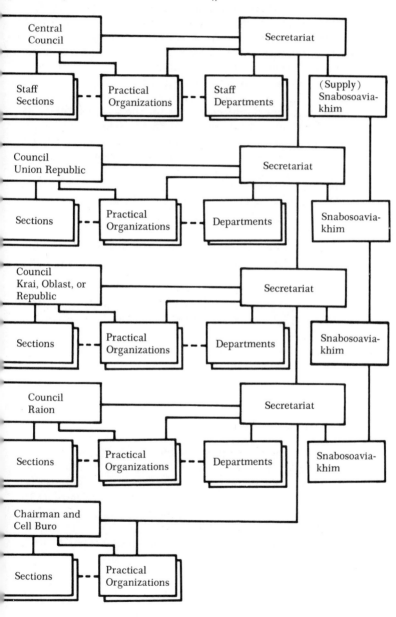

The mass of the membership was at the cell level; the bulk of work, therefore, had to be done at that level. The actual number of practical organizations at higher levels, especially above the raion, was not intended to be great. Second, the training and technical level of practical organizations sponsored by cell and raion was quite elementary. The oblast and republican councils sought to establish more advanced and specialized training, to engage in activities that produced cadres for the practical work at the lower levels. Third, land, buildings, rooms, and equipment were essential to the practical organization, but they were not always easily obtainable. Not infrequently at the cell and raion level practical organizations were a joint matter or a sort of "colonization" on some other organization's premises; schools, for example, sporting organizations, civil airfields, factories, territorial militia training points, and Red Army houses were wont to find themselves hosting an Osoaviakhim practical organization. If this *kustarnichestvo* characterized the lower levels, the same was not true at higher levels. In fact, the Society's right to engage in certain commercial activities at the higher levels encouraged an increasing number of distinct Osoaviakhim practical organizations operating as semi-autonomous firms.

The following list of practical organizations begins with the types that were simplest and most common and proceeds to the more complex. It is not complete in that it does not account for all the local innovations that flourished at one time or another, but it does include those that became standardized.

Circles. A small group of members choosing to study a certain topic or specialty was formed into a circle that pursued a series of planned discussions and lessons. The earliest and most numerous of these were circles of military knowledge (KVZ). They could operate with a few pamphlets and a discussion leader in almost any improvised meeting place. Or they could be highly sophisticated, requiring special equipment for teaching advanced courses.

In general the circles served to prepare members for more advanced work and training.

Corners.   Any public place in a factory or institute where wall newspapers were displayed and reading material was available might be used by Osoaviakhim to establish its own display of readings, simple equipment, and charts explaining military, aviation, and chemical matters. Factory clubs, Red Army day rooms, and similar places not infrequently housed Osoaviakhim "corners." The corners were used not only to post technical information but also to solicit new members.

Small-bore ranges.   These were training facilities for marksmanship. They were limited in size and could be constructed in school buildings, in attics, apartment houses, and in any other buildings where fifteen or twenty feet of range distance could be found. In order to use them on a year-round basis, they were normally put inside rather than outdoors.

Teams and detachments.   These were widely employed in air and chemical defense work both as training units and as operational units for the event of war and actual air attacks. The terms were also attached to marksmanship, aviation crop dusting, and pest control. The latter sold their services to collective farms and tried to make a profit to be turned over to the Osoaviakhim treasury.[8]

Training points.   The idea of a network of training points originated in connection with the territorial militia.[9] Osoaviakhim strived for a proliferation of its own training points and also inherited most of those of the militia. They were of a permanent nature, an area of land provided by factories, local soviets, MTS's, and other institutions, equipped with facilities for more advanced kinds of Oso-

[8] *Ustavnoi sbornik,* pp. 99-101.
[9] Frunze, *Izbrannye proizvedeniia,* p. 380.

aviakhim training. Some were fairly elaborate and maintained a staff of Osoaviakhim apparatus workers. Although military training points predominated, chemical, aviation, and naval training points also existed. As Osoaviakhim grew and developed regularity in its activities, the training point became one of the most important practical organizations. Found at the cell level initially, the raions eventually took them over entirely.

Clubs. Sometimes a permanent installation, sometimes simply an organization such as a marksmanship or sport club, the club concept was widely used. In aviation, however, it came to have a very particular form at the oblast and republican levels and embraced a complex array of facilities and activities.

Military stables. Notwithstanding the drive for motorization of all forces, the Soviet commanders believed that horse stock, even cavalry units, would retain a significant role in modern warfare. Certainly horse stock was important in Soviet agriculture. Osoaviakhim, therefore, engaged in the maintenance of military stables in the rural areas. A stable might fall under the control of a village cell or local Osoaviakhim council.

Defense houses. In the same way that the Red Army had developed a net of Red Army houses for education and recreation, Osoaviakhim built its own net of defense houses. They were meant to provide a place for seminars, lectures, films, and general propaganda work. Some were rather elaborate, at least in cost. The Ural organization was rebuked for planning to spend 2,000,000 rubles for a central defense house and was urged to construct several smaller raion defense houses with the same money.[10]

Schools. Only at the higher levels were schools organized. Some were of a permanent nature, for training persons

[10] *Osoaviakhim,* 17-18 (1930), 25.

in specialties such as flying, parachuting, and gliding. Both permanent and temporary schools were used to provide instructors for lower level practical organizations and cadre for the Osoaviakhim apparatus.

Para-military formations.   For more advanced military training, platoons, companies, and battalions were formed from the membership in cities and large industrial areas. Pre-inductees (youth subject to future call to service in the Red Army), veterans of the Red Army, and reserve command staff personnel made up these units. Their activities revolved around the training points and summer camps, and they joined the Red Army for short field exercises in the fall.

Camps.   After the training points became numerous, a net of camps was built near large cities and industrial areas. They provided facilities for more advanced military training but were hailed as combination recreational and military installations.[11] Workers who were members of the Society were encouraged to escape to these outdoor habitats during their vacations in order to enjoy the fresh air, physical training, and sporting activities.[12]

Laboratories and experimental plots.   Because Osoaviakhim was supposed to be spearheading the mastery and implementation of technology in Soviet society, it was appropriate to operate laboratories and experimental plots. The laboratories did not play a wide role, and one gains the impression that they lent more to Osoaviakhim appearances than to substantive work. The use of experimental plots, in contrast, was widespread in the late 1920's; they were used to demonstrate the advantages of chemical fertilizers and crop varieties.[13]

[11] L. Malinovskii, "Zadachi Osoaviakhima," *Voina i revoliutsiia*, 6 (1928), 11.

[12] *Osoaviakhim*, 15 (1930), 8.

[13] *Osoaviakhim*, 17-18 (1930), 4. Over 4,000 such plots existed in 1929.

Enterprises. Osoaviakhim was intended not only to support itself financially but also to contribute to defense sectors of industry, particularly aviation and chemistry. Commercial enterprises were considered among the ways to generate funds.[14] The types and sizes of enterprises varied greatly. The Osoaviakhim publishing house operated on a commercial basis, a practice that provoked complaints from the provincial membership about being forced to pay for Osoaviakhim texts and brochures. An all-union lottery system provided the monies to build and operate assembly plants for light aircraft production.[15] Varieties of enterprises proliferated at lower levels. The rural organizations were encouraged to cultivate "defense hectares" on a profit basis and allowed to keep 70 percent of the net income.[16] Aviation-chemical detachments organized and equipped for crop-dusting and pest control existed in the Ukraine, the North Caucasus, and Central Asia.[17] Collective and state farms contracted with these detachments for their services. Films and spectacles were presented for paid attendance, and numerous other small commercial endeavors took place, not the least of which was the illegal practice of distilling vodka in the name of assistance to chemistry. Many of the permanent practical organizations, training points, camps, and aeroclubs, for example, ran small enterprises such as a pig sty and dairy barn.[18]

With this survey of the component elements kept in mind for reference, let us now consider the pyramidal structure which contained them.

[14] *Ustavnoi sbornik,* p. 13.

[15] *Samolet,* 7 (1932), 9.

[16] *Osoaviakhim v kolkhoze* (Moscow: 1934), p. 152.

[17] See *Samolet,* 10-11 (1932), 1-5, for figures on the extent of this activity. In 1931, 248,900 hectares were reported cleared of pests and insects.

[18] *Samolet,* 2 (1936), 7.

Chapter VIII

The Hierarchy of Societies

General

Organizational jurisdiction in Osoaviakhim was delineated primarily by the "territorial" principle. The notable exception was the society of railroad and water communication workers, which established its network of organizations by the "line" principle. The remainder of Osoaviakhim societies, the large majority, strictly followed the Soviet territorial administrative districting, beginning at the all-union level, following the union republic and autonomous nationality boundaries, and adhering to the local oblast, okrug, and raion (city and rural) administrative divisions at the lower levels. Thus the Union Osoaviakhim shared the formal multi-republican, multi-national federal nature of the USSR. The RSFSR, the Ukraine, Belorussia, and the Transcaucasian republics each formally possessed a separate society within the Union Osoaviakhim. The nationalities within the RSFSR also enjoyed the form of a separate national society, but in the hierarchy these societies tended to rank with those of the krai and oblast level. In 1929, the member societies of the Union numbered 26.[1]

On the face of it, there seems to be no reason why Osoaviakhim could not have been organized on a functional basis or some other territorial pattern, a very appropriate alternative being the military district system (*voennye okrugi*) of the Commissariat of Defense. There are cogent considerations, however, that can be discerned

---

[1] *Osoaviahkim*, 16 (1929), 6.

for the solution that was chosen. First, if a functional division of Osoaviakhim's many tasks had been desired, there would have been little sense in amalgamating the predecessor societies that already enjoyed functional distinction. Implementation of the functional principle would have required further subdivision of ODVF, Dobrokhim, and VNO, not unification into a single society. The Osoaviakhim unification implied integration of organization, not differentiation, and the territorial principle was a logical basis for greater integration.

Second, if the Society was to retain its civil and voluntary character while occupying itself more and more with military activities, structuring it parallel with the Red Army districts would have been politically unwise. There were always some persons who argued that Osoaviakhim ought to abandon its public voluntary work and become simply the military reserve.[2] Symmetry between the Osoaviakhim hierarchy and the military districts might have encouraged such attitudes and perhaps could have led to informal bureaucratic groupings capable of threatening the public voluntary character.

Third, by building the organization along the state and party administrative lines, party supervision of Osoaviakhim was simplified. Responsibility for Osoaviakhim work could more easily and unambiguously be placed on the local party committees and the local soviets. Parallelism with the party also permitted more flexible use of the scarce party cadres. As it turned out, the discretion inherent in such local flexibility was used as often to dodge the responsibility for Osoaviakhim work as it was to insure its efficiency.

The Union Osoaviakhim

It has already been observed that the Union was federal in character. The explicit task of the Union was to unite "activity of separate independent societies of Osoaviakhim

[2] *Itogi IV Plenuma TsS Osoaviakhim* (Moscow: 1933), p. 45. Hereafter cited as *Itogi IV Plenuma*.

. . . by means of compiling and executing a general plan of work . . . assisting the strengthening of defense and aiding aviation and chemical construction through spontaneous public activity."[3] This statement, taken from the rules of the Union, expresses the ambivalent attitude of the leadership of all public voluntary organizations: spontaneity by the public and organizational control are desired at the same time, asked for in the same breath. The Union Osoaviakhim rules make it clear that control was preferred and would be required. On the other hand, a democratic structure for mass spontaneity was also prescribed.

The democratic structure actually amounted to a mechanism for delegating authority upward. Every member society was guaranteed representation in the all-union congress. The congress elected the Central Council, its presidium, and also a revision commission (see Chart I). Theoretically the congress approved all plans and policy decisions, but that right proved impractical to exercise, especially since there were only two congresses convened in the period before World War II.[4] Effectively, authority was surrendered to the Central Council and the presidium. Because the Central Council usually convened only once annually, the presidium was left more or less fully in control of the organization.

To exercise the central authority, the presidium needed administrative structures. The rules permitted it to develop two parallel staffs, one presumably made up of volunteers chosen from the Central Council and augmented with ordinary volunteer members who possessed useful expertise, and another full-time salaried staff, the secretariat. The superior authority of the secretariat staff was never in doubt; in fact, it remained a perennial problem to make the staff sections of the Central Council more than adjuncts of the secretariat and to get volunteers to take responsible roles in them.

[3] *Ustavnoi sbornik*, p. 11.
[4] The rules prescribed bi-annual congresses.

Although this delegation sequence insured the secretariat primacy, the annual plenums of the Central Council, including representatives from all the member societies, amounted to more than lifeless gatherings at which local power was renounced. They were extremely serious affairs, not meant to aggregate factional or local demands, but rather occasions for delivering candid harangues about the problems obstructing program implementation, for proclaiming "decisions" on how to correct dysfunctional behavior, and for morally obligating both the leadership and the mass membership to comply with the decisions taken.[5]

The centralization of authority is also evident from a comparison of the duties and rights of member societies. A member society had only two rights: its representatives could vote in all-union congresses and conferences, and it could withdraw its membership in the Union Osoaviakhim. The right to withdraw, however, was never exercised. At the same time, the Soviet government could arbitrarily liquidate either a member society or the Union Osoaviakhim. In contrast to these hollow rights reserved for the member societies, eight obligations were placed on them. Essentially these obligations amounted to abiding strictly by central directives, rendering extensive information on local activities to the center, and contributing to the Central Council a portion of the funds they raised.

The Republican Societies

The member societies of the Union Osoaviakhim were the republican societies, but they did not all keep step with the Union Osoaviakhim in prescribing their own formal structure. The First All-Union Congress of Osoaviakhim, it will be remembered, served to unify not the republican societies but two separate all-union voluntary societies, Aviakhim and OSO. At the time of the congress, January 1927, it was reported that the republican branches of Aviakhim and OSO were also making resolutions for

[5] In this respect they had something in common with the ancient Russian *zemskii sobor*.

unification similar to those approved at the First All-Union Congress.[6] Resolutions to unify did not mean that the formal structure for the new societies had been fully worked out. If it had been, it did not meet the approval of the Council of People's Commissars. The statutes for Osoaviakhim RSFSR received official endorsement only by October 18, 1928.[7] The Ukraine actually held the lead in this matter. The Ukrainian Council of People's Commissars approved the formal rules in time to have them registered with the NKVD on February 16, 1928.[8] Precisely when the other republics received approval of their rules is not disclosed in the available evidence, but the record of the Ukrainian case made it clear that the Ukrainian rules were the first. By 1935 the seven existing republics had regularized republican societies.[9]

Of the republican rules, only those for Osoaviakhim RSFSR are available. They are in two versions, the initial version of 1928 and a modified version of 1931, which replaced the former. We are obliged, then, to take the Osoaviakhim RSFSR rules as the general republican case for descriptive purposes.

The republican organization was by and large a copy of the Union Osoaviakhim. The congress, the council, the presidium, and the secretariat level were the representative and executive organs. A revision commission for checking and control was found there also. The operational organs, sectors, sections, and commissions mirrored the departmentalization of the Union Osoaviakhim. And they, like their Union counterparts, had to deal with subordinate levels through the apparatus of the secretariat. Supply of materials and equipment was the business of the republican Snabosoaviakhim, which enjoyed the same juridical and commercial bases as Snabosoaviakhim USSR.

The general and specific tasks assigned to the society

[6] *Pravda*, January 25, 1927.   [7] *Ustavnoi sbornik*, p. 22.

[8] *Ibid.*, p. 38.

[9] Boris Leont'ev, *Vooruzhennyi narod* (Moscow: 1936), p. 70.

were for the most part identical with those for the Union. The similarities were to be expected in view of the dictates in the Union rules that member societies make their activities and programs support the all-union plan. The characteristic distinction of the republican rules is greater specificity. For example, the conditions for membership were more discriminating. Fourteen was the minimum age for joining. Persons who had been deprived of voting rights or who had been limited in other rights as the result of criminal court proceedings could not become members. In the 1931 version, this sort of discrimination was more fully spelled out for "class aliens" and their children. The membership dues were clarified according to a progressive income scale.

Guidance for local organizations, krai, province, oblast, uezd, and raion, even for the cells, was provided on matters of procedure and operations, sometimes in detail, sometimes merely adumbrated. Expulsion of a member, for example, was explained as the prerogative of the cell general meeting, and the process of appeal was also elaborated. In contrast, the matter of organizational income, although outlined by category, was more general. Also, the executive and supervisory roles of the intermediate local organs (krai, oblast, raion, etc.) as well as the cell were outlined.

Of particular interest is the requirement that every local organization had to register with the local office of the NKVD and render a considerable amount of information on its size and activity.[10] Formal police monitoring was thus extensive, including even the Osoaviakhim cell. This requirement was not stated in the rules but rather in a law promulgated by the government of the RSFSR for all non-profit societies.

A rather clear picture of the formal structure, goals, and operational procedures can be derived from the republican statutes for Osoaviakhim. This result was intended by the authors because the rules were meant to

[10] *Ustavnoi sbornik*, p. 39.

be read and understood by the majority of the membership, which the leadership had described as culturally
backward. The rules were to guide this mass in organizing
itself to achieve a fairly complex array of aims.

The Local Organizations

In the union republics, local organization followed the
territorial principle down to the cell. In the large societies,
the RSFSR and the Ukraine, four lower levels of local
organizations existed until 1930-31 (see Chart I). The
oblast (and krai) level embraced several okrugs. The
okrugs were divided into raion or volost organizations,
which directly supervised the cells. A reorganization in
1930-31 eliminated the okrug organizational link,[11] but the
oblast and raion links gained importance.

The hierarchy of local organization was not always uniform in the smaller republics. Belorussia's republican society, for example, dealt directly with the raion level and
had no intermediate organizational strata.[12] Although
specific information on Central Asian and Transcaucasian
local structure is very limited, it most likely varied with
the local conditions of the soviets and party structure. The
overwhelming majority of the membership and activity
was at first restricted to the large cities and industrial regions, or, in other words, primarily confined to the RSFSR
and the Ukraine. In the first few years after 1927, then,
their local structure may be said to be typical of most
local organizations.

The single exception to the territorial structure of the
local organizations found in the Osoaviakhim organs was
for railroad and water transport workers. The functional
principle for subordination was deemed more appropriate
because "rail and water transportation is a single organism,"[13] especially from the point of view of defense preparedness, so it was argued. The section for rail and water

[11] *Osoaviakhim*, 23-24 (1930), 14.
[12] *Sputnik Osoaviakhim* (Moscow: 1936), p. 58.
[13] *Ustavnoi sbornik*, p. 42.

transport at the Central Council Osoaviakhim USSR and the Central Council Osoaviakhim RSFSR directly supervised the local organs of the Society that were composed of transport workers. At the oblast level, when such a region had a large transportation center, a transportation section was included in the oblast (krai, province) Osoaviakhim council. Instructions and directives for transport work, nevertheless, came to this section directly from the transportation section of the Central Council of the Union.[14]

Below the RSFSR and oblast level, the line principle applied completely, rail and water transport line organizations being composed of "point" and cell organizations.[15] The training activities of the line organization retained a certain uniqueness as well. The points and cells placed major training emphasis on defense against air and chemical attack on communication routes as well as on methods of hasty repair of bomb damage and restoration of route service during war time.[16]

The Primary Organization

The cell, of course, was the link in the organization that embraced the mass membership. Its size could vary greatly, including as many as two hundred or more members. The minimum number was initially set at three, raised to ten in 1931, and reduced to five in 1936.[17] The "general meeting" of the cell, the gathering of all the membership, elected the executive personnel, who led the cell work, and presumably approved work plans by voting on them.

[14] *Ibid.*, pp. 44-45.   [15] *Ibid.*

[16] M. N. Kuznetsov, *Protivovozdushnaia oborona i protivokhimicheskaia zashchita na zheleznodorozhnom transporte* (Moscow: 1938). This is a textbook on defense of railroads against air and chemical attack which also provides considerable information on the organization of the line, point, and transport cell of Osoaviakhim.

[17] *Ustavnoi sbornik*, p. 49; *Spravochnik aktivista*, p. 87; Leont'ev, *op. cit.*, p. 70.

Larger cells elected a buro in addition, consisting of three to nine members. Large cells also elected a revision commission; but, if they were small, less than fifteen members, a plenipotentiary to the raion revision commission was elected instead.[18]

As reorganization and change took place throughout the 1930's, this cell structure altered slightly and titles were changed (the secretary became the responsible secretary, the cell became the primary organization). Generally the cells were formed on a territorial basis, but as the Five Year Plans got under way, they were shifted everywhere possible to the "production principle." Persons who worked together on the same shift in a factory, on the same brigade on the collective farm, joined the same cell. Having the same schedule of free time and holidays, they could more easily be brought together for the increasingly complex training of degassing teams, rifle squads, air observation teams, and so on.

Initially the cell organization did not include staff sections such as were found at the higher levels. Instead, "deputies" were appointed in large cells to look after particular work specialties. By 1930, however, the staff of the cell was becoming more formalized. A minimum of five sectors of work was required: 1) organization; 2) agitation; 3) military; 4) marksmanship; 5) sponsorship; or in the case of rural cells, chemicalization of agriculture.[19] Persons of appropriate expertise in the community, who were not Osoaviakhim members, could be asked to work with a sector of cell work.

Mass training was done in practical organizations. From 1927 to 1930, they amounted primarily to circles, small bore-ranges, corners, and experimental plots and shops.[20] The circles could be of any type, military, chemical, aviation—a discretion giving the cell considerable flexibility in choosing its posture for operations. Reorganizations modi-

[18] *Ustavnoi sbornik*, pp. 50-52; *Spravochnik aktivista*, pp. 71-79.

[19] *Spravochnik aktivista*, p. 92.

[20] *Ustavnoi sbornik*, p. 56.

fied this mix somewhat in the 1930's, but essentially the practical organizations remained the same.

Membership

Four categories of membership are discernible. First, there was the ordinary member, at least 14 years of age, a voluntary joiner, dues payer, and participant in the Society's activities. The rules of the organization prescribed for him a variety of rights and obligations, the latter outweighing the former in number and scope. Among this kind of membership a special category existed for the more enthusiastic, the *aktiv*. In Osoaviakhim this status was formal. Cells awarded it to individuals with the approval of the general cell meeting in accordance with criteria prescribed by the Central Council.[21] A member, or an entire "collective" of members, could be awarded the status if some unusual feat of work had been accomplished for the Society. The logic of this distinction in membership was clear enough. It was a gambit to split the ranks of the apathetic masses and to generate a source of leadership personnel for expanding or simply continuing operations.

In practice the *aktiv* composed only a small fraction of the general membership and was meant to be exploited in every way possible as instructor cadre. For example, the Zamoskvoretskii raion in 1928 had 323 *aktiv*, all party members. The raion's uncertain count of total membership was 47,000, making the *aktiv* amount to less than one percent of that number.[22]

"Juridical members" composed a third category. All Soviet institutions, firms, trade unions, and public organizations could join Osoaviakhim in this capacity. They paid considerably higher dues and received more limited voting

[21] *Ibid.*, p. 59.

[22] *Otchet o dokhodakh i raskhodakh Zamraisovet Osoaviakhima za vremia s 1 oktiabria 1927 g. po 1 oktiabria 1928 g.* (Moscow: 1929), pp. 8-9.

rights than the individual member.[23] The object of this kind of membership from the Society's viewpoint was to secure greater financial resources, but plants and factories often stood to gain something in return for their contributions. Osoaviakhim brigades were mobilized for shock work to overcome production halts and to help in other ways through donation of their labor on weekends, after regular work hours.[24]

Finally, the salaried workers composed a group that held individual membership but also enjoyed a special status. Although relatively small in numbers, they could be found in the raion councils and training points. The size of this group, its cost in salaries, and its role vis-à-vis the voluntary membership formed a central problem for the organization.

An additional group that enjoyed what might be called adjunct membership deserves mention. Youth not yet 14 years old, the minimum age for ordinary membership, were not neglected. An affiliate society, "The Young Friends of Osoaviakhim," fully managed by Osoaviakhim cells, strived to embrace broad masses of children in its ranks.[25]

Recruitment

Although Osoaviakhim, through its recruitment programs, aimed to include a major part of the population, its recruitment criteria were hardly indiscriminate. The Osoaviakhim rules denied membership, as has already been mentioned, to anyone who had been restricted in his individual rights as a result of a court action as well as anyone who had been deprived of his voting rights. Additionally, members under 18 years of age were not eligible for election to an office or post in the Society. These legal criteria, however, do not disclose far more significant ones which can be gathered from recruiting policies.

[23] *Spravochnik aktivista*, pp. 250-53.
[24] For an example, see *Khimiia i oborona*, 6 (1934), 18-19.
[25] *Spravochinik aktivista*, pp. 199-205. This source includes the rules for "The Young Friends."

Social class was the most general of these and involved several distinctions. In the predecessor societies, little seems to have been said about class in an explicit way. By the 1930's the cries became shriller for class watchfulness and alertness to prevent "right wing opportunism." Spokesmen at the Second All-Union Congress of Osoaviakhim had taken notice of the danger, probably in connection with collectivization difficulties and the factional struggle between Stalin's clique and those sympathetic with Bukharin.[26] The II Plenum of the Central Council in 1931 took resolutions to prevent class aliens from penetrating into the ranks of the apparatus and the *aktiv*.[27] Molotov rebuked the III Plenum in 1932 for, among other things, neglecting the class criterion,[28] and Eideman declared that class vigilance was a *leit motiv* of the IV Plenum.[29] The culmination in the ensuing campaign against class aliens came in the winter of 1935-36, when Stalin ordered an exchange of membership documents for everyone in the Society. The purge of "undesirable elements" was not restricted to class aliens, and it is instructive to notice that "thieves, criminals, and class aliens" are grouped together in Stalin's decrees and are associated with extraordinary levels of financial corruption in the Society. In other words, the class criterion could be used to label anyone pressing his own ends at the expense of the organizational goals. Budennyi's speech to the IV Plenum in 1933 provides a vivid example. A state farm, he declared, lost 833 horses in one summer by working them to death. How to explain such a tragedy? Exactly 192 ex-kulaks worked on the farm. Their presence alone, insisted Budennyi, was responsible. In another place not one of 36 tractors was operative. Why? Two ex-kulaks were found in the local party cell![30]

This, of course, was not the only use of the class criterion. Osoaviakhim leaders remained continually sensi-

[26] *Osoaviakhim*, 17-18 (1930), 4.
[27] *Osoaviakhim na novom etape* (Moscow: 1931), pp. 18-19.
[28] *Khimiia i oborona*, 7 (1932), 1-2.
[29] *Itogi IV Plenuma*, p. 11.   [30] *Ibid.*, pp. 36-37.

tive to the social structure of the membership as a whole. Typical of this attitude is a discussion in 1929 of the necessity to achieve a social mix by the end of 1933 in which the proletarian element would exceed 40 percent.[31] In 1928 it has been only 35 percent, while peasants composed 28 percent of the total. Close watch of the class composition was meant to be facilitated by regular reports from every cell. In 1933 the Central Council standardized the accounting procedure for social composition of the membership by requiring a report every six months from every cell.[32]

The industrial and office worker elements had predominated easily in ODFV and Dobrokhim because these societies had an orientation that was more industrial than military or agricultural. Recruiting also proved easier in urban areas. From the first, therefore, the Society had a strong urban membership profile. But the mass of the Soviet population remained in the village. Osoaviakhim's aspirations to militarize the masses, then, had to include the villages if they were to be realized.

In the rural areas, recruitment followed the collectivization front. Osoaviakhim was meant to help advance that front but, more important, to play a role in consolidating the "socialist sector" of the village. B. Kolesnikov, who specialized in Osoaviakhim rural organization, provided detailed guidance for an "inkspot" recruitment program in the village. The Machine and Tractor Stations were to serve as the inkspot centers. Great care was to be taken to enlist *aktiv* who were unambiguously on the side of the collectivization, and the cell and council leadership had to remain "protected," or controlled, by the MTS citadel.[33] Thus recruitment in the countryside was not an indiscriminate matter of enlisting vast numbers but rather a program for making membership signal an individual's commitment to the regime's policies for social and economic change.

[31] *Osoaviakhim*, 16 (1929), 6.   [32] *Itogi IV Plenuma*, p. 44.
[33] B. Kolesnikov, *Osoaviakhim v derevne* (Moscow: 1933), pp. 44-48.

An implicit bias in Osoaviakhim's recruiting policy was the preference for youth. Certainly, persons of all ages were encouraged to join, but the entanglement with the Komsomol and the responsibility for pre-inductee military training provided a youthful accent to the membership profile.

The Society made explicit the aim of drawing large numbers of women into its ranks. In 1928, 700,000 women composed 17.5 percent of the total membership.[34] The Second All-Union Congress of Osoaviakhim underscored recruitment of females as a high priority task, and a goal of 32 percent was set for 1933 as the portion of women in the Society.[35] As it turned out, only 25 percent was realized.[36] Women could participate in most branches of Osoaviakhim work, even military training, and not a few became pilots and parachutists, as well as international competitors in rifle marksmanship.[37]

The national minorities were a special target for recruitment but not one marked by success. The Red Army had run up against language, cultural, and political obstacles in most of the nationality regions but overcame them significantly only in Belorussia and the Ukraine.[38] Osoaviakhim and its predecessors certainly could not avoid similar barriers in their campaigns to allocate new technical and military skills in those regions. At the First All-Union Congress, representatives from the national minorities complained bitterly and insisted that special programs had

[34] *Spravochnik Osoaviakhima po podgotovke trudiashchikhsia zhenshchin k oborone* (Moscow: 1930), fold out chart without a page number.

[35] *Osoaviakhim*, 17-18 (1930), 31.

[36] Leont'ev, *op. cit.*, p. 33.

[37] See *Spravochnik aktivista*, pp. 261-63, for a list of military duties for which women were trained. See *Osoaviakhim* 17-18 (1930), 30, for examples of women's marksmanship activities.

[38] Sidnev, "Prizyv natsional'nostei," *Voina i revoliutsiia*, 5 and 6 (1927), 113-24; 66-80. This two-part article attempts a comparison of pre-revolutionary and Soviet experience with the national minorities in the military.

to be devised if they were to cope with illiteracy as high as 95 percent in some cases. In no event, they argued, could they be expected to meet the same demands from the center as were placed on the local organizations in other areas.[39] Not a great deal of information is available on the progress Osoaviakhim made in the minority regions, but one may conclude from the resolutions of the VI Plenum of the Central Council (1935) that results disappointed the center. The poor quality of work among national minorities was described as "one of the most serious deficiencies" in the Society.[40] Because minority ethnic groups predominated along much of the Soviet frontier, the regime took a special interest in their loyalty and defense preparedness.[41] But whether or not proportionate results were achieved remains unclear.

Other less general criteria for recruitment might be isolated by studying the available records of local organizations, but those mentioned here suffice to demonstrate that recruitment policies were based on (a) securing a nucleus of *aktiv* for use as cadre, (b) an emphasis on youth, (c) thorough-going political support for the Stalinist programs after 1927 (by worker and rural socialist elements), which frequently meant simply the absence of personal corruption and misappropriation in the local organizations, (d) attracting female membership, and finally (e) drawing people away from traditional cultural patterns by engaging them in the technical and social aspects of modern military requirements.

[39] *Pravda*, January 20, 1927.

[40] *Itogi VI Plenuma*, pp. 51-52.

[41] *Spravochnik aktivista*, pp. 175-181. This handbook goes into some detail about the higher levels of discipline and training expected in the border regions.

Such a society [ODVF] must be linked to the trade unions in a firm manner, to the Commissariat of Education and the local Soviets. . . . Without active and conscious—technical, economic, and military—interest in aviation on the part of the working masses, we can have no serious and lasting success in this area.

Trotsky, *Pravda*, March 4, 1923.

Chapter IX

Linkages with Other Organizations

The Party

Perhaps what has been assumed heretofore about party-Osoaviakhim relations needs to be made explicit. Osoaviakhim could not challenge the party on policy decisions. Party control at the top remained beyond question although every level of Osoaviakhim did not always adhere strictly to the value preferences of the party's central leadership as criteria for organizational and individual behavior. To elaborate this point, we need to review the party values that Osoaviakhim was expected to instill, the party structural relations with Osoaviakhim, and some of the conflicts manifested in the structural relations.

The party elite unanimously placed high value on military power. Quarrels arose only on the question of how to maximize, or at least to satisfy, this value preference in an environment of terribly scarce resources. The party also valued literacy, modern industrial skills, and the habits of disciplined behavior engendered by military training. Osoaviakhim was viewed as a "transmission belt" for realizing these values.

To make certain the transmission belt was fully developed and that it did not remain motionless, party cadres had to have the levers for manipulating the Society. At the Union level, control was implemented just as it was in other institutions in society. Behind the appearance of popular membership representation in the Union congress, the rules permitted the presidium and the secretariat apparatus to monopolize the decision-making and information channels of the Society. The Bolshevik technique of control at the top of non-party institutions has been widely studied and should detain us here only momentarily.[1]

First, concerning the manner in which the mass voluntary societies were established, the pattern for Osoaviakhim and its predecessors followed remarkably the technique, described by Philip Selznick, which non-ruling communist parties use to manipulate "peripheral organizations."[2] What Selznick calls an "initiating nucleus," *Pravda* referred to as "the initiative of a group" for founding ODVF.[3] Initiative groups of party members responded in the Ural, the Ukraine, and elsewhere, taking their cue from Moscow. The chairman, the general secretary, the presidium membership, the chiefs of the staff sections, all such posts were monopolized by party members. The secretariat apparatus of Osoaviakhim was overwhelmingly dominated by party members.[4] Selznick's characterization, however, applies to peripheral organizations that enjoy a sufficient base of popularly shared organizational values to provide most of the energy, funds, and lower level leadership necessary for organizational pursuit of goals. In the Soviet Union, in contrast, where the party enormously hastened efforts in modernization, the base of popularly shared values for Osoaviakhim was inadequate for self-sustained operations. In the social and economic upheavals of the period 1927-1939, individuals were not likely to allocate their scarce income and leisure time to defense activities without strong inducements. If the top of the organization could be held fairly easily to the party's value system, the lower

---

[1] For general studies on Bolshevik rule, see Merle Fainsod, *How Russia is Ruled* (Cambridge: Harvard University Press, 1956); John N. Hazard, *The Soviet System of Government* (3rd ed. rev.; Chicago: The University of Chicago Press, 1964); Leonard Shapiro, *The Communist Party of the Soviet Union* (New York: Random House, 1960).

[2] *The Organizational Weapon* (Glencoe, Ill.: The Free Press, 1960), pp. 114-26.

[3] September 18, 1923.   [4] *Pravda*, January 25, 1927.

echelons could not. There the party faced not a rebellious membership but an apathetic one.

The party links with the lower levels of Osoaviakhim were essentially the same found between the party and the local soviets, the trade unions, schools, enterprises, collective farms, and so on. Party members, to the degree they were available, occupied the key positions down to the cell in some cases. Local party committees presumably provided cadre, such as organizers and instructors, to insure the execution of Osoaviakhim programs. Until 1935 the local party committees retained the discretion as to how many and which of their *apparatchiki* were assigned to voluntary defense work. The most characteristic feature of the local party relationship with Osoaviakhim was disinterest which led to serious neglect. If the party is seen as an aggressive cadre penetrating and dominating all institutions of Soviet society, the image usually portrayed, the case of Osoaviakhim is somewhat anomalous.

Voroshilov told the First All-Union Congress of Osoaviakhim that the party rank and file was "cool" toward the Society.[5] The manifestations of this widespread attitude led to testimony by a fraction of the Central Council of Osoaviakhim before the Bolshevik Central Committee in March 1928. The Central Committee was sufficiently disturbed to issue a decree to all local party committees, "On Osoaviakhim Work."[6] The wording of the decree, nevertheless, suggests that the center either hesitated to put its full authority at stake on the issue or considered it a low priority matter. It went only so far as ". . . to propose to party committees that they assign comrades to work in Osoaviakhim organs who could actually take active part in this work, freeing them from all other kinds of party and public tasks." The party committees took the communication quite literally as only a suggestion. In its report to the XVI Party Congress, the Osoaviakhim delegation complained that the decree of March 19, 1928, had gone largely unheeded.

[5] *Pravda*, January 27, 1927.   [6] L. Borisov, *op. cit.*, p. 42.

The general secretary of the Union Osoaviakhim, L. P. Malinovskii, left no doubt about the seriousness of the problem.[7] He accused local party committees of a general feeling expressed in the guidance one party committee had given to an Osoaviakhim leader upon his complaint of party neglect: "live the best you can—we are not interested in you." Moreover, Malinovskii declared that the view of Osoaviakhim as a "parasite" on the party had to be changed to a perception of it as a lever for public work and socialist construction. He could cite the XV Party Congress's resolution that Osoaviakhim was, in the party elite's view, "one of the most important institutions of Soviet society," not least because it contributed simultaneously to military and civil aspects of socialist construction. Because Osoaviakhim had taken more military responsibility ". . . with the agreement of the military department," local party attention to the Society was not a trivial matter.[8] Yet the local committees everywhere in the USSR were not even wont to check Osoaviakhim compliance with directives from the center. Furthermore, party committees habitually took the active elements from Osoaviakhim, when they appeared there, and moved them to other public work. Cell secretaries were replaced three to

[7] *Osoaviakhim*, 17-18 (1930), 7-10.

[8] Erickson, *op. cit.*, p. 308, concludes that Eideman's assumption of the chairmanship of Osoaviakhim in 1932 meant that the RKKA took "permanent responsibility" for the Society. Insofar as this conclusion implies RKKA control over Osoaviakhim, it is misleading. The military was forced to support with expertise and equipment Osoaviakhim's accretion of the territorial militia's role as a military mobilization base. At the same time, Osoaviakhim retained its own apparatus as well as its formal representative and voluntary character, thereby blocking the aspiration of the military leadership in the mid-1920's to use the policy of "militarization of the entire population" for expanding Red Army influence. The militarization policy was pursued, but control did not reside with the Red Army. Rather the military was forced to play the game by the rules of a mass voluntary society.

five times a year in many cases. The doors of raion council offices were known to be closed for months at a time in the Crimea and the Ukraine, a circumstance primarily due to party committee brigandage of Osoaviakhim leadership.[9]

An article by the deputy chairman of the Union Oso-aviakhim, N. Semashko, preceded Malinovskii's rebuke with many of the same charges but included a report of remedial actions taken by the central committee of the Ukrainian communist party.[10] Nine points of the instructions to local committees demanded assistance to Osoaviakhim, especially in rural areas, and set a date three months hence for progress reports.

The Osoaviakhim press reflected a regular concern with the problem of party reticence to commit time and resources to Osoaviakhim, at least until 1937, when eulogies to Stalin had replaced everything but technical articles. Documents from the Smolensk party archive reveal the genuineness of the problem. In August 1935, a secret decree went to all oblast committees from the Central Committee of the CPSU and the Council of People's Commissars. Signed by Stalin and Chubar, it outlined an extensive reorganization of the Osoaviakhim apparatus, a purge of the entire membership, and some specific instructions on local party committee links with Osoaviakhim. The local committees' discretion in allocating resources and personnel to Osoaviakhim was sharply curtailed. The party's command-line responsibility for voluntary defense work was placed personally on the second secretaries of the krai, oblast, raion, and city party committees. In turn, all chairmen of raion and oblast councils of Osoaviakhim were made "nomenclature" members of the raion and oblast party committees. Osoaviakhim was designated as "the most important form of public work" for the party.[11]

[9] *Osoaviakhim*, 17-18 (1930), 6-7.

[10] *Ibid.*

[11] WKP-186, pp. 210-19. The Smolensk archive is on microfilm. Documents are arranged in folders, each folder having a WKP number. The pages in each folder are numbered in pencil in the order that they were filmed. Professor Fainsod's

The decree makes it clear that the local party officials had ignored Osoaviakhim for years. With collectivization more or less complete and the Second Five Year Plan under way, time had perhaps been found to focus on heretofore neglected endeavors. If the image of war preparations in the West had been overdrawn in the past, Hitler's consolidation of power had given it increasing validity, probably making mass military training a matter of greater priority from Stalin's point of view. There are other reasons, to be discussed later, concerning the progression of bureaucratization in Osoaviakhim, reasons making it unlikely that such instructions could have been even partially heeded by the local party organizations a few years earlier.

As it was, the response to the decree hardly amounted to rapid compliance. The following spring, in 1936, a letter from the Smolensk oblast committee went out to the raion committees complaining of the sluggish reaction. Many raions, it observed caustically, possessed only "paper" Osoaviakhim organizations; where organizations did exist, the purge (exchange of membership cards for all Osoaviakhim members) was being carried out slowly in a "formal manner" rather than in the proper spirit of ridding the Society of unsavory elements.[12]

Two of the raion committee protocols reveal something of the action at the local level. The Medgorodok party committee had planned a conference of Osoaviakhim workers in late July 1936. It did not take place because no preparatory work was done and communists avoided commitment to attend. The committee chairman postponed it until August 13 and made the committee members responsible to spread the news by word of mouth

---

index, located on the first reel, showing where each folder is located in the 67 rolls of microfilm, makes it possible to find a reference when the WKP number and the page are cited.

[12] Columbia University Microfilm T-88, Item No. 921-24, p. 63. This set of three rolls of microfilm contains Smolensk archive materials but is separate from the main group of documents catalogued under T-87.

among party members that they all were obligated to attend.[13] The Upolkomzag party committee discussed Osoaviakhim work several times in January 1937, revealing a picture of disintegration of some cells, serious difficulties with migratory worker membership, and neglect by party members.[14]

This sampling of party records certainly does not justify the generalizations about the Union-wide response to Stalin's decree, but it does indicate that the party center could hardly count on a uniformly vigorous execution of directives at the lowest levels and that in some places no execution took place at all. It must be remembered also that Smolensk had no metropolitan and industrial centers like those around Moscow, Leningrad, the Urals, and in the South, areas where Osoaviakhim first expanded and displayed the most ability to attract favorable attention in the Osoaviakhim press.[15] The Smolensk example perhaps reflects accurately the conditions in the rural regions where the Society had always remained weak.

The Trade Unions

Formally speaking, the trade unions were to use Osoaviakhim as a vehicle for teaching basic military skills to the toiling classes.[16] The Osoaviakhim councils at all levels provided formal representation for the labor unions in the Society. The Central Council of the Union Osoaviakhim always included trade union leaders among its members, and, at times, ordinary workers from factories were added to emphasize the workers' role in the Society.[17] Represen-

[13] WKP-109, pp. 81, 87.   [14] WKP-107, pp. 89, 92, 94.

[15] *Osoaviakhim, Samolet, Khimiia i oborona,* and *Voina i revoliutsiia.*

[16] *Pravda,* June 29, 1927. This was made abundantly clear in an editorial: "In the face of military danger the trade unions will become the mass school of military training of the proletariat." And further, "Build the ranks of Osoaviakhim!"

[17] *Khimiia i oborona,* 7 (1930), 20. Six workers were elected to the presidium of the Central Council at the III Plenum in 1932.

tation was not meant to be used to challenge or alter Osoaviakhim policies, but rather as a moral endorsement by
the trade unions of those policies and as leverage for securing support for Osoaviakhim programs from the workers.
In the first place this meant encouraging workers to join
Osoaviakhim; second, it consisted of contributing money
and physical resources to the Society.

All of the old ideological lore on the military question
for the working class was invoked to justify this kind of
role. The workers had to be masters of military skills on
a mass scale "without break from work." This phrase, used
endlessly in discussing Osoaviakhim programs, had its
origin in the VII Party Congress resolution that justified
a regular army for the exigencies of consolidating Soviet
rule but still maintained that the best army for a workers'
state would be based on military training *"in conditions
near their everyday labor."*[18] Osoaviakhim provided the
practical structure for implementing this concept. The
"healthy" feature of the military training program was, of
course, the alleged bond it forged between the civilian
masses and the Red Army.

Two more interrelated arguments were used to persuade
the trade unions of the value of Osoaviakhim. All of the
Osoaviakhim literature intended for mass consumption
drew a picture of the USSR surrounded by a ring of capitalist states feverishly preparing for war.[19] The most elementary Osoaviakhim military training began with lectures aimed to instill this view of the non-Soviet world.

---

[18] *Vos'moi s"ezd RKP(b)*, Stenographic record (Moscow:
1933), p. 403. Italics in the original.

[19] See *Voina i revoliutsiia*, 2 (February, 1927), 21, for policy
on presenting war threats. An example of the proportion of
fabrication in this image is offered by Voroshilov's speech to
a conference in Leningrad in 1929. He declared that France
had over one million in military voluntary organizations, Italy
over two million, the United States had only 1,896,000, and
Great Britain had 7,788,000. *Stat'i i rechi* (Moscow: 1933),
pp. 297-98.

Second, the nature of modern war, much as Frunze had described it, made two factors urgent. First, the USSR had to build a military industrial base. To achieve this swiftly, manpower could not be idled away in the Red Army. Therefore, workers had to gain military skills as *vnevoiskoviki* (those trained outside regular military formations). Second, not only young males, but the entire population had to be trained for defense against aerial attack.

The trade unions were not always impressed by the cogency of these arguments. Spending preciously short hours of free time in defense training simply did not appeal to workers caught in the swirl of Soviet industrialization programs. Perhaps even more onerous from the view of the union leaders was the requirement to contribute funds for Osoaviakhim support. By 1930, the practice of granting 2 to 4 percent of the trade union cultural fund to Osoaviakhim raion councils became more or less mandatory.[20] A considerable portion of such donations was used to pay the salaries of the secretariat's apparatus, and the Red Army's newspaper did not sweeten this pill by complaining that salaries were far too low in the case of reserve officers serving as raion secretaries.[21] No less did the labor leaders detest the burden of Osoaviakhim membership dues. In the days of Aviakhim and the OSO, labor leaders had directed workers not to pay membership dues.[22]

A few years later, Osoaviakhim officials attributed four kinds of responses to labor unions. A few actually assisted in defense work. Others gave money and stopped at that. Still others remained indifferent to the Society. But there were not a few senior officials who actually impeded Osoaviakhim's programs![23]

The Osoaviakhim general secretary, L. P. Malinovskii,

[20] *Osoaviakhim*, 23-24 (1930), 14.
[21] *Krasnaia zvezda*, September 21, 1929.
[22] See Unshlikht's report to the First Osoaviakhim All-Union Congress, *Pravda*, January 19, 1927.
[23] *Osoaviakhim*, 17-18 (1930), 24.

admitted in 1930 that the quarrel with the labor unions was old and serious but also insisted that it had been finally decided by the exigencies of defense of the only socialist state in a hostile capitalist world.[24] His judgment proved overly sanguine. At the III Plenum of the Central Council of the Union Osoaviakhim in 1932, he found it again necessary to reproach the labor unions' uncooperative attitude and low level of participation.[25] By 1935, however, concern with labor unions had diminished greatly in published materials. In the record of the VI Plenum of the Central Council, held in that year, the only mention of them is in a resolution instructing them in a perfunctory manner to contribute 2 percent of their "means" to Osoaviakhim organs that train primarily workers.[26] Stalin's secret decree on Osoaviakhim in 1935, however, describes the trade unions as having acquiesced on the matter of financial contributions only to avoid wider involvement in defense work.[27] B. Leont'ev, a member of the secretariat apparatus, probably had the words of the decree in mind when he warned unions the following year, 1936, that they were obliged to follow the example of the metal workers and the electrical workers by supporting military training in more than a monetary sense.[28]

The linkage between the trade unions and Osoaviakhim, it seems beyond dispute, amounted to the imposition of a large voluntary organization on the union membership, an organization in which, at least in theory, trade unions could make direct contributions to defense. In reality Osoaviakhim was part of a system for compelling the union members to pay for their own military training. The trade union leadership did not submit to this system easily, but gradually the conflict was being resolved in favor of Osoaviakhim.

[24] *Ibid.*, p. 8.

[25] *Khimiia i oborona*, 7 (1932), 5.

[26] *Rabotu Osoaviakhima—na rel'si bolshevistskoi organizovannosti*, p. 58.

[27] WKP-186, p. 211.

[28] *Vooruzhennyi narod*, p. 44.

The Komsomol

The relation of the Soviet youth organization to Oso-aviakhim formally resembled that of the trade unions. Representation from the Komsomol was found in all the higher councils and, presumably, in all the subordinate councils. As in the case of the trade unions, the mass Komsomol membership was expected to join the defense society. Because of the Komsomol's youthful character, however, much of the membership was subject to obligatory military training and call up for Red Army service. Preparatory training in Osoaviakhim, it followed, was even more imperative for the Komsomolites. Not surprisingly, then, far greater pressure fell on the Komsomol to place its entire membership in Osoaviakhim. The formal exertion of this pressure came in two ways.

First, the Komsomol representation at the First Osoavia-khim All-Union Congress declared full support for the Society.[29] A short time later, a Komsomol Central Committee plenum pledged that 100 percent of the Komsomolites would become members of Osoaviakhim.[30] In fact, the requirement to participate in military training had been placed on the Komsomol as early as 1921, when its fourth congress made it a feature of the Komsomol rules.[31] The Soviet Navy, in particular, was made the object of Komsomol attention, and as the organizational control and discipline improved in the Komsomol, increasing efforts were made to exploit them in a "sponsor" role for military units and to prompt exemplary behavior from Komsomolites in the Red Army and Navy. They were intended to be the moral and spiritual pace-setters in military training. With the advent of the unification of all the voluntary societies in Osoaviakhim and the shift of program emphasis to more rigorous and sophisticated military training, Oso-aviakhim became one more structure in which the Kom-

[29] *Pravda*, January 18, 1927.

[30] *Osoaviakhim*, 17-18 (1930), 10.

[31] Ralph T. Fisher, Jr., *Pattern for Soviet Youth* (New York: Columbia University Press, 1959), p. 98.

somol could fulfill the obligation to participate in military training.

In 1931, at the IX Komsomol Congress, directions for participation in defense work were made more specific and demanding. Membership no longer sufficed. Every Komsomolite had to acquire a military specialty, a skill above the level of Osoaviakhim's elementary military training (e.g., vehicle driver, radio operator, parachutist, machine gunner, etc.).[32] Finally, in 1934, every Komsomolite was required to pass a military-technical test to prove his achievements.[33] Although these measures were intended to compel the Komsomol to become the elite and *aktiv* of Osoaviakhim, they also reflected Osoaviakhim's increasing institutional regularity and its standardization of achievement criteria. In the 1920's, Osoaviakhim simply could not have trained and uniformly tested the entire Komsomol membership.

The second means of urging Komsomol participation involved enticement, or reward. Unshlikht signed an order from the Revvoensovet USSR in December 1928, concerning incentives and privileges for Osoaviakhim members.[34] Anyone completing military circle first- and second-degree courses (second-degree courses included slightly more advanced training) received credit for one month of preinduction training (required for all youth of draft age by the military obligatory service law of September 18, 1925).[35] Those who mastered a military training specialty in addition to basic military skills were promised a direct assignment, upon induction into the Red Army, to a job requiring that specialty with whatever status the job might entail. Those who were serving in the capacity of *vnevoiskoviki* received credit for six months of assembly training (temporary periods on active duty required for *vnevoiskoviki*) if they completed the two degrees of military circle

---

[32] L. Borisov, *op. cit.*, p. 45.

[33] *Komsomol—boevoi drug DOSAAF* (Moscow: 1958), p. 15.

[34] *Ustavnoi sbornik*, pp. 76-77.

[35] See N. F. Kuz'min, *Na strazhe mirovogo truda*, pp. 34-35.

courses. Furthermore, no one participating in military circle training was subject to the Red Army call up in the year of his participation.

Neither obligations nor incentives motivated mass enthusiasm for Osoaviakhim membership. At the Second Osoaviakhim All-Union Congress in 1930, the Komsomol could only claim that 17 percent of its members also belonged to the voluntary defense society.[36] Later in the year, the general secretary of Osoaviakhim, Malinovskii, declared that the Leningrad Komsomol organization had not complied with a single Osoaviakhim directive. A year later, in the case of an Osoaviakhim training point near a Leningrad factory, improvement in the operation had only worsened relations with the local Komsomol leadership. Precisely why this result occurred, however, was not made clear.[37]

The voluntary image of Osoaviakhim's military training was apparently abandoned when Komsomolites availed themselves of the privileges of draft exemption through Osoaviakhim participation. In the Moscow oblast, an okrug council simply submitted a list of absentees from such training to the police.[38]

At the III Plenum (1932) of the Central Council, complaints of Komsomol apathy were still recorded, and at the IV Plenum (1933), the Komsomol secretary general, Kosarev, promised to overcome the low standards set by Komsomolites in Osoaviakhim.[39] At the VI Plenum (1935) critical attention to the Komsomol was mild in comparison with earlier times. Kaganovich did, however, emphasize the Komsomol's role in Osoaviakhim at the XVIII Party Congress in 1938.[40] Like the trade unions, the Komsomol had been entangled in Osoaviakhim, had experienced conflicts, but was hardly able to free itself from Osoaviakhim's

[36] *Osoaviakhim*, 17-18 (1930), 10.

[37] *Osoaviakhim*, 19 (1931), 13.

[38] *Osoaviakhim*, 17-18 (1930), 15.

[39] *Khimiia i oborona*, 6-7 (1933), 16.

[40] N. Markovin, *Osoaviakhim—moguchii rezerv Krasnoi Armii i Flota* (Moscow: 1938), p. 36.

embrace. Both organizations had been forced to supply Osoaviakhim with some of the most essential inputs: members and funds.

The Red Armed Forces

Osoaviakhim ties to the Red Army were of three types. First, high-ranking Red Army officers occupied posts in the organizational hierarchy. Second, every regiment of the Red Army had an Osoaviakhim cell.[41] Third, Osoaviakhim "assistance" to the Red Army brought the two structures together in a variety of activities.

Red Army officers, although always conspicuous on the Central Council, did not predominate there. A study of the membership of the presidium of the Central Council elected in 1932 will demonstrate this. Of all the presidiums, this is the only one for which institutional affiliation has been publicly indicated for all but one member. Of 46 members, five were clearly military officers. Eideman, chairman of the Society, Baranov, and Fishman were officers, although not identified as such. Five members are identified as belonging to the political-military administration of various departments of the armed forces. Belitskii was always associated with a military rank: most likely he was a political officer. Unshlikht, identified with *Gosplan*, had worked in the political-military administration for a number of years and also in the Cheka. Gorshenin, indicated as a member of the Komsomol central committee, was probably a political officer because he later is referred to as a colonel.[42] A total of 16 military and political-military officers, therefore, can be identified, or about one third of the membership. Of these, none could be considered among the most aggressive of the Red Commanders or among the most gifted of the ex-imperial officers. Baranov and Muklevich, Red Commanders associated with Frunze and very active in organizing the Red Air Fleet in the 1920's, were possible exceptions; but

[41] *Osoaviakhim*, 23-24 (1930), 19.
[42] *Samolet*, 2 (1938), 18.

strong personalities such as Tukhachevskii, Yakir, and Uborevich were conspicuously absent. In any event, the membership from the military-political administration, if subtracted from the military faction, takes away half of the military representation.

The picture is not greatly different for the incomplete membership information available on the presidium of 1927. Six officers among 17 members are found, and one of those, Voroshilov, hardly added strength to the military grip on Osoaviakhim. His special relation with Stalin was more important than his military ties. The presidium of 1935 did not add significant names from the military ranks. If one looks for continuity among the military representatives, Eideman, S. S. Kamenev, and the ornamental cavalryman, Budennyi, lasted at least until 1936. Kamenev died in that year. Eideman was shot in 1937. The obscure Komsomol leader, Colonel Gorshenin, became chairman of the presidium by 1938, perhaps in 1937.[43] Red Army control, if judged from this point of view, does not appear to have been a reality.

It would be highly instructive to know the military membership in the secretariat apparatus, but little comprehensive data are available. There is much to suggest that the reserve officers, who had been dropped from the Red Army during the rapid demobilization in 1921-1924, looked upon the lower level apparatus posts as a kind of patronage owed to them by the regime. It is doubtful that they, technically civilians, enhanced Red Army control in Osoaviakhim.[44]

At the top of the apparatus, Eideman was general sec-

[43] *Ibid.*

[44] See *Krasnaia zvezda*, September 7, 1929, for an interesting account of what the reserve officers believed they were due. Also see issues for September 10, 17, 19, and 21, 1929 for the variety of roles they were assuming in Osoaviakhim. Voroshilov had opened the door to the reservists at the First All-Union Congress of Osoaviakhim in 1927 by inviting them to participate instead of complaining about not being called up for training. *Pravda*, January 27, 1927.

retary until 1932 when he took the chairmanship of the
Central Council. L. P. Malinovskii, whose articles and
speeches gave him the image of a thoroughgoing Stalinist
apparatchik, took the general secretary post away from
the military. He had been Eideman's deputy secretary
since 1930 in any case. As Osoaviakhim experienced reorganizations and operational change, the articles dictating
new policy in uncompromising, imperative tones did not
come from military figures. They were signed by the professional party elite. N. Semashko, formerly the Commissar of Health, for example, scored the Society sharply in
1930.[45] At the III Plenum of the Central Council (1932),
Molotov gave the opening address, a scathing criticism. All
who followed him tried to maintain a similar tone.[46] Thus
it does not appear that the Red Army retained significant
leverage through the apparatus either.

The old Military Scientific Society cells, as long as they
were composed only of cadre officers—professionals in the
Red Army—enjoyed a modicum of popularity. The attitude
toward opening the cells to civilian mass membership has
been treated earlier in connection with the union of OSO
with Aviakhim. Many of the Red Army officers simply did
not care for mass voluntary organizations. Osoaviakhim,
nevertheless, maintained a network of cells throughout
the regular forces designed to perform two general kinds
of work. First, in the tradition of the VNO, they were to
conduct "military scientific" work. Scientific in this context meant essentially the application of Frederick Taylor's
ideas to problems of operations and training, but the results apparently remained insignificant. A cell secretary
pointed out in a letter to the former VNO journal, *Voina i
revoliutsiia*, that scientific research work made no sense
for the cells, that anything worthy of the name of scientific
rigor was beyond the intellectual level of the persons involved.[47] He received not encouragement but rebuke from
the editors for his well meant candor.

[45] *Osoaviakhim*, 17-18 (1930), 6-8.
[46] *Khimiia i oborona*, 7 (1932), 1-2.
[47] *Voina i revoliutsiia*, 1 (1930), 121-23. One can only be

The second type of work for the cells in the Red Army consisted of training cadres from among its ranks to return at the completion of their obligated army service to the civilian cells and practical organizations of Osoaviakhim. They were a source of *aktiv* that could bring knowledge of the changing technology in the regular forces to military training of the civilian masses. While there must have been some success in this endeavor, it hardly achieved the desired support within the Red Army. The cell of the 192d Infantry Regiment gained notoriety in the pages of *Osoaviakhim* for a year (1930) of inactivity before the "warm summer sun awoke the cell secretary from hibernation"![48] Not a few other cell secretaries, it was reported, also indulged in lengthy hibernations. At the II Plenum of the Central Council in 1931, it was admitted that work in Red Army cells was non-existent in most units.

A word of attention to the journal *Voina i revoliutsiia* is appropriate in connection both with the scientific work and the Red Army's interest in Osoaviakhim. Frunze initiated the publication in 1925 as the central organ of the VNO. Upon the Osoaviakhim unification in 1927, it became an Osoaviakhim journal but retained its professional military orientation. The first editors, Frunze, A. S. Bubnov, S. S. Kamenev, Tukhachevskii, Eideman, Yakir, and Klochko, were men with primarily a professional military interest. Upon Frunze's death, Voroshilov and Unshlikht joined the board of editors, which suggests that Stalin was making sure some of his reliable agents kept abreast of the editorial tone. In 1927, Yakir and Klochko, two of Frunze's aspiring Red Commanders, were dropped. For the first two years of its publication, the journal encouraged a vigorous interest among senior officers in the organizational developments within both the armed forces

---

reminded of Trotsky's strictures to those who insisted on the scientific nature of military affairs in Russia's backward conditions.

[48] *Osoaviakhim*, 23-24 (1930), 19.

and the voluntary defense societies. After the establishment of Osoaviakhim, however, attention to its organizational affairs fell to occasional short articles, finally in the 1930's to no attention at all. The striking change is perhaps indicative of the low level of involvement that senior military figures were allowed in Osoaviakhim policy affairs.

The journal, nonetheless, achieved impressive sophistication in matters of military and political history, strategy, operations, and tactics. Foreign literature received considerable space in reviews, bibliographical articles, and replies. Western military thought, technology, and economic organization obviously provoked keen Soviet interest. Many articles, although marred by religious deference to Marx, Engels, and Lenin, reveal a profound comprehension of many of the dimensions of war and politics that were to characterize the coming world conflagration.

A final point should be made on the role of Osoaviakhim organs in the Red Army and their connection with the larger society. As the modernization of the Red armed forces advanced in the shadow of successes in industrialization—achieving the capacity to provide modern equipment and technology to the military—the sophistication of Osoaviakhim's military work had to keep pace. Ex-Red Army men could alleviate this problem to some degree, but it was decided to detach elements of the regular forces for periods of direct assistance to Osoaviakhim training programs. The military expressed its distaste for this policy by failing to respond in many instances. Such passive resistance reached proportions wide enough to draw personal comment by Stalin in his secret decree of August 1935. He accused district and division commanders of formalism which effectively evaded orders from the Commissariat of Defense to render direct support.[49]

The third type of links between the military and Osoaviakhim includes those arising from Osoaviakhim activities aimed at direct support of the Red Army. For the most part they were not organizational ties but interorgan-

[49] WKP-186, p. 210.

izational points of contact that marked boundaries and overlap. Difficulties arise in defining them with precision because in fact they were not always clear and tended to shift from time to time. At the risk of imposing an image of tidiness that was not real, we can identify first, links and points of contact, and second, the functional boundaries marked by the links and points of contact.

Some of the links have already been mentioned. Men returning from military service were expected to take active roles in Osoaviakhim, especially its military training. The practice of assigning regular units to assist Osoaviakhim training also joined the two structures. Beyond these, other links developed in the practical organizations. The Red Army initially helped train a skeletal cadre of instructors that could meet the increased military training responsibility placed on Osoaviakhim.[50] Moreover, as Osoaviakhim built a larger network of training points and camps, Red Army officers were sought to command the more developed ones, especially the camps.[51] In like manner a network of aviation schools and aeroclubs was created, but the need for aviation instructors could not be met at first by Osoaviakhim cadre training. Flying and parachuting could hardly be taught by eager but ignorant *aktiv*. The Red Air Fleet had to supply both instructors and management for the incipient aviation program in Osoaviakhim.[52]

In 1927 Osoaviakhim began forming para-military units up to battalion in size. The units brought Osoaviakhim and the Red Army together each fall, when they participated in the Red Army district maneuvers. The Osoaviakhim "training formations," as they were called, apparently irritated the Red Army command as much as they allegedly helped. At least the critiques of their performance by cadre officers reveal more the image of a grand melee than of

---

[50] V. Konokotin, "K itogam chetyrekhmesiachnoi vnevoiskovoi podgotovki," *Voina i revoliutsiia*, 1 (1928), 79-85.

[51] *Osoaviakhim*, 21 (1930), 12.

[52] *Krasnaia zvezda*, September 19, 1929.

orderly tactical coordination in the autumn exercises.[53] But the seriousness of the critiques themselves suggests that the training formations were meant to endure.

Finally, Osoaviakhim participated in the annual call up for the Red Army recruits. At the assembly points, Osoaviakhim organizations were expected to agitate and propagandize the inductees, to assist them in entering the military in a proper mood.[54] Apparently the local *voenkomaty* of the Red Army appreciated this aid and sought it. One request in the Iarotsevskii Raion (Western Oblast, Smolensk) is interesting because of the channel through which it was made. The commander of the raion *voenkomat*, a certain Vensiatskii, dispatched a secret letter to the raion party committee asking assistance in the 1929 call up. He wanted to discredit rumors in the region to the effect that military service involved extraordinary hardship; also he wanted the party committee to instruct Osoaviakhim, as well as other organizations, to make the assembly of inductees as attractive and orderly as possible.[55] Perhaps Vensiatskii also dealt directly with Osoaviakhim leaders, but one may infer that he felt the party committee was the effective channel to Osoaviakhim when he wanted to compel it to respond.

The functional boundaries between the military and Osoaviakhim were defined by types of elementary and specialist military training allotted to the voluntary society. From the first, to be sure, the voluntary societies were conceived to straddle the traditional military-civil boundary, but as much as Aviakhim leaned toward the civil-industrial side, OSO leaned toward the military side. Unification of the two societies reinforced the straddle position. The story of Osoaviakhim thereafter is one of increasing encroachment on the military side.

Encroachment took place on two fronts. As new tech-

[53] *Krasnaia zvezda*, September 3, 1929; *Osoaviakhim*, 16 (1929), 8-10; 21 (1930), 3-5.

[54] *Krasnaia zvezda*, October 10, 1929. This source gives an example of how this was well done in one case.

[55] WKP-150, p. 64.

nology was mastered in the military, Osoaviakhim initiated and expanded programs for teaching the newly relevant skills. The most spectacular endeavor in this respect was the network of aviation schools and aeroclubs that trained fliers, technicians, mechanics, and parachutists. On the other front, Osoaviakhim took charge of a large sector of the basic military training that in most other states lies entirely within the sphere of the military establishment. The shift of this responsibility did not always work out smoothly. The support required from the Red Army led to disputes in which Osoaviakhim leaders rejected orders from the Revvoensovet, making it necessary for the military to communicate through the state executive bureaucracy.[56] At its height, Osoaviakhim had effectively replaced the territorial militia system. In the beginning, however, it had neither the organizational capacity nor the membership size to supplant the territorial militia; but by 1934 the Red Army began to dismantle the militia units or convert them into cadre units. Voroshilov signalled the general orientation for the Society's development at the First All-Union Congress of Osoaviakhim in 1927 by underscoring the new priority to be placed on defense work as compared with civil endeavors. His claim that the Society would rapidly increment the state's defense capacity may be viewed as simply a pre-emptive argument against the charge Trotsky, Zinoviev, and Kamenev were making in early 1927 that Stalin's faction had followed a policy leading to serious defects in the already precarious Soviet defense posture, although the series of ensuing Osoaviakhim programs suggests that there was more than a polemical intention behind Voroshilov's remarks.

It will be recalled that the concepts of *vseobuch* and *vnevoiskoviki* for training personnel without regular periods of service in cadre units had already been established as an adjunct to the militia system. Unshlikht's order in December 1928, mentioned earlier, disclosed an implicit policy of shifting *vseobuch*, or pre-inductee training,

[56] *Osoaviakhim*, 21 (1930), 12.

and the *vnevoiskoviki* to Osoaviakhim's area of responsibility. The Red Army had earlier that year conducted four months of training aimed at building an Osoaviakhim instructor cadre able to manage the new responsibility.[57] At the same time, Osoaviakhim was pressing a membership drive to draw in all the reserve officers and ex-Red Army men.[58] In 1930, Unshlikht outlined the direction of this policy in considerable detail.[59] He re-stated the old dilemma in the military question: how should resources be divided between contemporary force structures and what must be allocated to industrialization efforts that promised greater future defense capacity? The only way out, according to Unshlikht, was to keep the large majority of human resources in productive sectors of the economy. The party was implementing its allocation decision through three "links" in the defense establishment: regular forces, the territorial militia, and Osoaviakhim. The last link, he insisted, had to expand its role enormously, draw in the entire population, become the reserve of the Red Army, and supply it not only with fully trained recruits but also with personnel possessing specialist skills. Beyond that, Osoaviakhim had already taken the responsibility for continual retraining of the reserve officers in the new techniques and technology appearing in the Red Army. Unshlikht's article summed up much of the program adopted at the Second All-Union Congress of Osoaviakhim in February 1930.

To support the military training program, the network of training points was expanded to more than 2,000 by 1933.[60] As the number of Osoaviakhim camps also increased, the practice of taking groups away from their jobs in industry for short training periods became widespread.[61] Pilot training, too, had been more and more

[57] Konokotin, *op. cit.*

[58] *Pravda*, January 20, 1927. Unshlikht clarified this goal to the Osoaviakhim congress.

[59] *Pravda*, February 23, 1930.   [60] *Itogi IV Plenuma*, p. 3.

[61] In 1932, 400 camps were operative. B. Leont'ev, *op. cit.*, p. 2.

shifted to conditions that took the student pilot from his place of production work. The only sign of drawing back from the Osoaviakhim expansion program appeared in Stalin's secret decree in 1935.[62] Although defense work, according to Stalin, was to become more central in Osoaviakhim at the expense of civil endeavors, retraining reserve officers and NCO's and any other training requiring the individual to leave his place of employment in the economy was withdrawn from Osoaviakhim and transferred to the responsibility of the military department.

Two judgments about Osoaviakhim's relations with the armed forces seem justified. First, the voluntary society's hierarchy and control mechanisms remained independent of the military and firmly in the hands of the party apparatus even if the party apparatus at the lower levels found little time or interest in using those controls. If Frunze's Red Commanders had truly believed the military could increase its own influence over human and industrial resources by means of the voluntary societies, they were duly disappointed. Their concepts of mass militarization and of the implications of new technology for warfare were not cast aside but rather implemented under party tutelage.

Second, the boundary between the military department and the mass of the population remained very porous, a condition greatly facilitated by Osoaviakhim. In the mass voluntary society a modicum of "military literacy" (*voennaia gramotnost'*) could be imposed on the citizen without taking him into either the regular forces or the militia. At the same time, Osoaviakhim remained the gatekeeper by which citizens entering the regular forces increasingly had to pass.

Relations with other Public Institutions

It should be obvious by now that both the programs and membership structure of Osoaviakhim led to overlap with most major institutions in Soviet society. The state bu-

[62] WKP-186, pp. 210-11.

reaucracy, the school system, as well as all production enterprises were bound to find the defense society active on their physical premises and frequently within their sphere of administrative authority. Clashes were almost certain to occur in such circumstances.

Among the departments of the state bureaucracy, Osoaviakhim had formal relations with the People's Commissariats of Internal Affairs (NKVD) and Finance (NARKOMFIN). The Osoaviakhim rules required the Union to coordinate with the NARKOMFIN publication of information in connection with the responsibility for "public accountability."[63] It is obvious from Osoaviakhim periodical literature as well as from the Smolensk party archival material that the central finance offices watched over Osoaviakhim budgeting operations and occasionally made extra funds available for purchase of equipment and training materials.[64] The Osoaviakhim all-union lottery program, a significant source of income, required annual approval by the Council of People's Commissars. The finances, therefore, were controlled and coordinated as far as possible by the state bureaucracy. All Osoaviakhim organizations had to register with the NKVD. Furthermore, all programs, plans, and activities had to be reported in considerable detail to the local office of the NKVD.[65] The relation with the NKVD appears to have been primarily used to insure police veto power. That such control was exercised in a suspicious manner, even to the point of keeping weapons for military training in very limited supply, is indicated by Stalin's secret decree of 1935. At that time, the NKVD was instructed to loosen up its grip where it was impeding mass defense work, especially in rural areas.[66]

In the application of chemical fertilizers in agriculture, an activity begun by Aviakhim, the defense society ran

---

[63] *Ustavnoi sbornik*, p. 20.

[64] WKP-186, pp. 217-18; WKP-149, p. 500. The Roslavl (okrug) Soviet executive committee in 1930, for example, granted 420 rubles of state funds for purchase of gas masks.

[65] *Ustavnoi sbornik*, p. 29.   [66] WKP-186, p. 214.

into opposition from the Commissariat of Agriculture. A speaker at the First All-Union Congress of Osoaviakhim complained that agriculture officials insisted that fertilizer was none of Aviakhim's business.[67] This conflict was at least partially resolved when the Committee for Chemicalization, established in 1928 or 1929, took away from Osoaviakhim some of its operational responsibility.[68] In 1929, however, a deputy commissar of agriculture, a certain Kviring, was made a chairman of the Central Council staff section for chemicalization of industry and agriculture.[69]

The relations with the Commissariat of Education must have involved similar clashes. When Osoaviakhim began taking charge of obligatory military training (*vnevoiskoviki* and pre-inductee), a three-way problem in cooperation arose in the schools. All schools higher than the seven-year level were required to support the obligatory military training program. Two levels of courses, taught in either 120 hours or 180 hours—depending on the type of school—had to be provided. The military department, specifically the *voenkomaty*, supplied instructors and equipment for which the Commissariat of Education had to pay. Osoaviakhim took responsibility for all practical work, exercises, and training not presented formally in the classroom.[70] In an effort to make this multi-institutional system work, the Commissariat of Education placed one full-time worker from its office on an interdepartmental commission at oblast and krai level.[71] Presumably he was to insure coordination of this combined effort throughout an oblast or krai. Difficulties, nonetheless, were not to be evaded so easily in an operation supervised by three agencies. The behavior of a certain Golovanov, a military in-

[67] *Pravda*, January 20, 1927.
[68] *Osoaviakhim*, 17-18 (1930), 4.
[69] *Krasnaia zvezda*, September 27, 1929.
[70] *Spravochnik aktivista*, pp. 216-23; *Krasnaia zvezda*, September 12, 1929.
[71] *Spravochnik aktivista*, p. 222.

structor in the system, suggests the kind of conflicts that were likely to occur.[72] Because instructors were in short supply, Golovanov was able to sell his services to the highest bidder. The teknikums and more sophisticated institutions could afford to exceed the 120 ruble minimum monthly salary for military instructors.[73] Golovanov refused to work in the rural areas or the factory schools as long as teknikums would pay 400 rubles monthly. But that was not the only trouble with the "little dictator," Golovanov. Even in the teknikum, he reportedly obstructed Osoaviakhim endeavors by denying access to weapons and equipment except with his special permission. He insisted on keeping the keys to the equipment room in order to prevent indiscriminate entry. Although the account of this episode did not acknowledge it, maintenance of equipment, especially weapons, was dangerously poor in many cases, and directives to stop such neglect repeatedly came from the highest levels in Osoaviakhim. Golovanov was simply taking advantage of the ambiguities arising from the uncertain division of administrative responsibility and choosing to follow policies in a priority that pleased him. No doubt there were many such Golovanovs.

Factories, plants, and other institutions were no less obliged to share the costs for military training than the schools. The management of a factory was expected to take financial responsibility for the preparedness of its employees. The NARKOMFIN prescribed the amount to be paid into the local program of pre-inductees and *vnevoiskoviki*. In this respect, the plants, factories, and other institutions were involved in a three-way tangle analogous to that of the schools. But they frequently became more deeply involved in Osoaviakhim through juridical membership.

Institutions belonging to the Society in a juridical membership status paid several hundred rubles annual dues above the contributions for obligatory training.[74] The

[72] *Osoaviakhim*, 23-24 (1930), 19.
[73] *Spravochnik aktivista*, p. 223.   [74] *Ibid.*, pp. 251-52.

plants and factories did not always find such contributions unrewarded. Two possibilities existed, at least in principle. Osoaviakhim liked to make a great deal of its contributions to improved work discipline, health, and worker skill levels. Occasional "testimonials" by plant directors praise the educational and character building consequences of Osoaviakhim work among the employees.[75] A second kind of return for the plant director came in the form of free labor. Osoaviakhim shock brigades of workers were formed to help overcome halts, bottlenecks, and breakdowns in plant production.[76] Brigades worked after regular hours and on holidays. Although no evidence has been found that plant managers refused to support Osoaviakhim, one might suspect that they, like the trade union leaders, resented being forced to pay for voluntary defense work. Unlike the union officials, however, they did realize in some cases a return for their contributions, a fact perhaps explaining their apparent acquiescence.

Two intended consequences were realized from the policy of entangling Osoaviakhim with other institutions. The NKVD and NARKOMFIN links helped secure control at the center. Most of the other institutions provided access to resources, namely funds and members. The NARKOMFIN also provided limited financial support. But these consequences were purchased by accepting the dysfunctional behavior arising from ambiguous divisions of administrative responsibility.

[75] For an example see *Osoaviakhim*, 19 (1931), 13.

[76] For example, see *Osoaviakhim*, 19 (1931), 3-5; *Khimiia i oborona*, 6 (1934), 18. The latter source presents an example of how this kind of employment of the Society was expected to respond to control from the Central Council.

Part III
Osoaviakhim as an Economy

Chapter X

Resources—Organizational Inputs

Thus far we have viewed Osoaviakhim as an administrative and social structure. In this and the following section we shall see it as a production organization; that is, an organization taking a set of inputs (land, labor, and capital) and converting it to outputs that are presumably equivalent to attainments of organizational goals.[1]

From the earlier discussion of the considerations leading to the founding of mass defense societies, it is readily apparent that the Soviet leadership was seeking an inexpensive formula for militarization of the society. The old Social Democratic slogan, "an armed people," meaning universal military training "outside the barracks," which ostensibly would dissolve the odious civil-military dichotomy, had economic implications of cheapness that greatly appealed to the Bolsheviks. If acceptable levels of military preparedness could be maintained through a mixed system, a small cadre force structure backed up by vast reserves "outside the barracks," the defense budget could be largely committed to developing the technology for a potentially large motorized military capacity. And if one perceived, as Trotsky did very clearly and as Voroshilov later felt free to admit, that many aspects of military train-

[1] Philip Selznick, "The Foundations of the Theory of Organization," *Complex Organizations*, p. 20. Selznick suggests that organizations may be viewed analytically both as adaptive social structures and as economies.

ing, both skills and personal discipline, were as relevant for a modern industrial labor force as for a motorized army, the mixed system, by embracing a wider portion of the population, was more attractive.

A study of the resources committed to Osoaviakhim discloses how stubbornly the regime struggled to realize the low costs of such a defense policy. Although precise budget data are not available, or only very incomplete, sufficient evidence can be drawn together to suggest some cogent inferences. This can be done by searching out available information on four categories of resources: money, labor, land, and equipment.

Monetary Resources

The Osoaviakhim USSR rules outlined the general sources of finance for the Society's activities:[2]

1) membership dues
2) subsidies and donations from the state, party, and other institutions
3) campaigns for fund raising and lotteries
4) interest on the Society's capital
5) income from enterprises and property

At the cell level, the sources were generally the same:[3]

1) membership dues
2) special collections and donations
3) income from public performances, lectures, and voluntary self-taxation
4) sale of literature and badges

The intermediate levels of the hierarchy, raion, oblast, and republic, had primarily the same prescriptions for income. (See Chart V for an example of a raion council's income.) These general sources were established in 1927-1928, and their general scope remained the same throughout the

[2] *Ustavnoi sbornik*, p. 20.
[3] *Ibid.*, p. 56.

CHART V

Zamoskvoretskii Raion Council, Osoaviakhim: Report of Income

Fiscal Year: October 1, 1927–September 30, 1928
Source: Zamoskvoretskii raionnyi sovet, *Otchet o dokhodakh i raskhodakh Zamraisoveta* (Moscow: 1928), p. 26.

Item	Source of Revenue	Planned		Actual	
		Rubles	*K*	*Rubles*	*K*
	Balance carried forward			1,427	53
1	Membership dues	5,250		6,472	
2	Sale of property			55	50
3	Sale of membership cards	250		408	81
4	Sale of lottery tickets	2,125		1,219	52
5	Sale of jubilee badges	750		564	52
6	Sale of port cigars			31	86
7	Debts paid on membership and other badges			301	75
8	Debts paid on literature	462	50	82	26
9	Films, concerts, spectacles	1,200		4,109	56
10	From doubtful debts	150		102	44
	Totals	10,187	50	14,784	14

1930's, but the proportions and means in each category varied as the organization was built out from the center and as the practical organizations became vital. To the degree possible, of course, all subunits in Osoaviakhim were expected to be financially self-supporting.

Some idea of both the proportion of various sources of income and the fraction of the subsidy from the top, or from the state, can be derived from summary information on the 1929-1930 budgets of the oblast, krai, and republican societies. Of those that rendered complete financial accounts to the Central Council, the sources of income by percentages were:[4]

[4] *Osoaviakhim*, 28-29 (1931), 24-25.

Dues	7.1%
All-Union Lottery	16.3
Supply sales and practical (commercial) activity	28.1
Donations, grants from the Central Council	23.4
Grants from the trade unions and economic firms	18.9
Other	6.2

If donations and grants from the Central Council and "other" are considered sources from "above," or from the state budget, then about 30 percent of the income amounted to state subsidy. But since the Central Council's income was mainly derived from the local societies, it becomes clear that the real percentages from the state budget had to be less than 30 percent. To be sure, the grants to Osoaviakhim from trade unions and economic firms potentially deprived the state of that amount of income and, therefore, were effectively state subsidies. The important point for our analysis is the degree to which transfer of funds for voluntary defense work took place locally as opposed to transfers by way of the state budget. Obviously Osoaviakhim depended for the majority of its financial resources on what could be generated locally. It is instructive, then, to examine each of the local sources in some detail.

Dues were required from every member, both real persons and juridical persons. A small initial sum (20 kopecks in 1928; one ruble in 1936) was paid for joining, and thereafter an annual rate applied for maintenance of membership. In 1928 the dues rate amounted to less than one tenth of one percent of a member's income:[5]

1) Soldiers, farm laborers, unemployed, pioneers, students in trade schools.   .10 rubles
2) Peasants, students with stipends.   .30
3) Workers, office workers, military officers with a monthly income of less than 75 rubles.   .60

[5] *Ustavnoi sbornik*, p. 27.

4) Persons with monthly incomes above
75 rubles.   1.20

In 1929 the third and fourth categories were increased slightly.[6] By 1936 the rates had advanced sharply:[7]

1) Anyone with an income below the
minimum taxable level.   1 ruble
2) All those with monthly incomes up to
300 rubles above the minimum taxable
level.   2
3) All others.   3

It would be misleading, of course, to suggest a precise increase in the real dues rate. The economy experienced inflationary pressures in these years (1927-1936), and the income of industrial workers had been bid up somewhat due to competition in the Soviet labor market. In spite of the diverse conclusions found in the literature on Soviet index numbers during the First and Second Five Year Plans,[8] the rate of increase in dues, especially in the lower categories, of ten and three times (.10 and .30 divided into one ruble) in six or seven years was probably greater than the rise in personal incomes. And the bulk of the membership fell into the lower categories.

Juridical members paid dues at a rate based on the

[6] From .60 rubles to .80 rubles for workers and 1.50 rubles for those with monthly incomes between 75 and 150 rubles. Those with incomes above 150 rubles paid two rubles. *Krasnaia zvezda*, October 1, 1929.

[7] WKP-186, p. 217.

[8] Abram Bergson (ed.), *Soviet Economic Growth* (Evanston, Ill.: Row, Peterson and Company, 1953); A. Bergson, *The Real National Income of Soviet Russia Since 1928* (Cambridge: Harvard University Press, 1961); Alexander Gerschenkron, *A Dollar Index of Soviet Machinery Output, 1927-28 to 1937* (The Rand Corporation, 1951); Naum Jasny, *Soviet Industrialization, 1928-1952* (Chicago: The University of Chicago Press, 1961); Franklyn D. Holzman, *Soviet Taxation* (Cambridge: Harvard University Press, 1962); and others.

CHART VI

Zamoskvoretskii Raion Council, Osoaviakhim: Report of Expenditures

Fiscal Year: October 1, 1927–September 30, 1928
Source: Zamoskvoretskii raionnyi sovet, *Otchet o dokhodakh i raskhodakh Zamraisoveta* (Moscow: 1928), p. 27.

Item	Nature of Expenditure	Planned		Actual	
		Rubles	K	Rubles	K
	General Expenses				
1	Employees' salaries	3,297	96	3,571	27
2	Social insurance and cultural needs	453	37	355	07
3	Office expenses	180		220	92
4	Postal and telegraph	350		388	43
5	Organization and agitation	1,100		911	10
6	Street car fares and travel costs	300		61	94
7	Costs for distribution of lottery tickets	1,030		503	04
8	Housekeeping and utilities	530		529	40
	Expenses by sections and campaigns				
9	Women's section			5	
10	Aviation sport section			172	
11	Organization section			10	
12	Marksmanship section	2,946	17	368	90
13	Chemical and air defense section			45	53
14	Military training section			1,582	31
15	Agitation section			2	75
16	Cost of Komsomol parade			153	28
17	Cost of Defense Week			184	29
18	May First Celebration			6	56
19	Write-off of accountable sums			733	57
	Totals	10,187	50	9,805	36

CHART VII

Percentages of the Funds Retained by Osoaviakhim Cells

Source: *Ustavnoi sbornik; Spravochnik aktivista Osoavia-khima*; and Smolensk Party Archive, WKP-186.

Sources of Income	1928	1931	1936
1. Initiation dues	50%	50%	0%
2. Membership dues	50	35	30
3. Donations, collections	50	100	0
4. Spectacles, performances, lectures, self-tax, and production activities	100	100	100
5. Union lottery	10	12	10
6. Sale of literature and badges	100	100	100
7. Special campaigns	0	0	0
8. Trade union contributions	?	100	100
9. Payment from firms and institutions for military training of employees	N/A	N/A	100

total production of the firm or institution concerned.[9] The precise amounts were negotiated in individual cases with factory or institution directors. This method of deriving contributions directly from firms was supplemented in the mid-1930's with direct grants by such institution employees. In addition, juridical members' dues became limited to sums not greater than 10,000 rubles, and they were usable after 1935 only for designated training activities such as aviation clubs, defense houses, and naval stations.[10]

Osoaviakhim's demonstrated ability to collect dues remained unimpressive. Fifty percent was the usual fraction, varying between town and country, and sometimes falling below one-half on an all-union basis. At the Central Council plenum in April 1928, it was admitted that

[9] *Spravochnik aktivista*, pp. 250-53. A range of corporation rates from 10 to 250 rubles is outlined in this source.
[10] *Itogi VI Plenuma*, p. 50.

CHART VIII

Hierarchical Distribution of Membership Dues

Source: *Ustavnoi sbornik; Spravochnik aktivista Osoavia-khima*; and *Sputnik Osoaviakhima.*

	1928		1931		1936	
	Initiation	Annual	Initiation	Annual	Initiation	Annual
Primary organizations, "Cells"	50%	50%	50%	35%	—	30%
Raion organizations		25		30	30	50
Oblasts, krai, republics, autonomous republics		20		30	30	15
Central Council, Osoaviakhim USSR	50	5	50	5	40	5

only 50 to 60 percent of the members paid dues.[11] In 1932, the Central Council's expert on finances, Loktev, said that some organizations failed to collect as much as 60 to 70 percent of the annual dues. Nizhenovgorod collected only 33 percent in 1931; Leningrad–81 percent; Central Asia–60.7 percent.[12] According to the rules, persons failing to pay dues for six months automatically lost membership. The desire to expand the Society, however, probably worked against the exercise of this regulation. As much can be gathered from Stalin's decree in 1935, which emphasized that no one could be a member without paying dues promptly.[13] Such emphasis was superfluous if the rules were being applied.

The large percentages of members evading payment of

[11] *Ustavnoi sbornik,* p. 4.
[12] *Khimiia i oborna,* 3-4 (1932), 33.
[13] WKP-186, p. 212.

dues is indicative of the vast disorder and irregularities so characteristic of the lowest levels of the organization. But when the severe economic conditions surrounding the individual Soviet consumer during the First Five Year Plan are considered, it is perhaps amazing that half of the membership could be induced to relinquish even petty sums to Osoaviakhim.

Next let us examine income derived from fund-raising campaigns. They were the first and oldest form of income for voluntary defense societies. ODVF's foundation in 1923 had been the excuse for a flurry of campaigns and fund-raising tricks lasting throughout the spring, summer, and fall. One of Trotsky's addresses to the ODVF in its first weeks of expressed concern that no more than a "straw fire" of fund-raising activity would come of the plans for organizing mass military training and educational work.[14] Although Trotsky's fears were not realized, public collections and special purpose fund drives remained an important source of income.

The annual All-Union Lottery, begun in 1927 and continued without interruption, was extremely successful. It produced a net income of 1,500,000 rubles in 1929.[15] After announcing the very precise figure, 10,726,566 rubles, as the lottery income in 1931, the Union Osoaviakhim set a target of 50,000,000 rubles for 1932.[16] In 1935 the lottery produced 70,000,000 rubles, a sum larger than the entire Union Osoaviakhim budget for 1931 (55,400,-000 rubles).[17] The largest share of the proceeds of the lottery went to the Central Council, 59 percent in 1931. Cells kept 10-12 percent; raion councils took 18 percent; and 11 percent was left for the oblast level.[18]

There were also special-purpose funds. The dirigible fund provides an example. By the end of 1931, it amounted to more than 17,000,000 rubles.[19] This sum was broken

---

[14] *KVR*, Vol. 3, Bk. 2, p. 182.
[15] *Osoaviakhim*, 16 (1929), 19.
[16] *Osoaviakhim*, 24 (1931), 1.
[17] *Ibid.*, p. 6.   [18] *Ibid.*, p. 1.
[19] *Osoaviakhim*, 31-32 (1931), 1.

into fractions that were earmarked for dirigibles with specific names, a technique obviously intended to provide the donors with concrete symbols for their sacrifices. When possible, some act by the capitalist world, which could be presented as perfidy and warmongering, was used as the ostensible purpose for donation. The first detachment of airplanes, it will be recalled, was bought by ODVF contributions in 1923 and named "Ultimatum" in mockery of the Curzon ultimatum of May 2, 1923, which expressed British displeasure over Soviet actions in Central Asia.[20]

A similar linking of Osoaviakhim funds and activities directly with particular episodes in Soviet foreign affairs was attempted in June 1927. A special fund, entitled "Our Answer to Chamberlain," was established to buy a squadron of aircraft. Within a few weeks over 11,000,000 rubles were collected.[21] The occasion of the British government withdrawing its *de jure* recognition of the Soviet government was being exploited in this case. In a like manner, 8,000,000 rubles were collected for the Soviet Special Far Eastern Army in 1929 and 1930. Trouble with China in the summer of 1929 provided the ostensible motivation for the several campaigns that yielded this money.[22] From the founding of Osoaviakhim, the rules had allowed for a reserve fund. It came to be called the defense fund and was fed both by budget transfers and by fund drives. By 1931 it amounted to 27,000,000 rubles.[23]

The Union Osoaviakhim was by no means the only level in the hierarchy that could initiate campaigns. All levels, especially the cells and raion councils, were called on repeatedly to execute their own fund drives in support of local Osoaviakhim programs. The lottery, however, remained a Union Osoaviakhim prerogative, and even then

[20] See Fischer, *The Soviets in World Affairs*, I, 433-35, for background on the Curzon note. See Trotsky, *KVR*, Vol. 3, Bk. 2, p. 103, for background on the naming of the airplane detachment and its connection with stimulating domestic concern over Soviet military-technical backwardness.

[21] Borisov, *op. cit.*, p. 41.   [22] *Ibid.*, p. 43.

[23] *Osoaviakhim*, 21 (1931), 13.

it had to be approved anew each year by the Council of People's Commissars.[24]

Sometimes fund drives were coordinated with membership campaigns and concentrated for a few days on an all-union basis. In the summer of 1927, a "Defense Week" was organized, a week of shows, demonstrations, and activities aimed at raising money and membership. In 1930 a ten-day period (*dekada oborony*) was used in the same manner.[25]

Another important source of funds at every level included both "production" and "commercial" activities. The commercial endeavors varied almost as widely as the imaginations of the local and central leaders but can generally be grouped into two types: sale of material *within* Osoaviakhim and sale of goods and services *outside* the organization.

The supply system, embodied in Snabosoaviakhim, operated on the *khozraschet* principle. A local council or cell buro got as much supply as it could purchase with its own funds. Snabosoaviakhim tried to meet its own costs and manage a small profit. But Snabosoaviakhim, as well as the local organizations, was given to the use of contracts with private entrepreneurs in localities where its own apparatus remained weakly developed. At first the leadership in Moscow had vehemently defended such modes of operation. In the debate at the ODVF First Oblast Congress in the Tartar Autonomous Republic in 1924, a local leader, Kononov, complained about having to purchase instructional literature from NEP-men. He even suggested that the money might better be spent on another instructor's salary rather than on pamphlets in the Russian language, which Tartars could not read. Ganeev, an *apparatchik* from Moscow, answered that the Society's press operated on the principle of *khozraschet* (presumably a virtue) and that the commercial system of distribution was necessary in order to force the oblast society to overcome its indebted-

[24] *Ustavnoi sbornik*, pp. 131, 151.
[25] Borisov, *op. cit.*, p. 44.

ness.[26] The practice of making users pay for all literature endured after all the NEP-men had disappeared. In fact, the sale of literature for a profit at every level reflected a fraction of the budgetary receipts.[27]

Commercial endeavors of greater importance were those selling services outside Osoaviakhim, because they produced more income. It is impossible to know and list every type of enterprise, but a few examples will reveal their nature and general extent.

Chemical-aviation detachments performed rodent and insect control for collective and state farms on a contract basis. Profits were limited to 20 percent but the detachments were not supposed to operate at a loss.[28] In the matter of insect control, Osoaviakhim expanded the area maintained from over 10 million hectares in 1927 to 248 million in 1932.[29]

Another enterprise, one peculiar to rural organizations, was the system of "defense hectares." Some state and collective farms set aside a few hectares of arable land to be cultivated entirely by Osoaviakhim personnel. The local cell and raion organizations retained as much as 60-70 percent of the income from the produce.[30] By 1932, over 400,000 hectares of grain land had been placed in cultivation by Osoaviakhim cells.[31]

[26] Pervyi oblastnoi s"ezd ODVF, Tatrespubliki (Kazan: 1924), pp. 36, 41.

[27] Otchet o dokhodakh i raskhodakh Zamraisoveta Osoaviakhim, p. 26. The source shows the planned and realized receipts on literature sales for 1927-28. See Osoaviakhim, 17-18 (1930), 1; and 3-4 (1932), inside the front cover, for examples of instructions to cells for purchase and sale of journals. Spravochnik Osoaviakhim po podgotovke trudiashchikhsia zhenshchin k oborone, pp. 117-25. This provides a price list for Osoviakhim materials and texts.

[28] Ustavnoi sbornik, pp. 99-103.

[29] Samolet, 10-11 (1932), 1-5.

[30] Osoaviakhim v kolkhoze, p. 152.

[31] Osoaviakhim, 21 (1931), 13. This figure was a projection

Osoaviakhim production efforts in the cities retained some of the character of the NEP period. All cells and raion councils were permitted to make money from showing slides and films, staging entertainment performances, presenting lectures, exhibits, and so forth, but these activities could be used for educative purposes as well as for sources of income. The spirit of the Osoaviakhim rules was clear in this respect, but the rate of organizational expansion demanded by the center could hardly be supported on such a marginal source of revenue. Many commercial activities, which had nothing to do with defense, were tolerated at first. For example, barbershops, cafes, sewing shops, photograph shops, production of powder, and boot making were typical enterprises. During the First Five Year Plan, the revision commissions throughout the hierarchy were instructed to end all such ventures, to destroy all traces of the "NEP spirit."[32] The action by the revision commissions, nevertheless, hardly snuffed it out. According to Stalin and Chubar in 1935, such commercial activity had flourished regardless, but was to be tolerated no longer. The secret decree to the local party committee in August demanded an abrupt halt to all commercialism except that directly related to defense work.[33]

Financial receipts also came in the form of grants. The Central Council frequently made funds available to the local organizations for special purposes. In the early 1930's, these sums amounted to tens of millions of rubles for construction of training facilities. The Society's budget for 1932 set aside 42,000,000 rubles for construction alone.[34]

Naturally most transfers of funds from the center to local organizations were made for special purposes and

---

based on land already committed. In 1931, 400,000 hectares were harvested.

[32] *Pervoe vsesoiuznoe soveshchanie revizionnykh komissii soiuza Osoaviakhima SSSR, 1931 g.* (Moscow: 1931), p. 28. Hereafter cited as *Pervoe vsesoiuznoe.*

[33] WKP-186, pp. 212-16.

[34] See *Osoaviakhim*, 28-29 (1931), 5.

amounted not to income for the Society as a whole but simply reallocation of income within the organization. To the local leaders, nevertheless, such money looked like income, and many of them incurred debts in the belief that the center would always provide the necessary subsidies.[35]

The degree to which the state put funds at Osoaviakhim's disposal is not known, and the information on the Central Council's budget is too limited for precise estimates. It is, nonetheless, possible to argue that direct budget transfers were small. Two reasons encourage this conclusion. First, the ethos the party desired to encourage in the voluntary societies was one of thrift, self-sufficiency, and ingenuity both in technical innovations and in finding resources. To put large sums in Osoaviakhim's account would have undermined this aim and exacerbated the problem of finance discipline. Second, larger and larger sums of money were falling into Osoaviakhim's hands directly from factory and plant budgets. The labor unions always were supposed to donate 2 or 4 percent of their cultural fund and later 2 percent of their entire income to Osoaviakhim military training. As the responsibility for *vseobuch* and *vnevoiskoviki* was transferred to Osoaviakhim, and as the local organizations developed the facilities to carry out such training on a large scale, many institutions such as factories, public organizations, and cooperatives made yearly grants to Osoaviakhim for military training of those among their employees who were subject to *vseobuch* and *vnevoiskovaia podgotovka*.[36] Also, local Soviet organs helped pay for water, electricity, and other utilities required in Osoaviakhim training points, camps, and other installations.[37] There was, therefore, a considerable flow

[35] *Pervoe vsesoiuznoe*, p. 28; *Khimiia i oborona*, 3-4 (1932), 33. Loktev, the financial expert for Osoaviakhim, complained frequently of this local "dependency" attitude toward the center.

[36] WKP-186, p. 217. The NARKOMFIN supervised the terms of these transfers.

[37] *Ibid.*, p. 219.

of funds from public and economic institutions laterally to Osoaviakhim organs. It seems the central leadership preferred this arrangement to one of handling the transfer at the level of the state budget and the Central Council of Osoaviakhim.

Exceptions did exist. Pilot training only began on a significant scale in the 1930's. As the system of aviation schools changed to a network of "clubs," the center took more financial responsibility for pilot training.[38] By 1938 the aviation training finances were entirely controlled by the center with little or no dependency on local contributions.[39]

Members as Labor and Raw Material

Members were Osoaviakhim's major source of labor. Criteria and patterns of recruitment have already been discussed, but a few more remarks can be made from the viewpoint of members as "labor inputs" and as "goods in process."

First, recruiting was perhaps the Society's most important resource procurement activity. The success of the organization depended on bringing millions of people into Osoaviakhim's ranks. As raw material, the member potentially brought with him a capacity to pay dues, to be a subject of the Society's training programs, and, if successful in training, to become an *aktivist*, an instructor, a cadreman of one kind or another. In these latter roles he is more accurately classified as labor. Furthermore, he could use his free evenings and holidays to work on Osoaviakhim projects: building training points, camps, and working in shock brigades that tried to expedite chemical, aviation, and defense industrial production. When he was not engaged in this sort of labor contribution (by way of *subbotniki*, a term referring to holidays spent working for no wages), he could revert to the role of "goods in process" by acquiring skills through the training programs which

[38] *Ibid.*, p. 217.
[39] *Samolet*, 2 (1938), p. 19.

would increase his skill as a modern industrial or agricultural worker as well as a modern soldier.

Naturally, every Soviet citizen was not an equivalent unit. Youths were preferable to the aged, the urban worker worth more than the peasant, especially the non-collectivized peasant. Priorities in recruiting reflected these preferences. The Komsomolite and trade union member became the primary recruiting targets. In the village the MTS membership, then the collectivized peasants were sought. Everywhere the veterans of Red Army service were looked upon as the most promising source of Osoaviakhim *aktiv* and instructor cadres. The military section of the Nizhegorodskii Province Osoaviakhim Council, for example, was tediously explicit in a free (sic!) brochure on the matter of reserve officers as an important element in the Osoaviakhim military program.[40] Perhaps the recruiting preferences for the industrial worker and urban population are evident from the initial strength of the Osoaviakhim organization in the urban regions, but one must not overlook the fact that this was partly a reflection of the difficulties in building the organization in the remote rural areas and the relative ease with which the city population could be coerced to join. The ODVF membership in Kazan and the surrounding territory provides an example. While the city organization had 210 cells and 25,799 members, the canton towns (*kantonie goroda*) and the villages added only 10,000 more members.[41] In the Western Siberian Krai, an Osoaviakhim congress in 1931 reported a doubling of membership to 360,000, but at the same time it was admitted that little progress had been made in the socialist sector of the village.[42] The Western Oblast (Smo-

[40] *Voennaia sektsiia, Nizhegorodskogo gubernskogo soveta Osoaviakhima: Osnovnye tekushchie zadachi po voennoi podgotovke* (N-Novgorod: 1929), pp. 1, 11-15. Hereafter cited as *Osnovnye tekushchie zadachi*.

[41] *Pervyi oblastnoi s"ezd ODVF, Tatrespubliki*, p. 26.

[42] *Sbornik reshenii I(III) kraevogo s"ezda Osoaviakhima Zapadnoi Sibiri (25-29 aprelia 1931 g.)* (Novosibirsk: 1931), pp. 11-13.

lensk) as late as 1936 had only a very limited membership in the rural areas.[43]

Recruitment for the Society at large naturally became the main operational concern during the first years of the Society. Until large numbers of members were drawn into the organization's control, the scope of all other activity had to remain limited. A Soviet student of Osoaviakhim's development declares that membership drives, propaganda, and fund raising were the major activities until 1929-1931, giving the Society at first only an agitational character.[44] There is some truth in this. A reorganization was undertaken in 1930-1931 to improve the administration at the local level, but the naked agitational feature hardly receded with respect to recruiting.

In 1929, the following control figures for the First Five Year Plan were advanced:[45]

1928	4,000,000
1929	5,000,000
1930	6,150,000
1931	7,450,000
1932	8,900,000
1933	10,000,000

By 1930 the control figures had been revised upward:[46]

1930	6,755,000
1931	9,030,000
1932	12,300,000
1933	17,000,000

The leadership remained worried about the social composition and strove to increase the proportion of workers in the Society. Chart IX shows the percentages of peasants

[43] Columbia Microfilm, T88, Serial 1, Item No. RS921-924, p. 63. A secret letter to the raion committees bitterly decried the falsification of rural recruiting results and programs for Osoaviakhim work.

[44] Borisov, *op. cit.*, p. 41.

[45] *Osoaviakhim*, 16 (1929), 6.

[46] *Osoaviakhim*, 17-18 (1930), 31.

and workers for 1929 and 1931 as well as the proportions planned for 1933. Actually, the peasantry was showing a slight gain by 1931, but as the collectivization program succeeded, and the entire population was embraced by socialism, the peasant-worker dichotomy became less

CHART IX

Social Structure of Osoaviakhim

Sources: *Osoaviakhim* 16 (1929) and 17-18 (1930); *Spravochnik aktivista.*

Social Class	1928 (actual)	1931 (actual)	1933 (planned)
Workers	35%	35%	41%
Peasants	28	34	35
White collar or office workers	26	17	9
Others, including students	11	14	15
Percentage of the total membership which was military	8.5%		2.5%
Percentage of the total membership which was female	17.5%		32% (Never realized)

meaningful. After all, the entire population was Osoaviakhim's appropriate concern if the entire Soviet population was to be militarized.

The First Five Year Plan goals for Osoaviakhim recruitment included raising the fraction of the total population in its ranks from 2.6 percent to 6.2 percent. About 50 percent of all workers in the USSR were to be recruited. The number of women was to be increased from 17.5 percent to 27 percent. Although military membership was to rise in real numbers, the percentage was expected to drop from 6.5 to 4 percent.[47]

In 1928 only 25 percent of the membership was report-

[47] *Osoaviakhim*, 16 (1929), 6.

edly engaged in Osoaviakhim practical work, that is, training circles and the like. It was planned to maintain at least
that level during the rapid membership expansion.[48] Most
of the remaining 75 percent, however, was expected to
be involved in the agitational and propaganda work of the
cells.

All did not proceed according to plan. At the III Plenum
of the Central Council in 1932, the Society boasted that
12,000,000 members were in its ranks. With vitriolic candor the Osoaviakhim USSR Chairman, Eideman, told the
plenum that the membership figure was illusory.[49] Investigations revealed, he declared, that it was 50 or 60 percent
larger than the effective membership, and that the most
optimistic accounting allowed for only 7 to 8,000,000.
Three years later Stalin and Chubar criticized the reported
figure of 13,000,000 members in metaphorical language
designed to implement a complete exchange of individual
membership cards—in other words, a purge of the Society.
They described the figure as "swollen with moisture,"
"overblown," and simply a "paper figure."[50]

Regardless of the misleading nature of the membership
figures, the Society maintained steady growth in numbers.
The only occasion of an absolute decrease in membership
was in 1927 when the predecessor organizations were combined to form Osoaviakhim.

Land and Installations

Although these resources might seem negligible or obtainable by state edict, the case was often otherwise.

The problem of space for practical organizations was
especially acute in the period of the First Five Year Plan.
Study circles certainly could not accomplish all of the
educational objectives of Osoaviakhim programs. Marksmanship training required ranges; small tactical exercises
required open spaces; aviation and gliding required land-
ing fields.

[48] *Ibid.*   [49] *Osoaviakhim,* 7-8 (1932), 5-12.
[50] WKP-186, p. 210.

Reports of conflict over the control of rooms, buildings, and grounds for Osoaviakhim programs can be found occasionally in Osoaviakhim journals. In Leningrad, for example, the trade unions at one factory had taken over the rooms originally allocated for Osoaviakhim circles.[51] Similar occurrences were reported from Moscow.[52] Speaking to the First All-Union Conference of Revision Commissions, the specialist on revision work, Tsernes, declared that many local organizations of the Society had not yet learned to fight for their share of the "means" from the trade unions, schools, and factory management.[53]

One aspect of acquisition of land and facilities by Osoaviakhim remains unclear but of some interest. The concept of "training points"—locations equipped to support intensively scheduled and more sophisticated military training—apparently originated in the territorial militia system. Frunze had desired sites for militia training down to company level, particularly for pre-inductee training (*vseobuch*). He reported to the III Congress of Soviets, May 1925, that about 4,500 training points had been constructed, too few to meet the territorial needs.[54] As Osoaviakhim took responsibility for pre-inductee training, it may have also received control of some territorial militia training points. If this was so, the number must have been small because Eideman reported that the Osoaviakhim net of training points in 1933 had only reached 2,000.[55] In one case at least, the military department turned over property to Osoaviakhim. The Nizh-gnilovskii airdrome near Rostov, formerly a military airfield, became the location of an Osoaviakhim aviation school.[56]

The construction program, begun in 1928 and pressed at a furious pace until the mid-1930's, was the most fundamental aspect of land and installation inputs for the Society. It moved forward on three general fronts, construc-

[51] *Osoaviakhim*, 19 (1931), 13. See *Osoaviakhim*, 17-18 (1930), 14, for a report of this as a general problem.
[52] *Osoaviakhim*, 19 (1931), 14.
[53] *Pervoe vsesoiuznoe*, p. 27.
[54] *Izbrannye proizvedeniia*, p. 427.
[55] *Itogi IV Plenuma*, p. 3.   [56] *Samolet*, 1 (1932), 10.

tion for military training facilities, for aviation training, and for chemical and air defense work. The military construction program received the strongest impetus, followed by the aviation network and installations for chemical and air defense work, the last always being the "weak sector" in Osoaviakhim's overall program.[57]

The military program had the aim of providing a net of training points and camps at which most of the Society's military training would take place. Training points operated year round, while camps, fewer in number but more elaborate in size and facilities, became the sites for summer training and periodic assemblies of Osoaviakhim military formations.[58] An allied facility for general use by the Society, especially for mass propaganda work, was the net of defense houses. They were built first in urban areas, then in smaller towns and cities.

The aviation program was tied to aviation schools. These installations housed facilities for all aspects of aviation training to include gliding, pilot training, parachuting, and technician and mechanic training. In a reorganization in the 1930's, they were renamed aeroclubs, but the installations remained essentially the same. A system of ancillary installations, gliding stations, and parachute towers was wider spread, but the core of the aviation program remained the aviation schools (aeroclubs).[59]

Chemical and air defense work failed to advance beyond the level of "circle" training until 1933, when stric-

[57] See *Khimiia i oborona*, 15-16 (1932), 1-2, for a discussion of the lag in chemical work.

[58] See L. P. Malinovskii, "Zadachi Osoaviakhima po voennoi podgotovke v letnii period," *Voina i revoliutsiia*, 6 (1928), 3-12; and S. M. Belitskii, "Boevaia podgotovka Osoaviakhima," *Voina i revoliutsiia*, 8-9 (1932), 144-49. These articles outline in brief form the development of fixed installations for military training. Also see N. Markovin, *Osoaviakhim—moguchii rezerv Krasnoi Armii i Flota*, pp. 26-29, for a later account, describing the completed system.

[59] For the outlines of the development of aviation installations, see *Samolet*, 10-11 (1932), 2-4; 9 (1936), 1; 2 (1938), 18-19.

tures from above called for more advanced programs. The earlier enthusiasm over pest control work and fertilizer applications did not suffice to appease the center. The problem for the chemical and air defense work was not so much construction of facilities as it was the creation and operation of chemical and air defense staff sectors on Osoaviakhim councils, especially at the raion level.[60] Most formal training could be conducted at the military training points, but there was some construction of special chemical training points.[61] In the late 1930's, Osoaviakhim began attempts to build a network of Air Observation, Notification, and Communication Points (VNOS).[62] No evidence exists to judge how extensively the system was developed.

A general impression of the physical scope of the construction programs can be obtained from the following incomplete figures. They reflect the growth trends in installations of the key types, types on which most of the training programs depended:[63]

| | Years | | | | | | | |
	1928	1929	1930	1931	1932	1933	1934	193
Training points				500	1,071	2,000		
Camps	none			176	400			
Aviation schools	2	4	8	27	29	33		15
(Aeroclubs, 1936)								
Defense Houses		65	100	278		2,000 (planned, probably not achieved		

[60] See *Khimiia i oborona*, 6 (1934), 19-21, for the results of a broad investigation into local work in chemistry and air defense.

[61] *Itogi IV Plenuma*, p. 3.

[62] E. F. Burche, *Kak raspoznavat' vozdushnogo vraga* (Moscow: 1937), pp. 11-19. This volume explains the desired system of aerial warning installations for the border regions, rail lines, and major cities, and provides details on the equipment used in standard installations.

[63] Leont'ev, *op. cit.*, pp. 13-14, 24; *Osoaviakhim*, 17-18 (1930), 25-26; *Samolet*, 9 (1932), 1; *Pervoe vsesoiuznoe*, p. 22.

To be sure, many other installations are not accounted for here. The construction plan, as discussed in 1931, envisaged naval stations, gas and bomb shelters, ranges, stables, warehouses, and even living quarters for Osoaviakhim *apparatchiki*. No figures, however, are available for these categories, but one should not expect that, if the figures were on hand, greater exponential trends would appear than those revealed above. In all likelihood, they would be lower because they did not receive as much emphasis in the Osoaviakhim press.

The development of training installations never fully satisfied the leadership's aspirations. This can be inferred from the number of training points, probably the most crucial installation for Osoaviakhim programs in general. One training point in Leningrad had 200 persons on the rolls.[64] Another in Moscow had about 1,000.[65] If the larger number is used as an average, 2,000 training points accommodated 2,000,000 members. Eideman had conservatively set the membership at 7 to 8,000,000 in 1932. Thus there were by no means enough training points to accommodate more than one-fourth of the membership. It is also doubtful that the number of training points greatly increased beyond 2,000. In 1935, in the wake of Stalin's crackdown on the Society, Osoaviakhim was more occupied with consolidating its ranks than with expanding its facilities.

To measure construction by numbers of installations is not to demonstrate fully what was accomplished. Descriptions of the installations themselves can provide a more valid view of their modesty as well as a keener perception of the primitive and improvised character of many of the Society's endeavors.

A training point in Moscow, considered successful in its work, had for indoor facilities a few rooms of the "House of Peasants." A rotating guard detail of five members secured the point when it was inoperative. The inventory of equipment, other than graphic aids and literature, included

[64] *Osoaviakhim*, 19 (1931), 13.
[65] *Ibid.*, p. 14.

two machine guns and 337 rifles of World War I vintage.[66]

An aeroclub in Podolsk, Moscow Oblast, was much more elaborate. In 1935 it had the following material:

one glider hangar
gliders (number not given)
three wooden houses
one parachute tower
one garage
one stable
one cow barn
one pig sty
one tractor
two trucks
12 hectares of grain
two horses
10 cows
12 calves
nine pigs

On a budget of 180,000 rubles and with a full-time salaried staff of 47 persons, the club trained 202 glider pilots and 28 parachutists in 1935. Over half the budget went to salaries for the staff.[67] The agricultural items give some notion of the mix of resources used by Osoaviakhim practical organizations to support programs by their own "means" (*sredstva*).

Equipment

Part of the apparatus, Snabosoaviakhim, formally retained the responsibility to provide equipment for activities that could not be found locally or fabricated by the users. The evidence on supply of equipment is sparse, largely found in complaints about shortages, but some significant outlines are discernible.

First, Snabosoaviakhim was notoriously poor in performing its role. It suffered from an insufficiently developed net

[66] *Ibid.*   [67] *Samolet*, 2 (1936), 7-8.

of distribution points at first and also attracted profiteers, swindlers, embezzlers, and those of the "NEP spirit." Second, equipment of the modern sort simply was not to be found before Soviet military industries acquired the capacity to produce it. Even then it remained difficult for Osoaviakhim to compete with the Red Army in procurement. New small arms, new gas masks, parachutes of the latest design, things of this kind usually found their way into Osoaviakhim after the Red Army had received the lion's share and had developed techniques for training personnel to use them. Another problem with equipment derived from the cultural gap. Poor care of small arms, in particular, caused shortages and frequent breakdowns in marksmanship programs. Finally, Osoaviakhim made unusual efforts in some instances to produce its own equipment in plants owned and managed by the Society. Some examples of these characteristics of equipment supply are instructive.

Even when equipment was in Snabosoaviakhim's possession, it did not always receive appropriate distribution. An *Osoaviakhim* editorial in May 1930 reported that many cells actually had excesses of equipment that other cells sorely lacked.[68] A ludicrous incident occurred in the Ural organization when it was decided to "militarize" hunters with more rifles and ammunition. A requisition was made through the Snabosoaviakhim channels. Promptly the Ural society received 17,000 fishhooks at a cost of 210.10 rubles and 178.50 rubles worth of fishing tackle![69] In chemical work, which received extra attention after 1931, cells were encouraged to telegraph the center when supply deficiencies were totally disrupting programs such as gas mask training.[70] The II Plenum of the Central Council in 1931 found time to enumerate systematically the administrative problems in Snabosoaviakhim and to present recommendations for remedial actions. Lack of planning, in-

---

[68] *Osoaviakhim*, 15 (1930), 1.

[69] *Osoaviakhim*, 23-24 (1930), 19.

[70] *Khimiia i oborona*, 1 (1932), 21.

competent personnel, local obstructionism, poor accounting techniques, and weak central management numbered among the inadequacies. The recommended remedies mainly involved tightening control procedures, planning, and procurement of the most advanced models of equipment.[71]

Rifle supply maintenance remained a serious problem, never completely solved. The woes of shortages, broken sights, and rusted bores were sung loudly in 1929,[72] and Eideman found it still necessary in 1932 to regale the III Plenum about the results of investigations into small arms procurement and maintenance.[73] Dirty weapons, thrown in piles, were found everywhere investigators looked, even in organizations where agitators were shouting "hallelujahs" about "mastery of technology." Some organizations sold their small arms to private citizens, which enraged Eideman. The problem remained sufficiently serious to elicit Stalin's threatening words in 1935.[74]

Unless such proportions of neglect and misappropriation could be stopped, inputs of equipment would contribute little to the achievement of organizational goals. There was good reason to worry because, during the First Five Year Plan, 30 percent of the budget at all levels in the Society was being spent for equipment.[75]

More spectacular but less significant for equipment supply were Osoaviakhim ventures in operating its own factories. A writer in Western Europe, who took cursory note of Osoaviakhim, declared in the late 1930's that its supply was enormous and that the Society had its own industrial plants to insure an abundance.[76] The basis for

[71] *Osoaviakhim na novom etape*, p. 38.

[72] *Osoaviakhim*, 16 (1929), 11.

[73] *Osoaviakhim*, 7-8 (1932), 7.

[74] WKP-186, pp. 210, 214.

[75] *Pervoe vsesoiuznoe*, p. 47.

[76] N. Basseches, *The Unknown Army* (New York: The Viking Press, 1943), translated by Marion Saerchinger, pp. 162-63.

this assertion was not explained, however, and it was probably an exaggeration.

One notable endeavor, nevertheless, is of interest. The aviation industry apparently was slow in supplying Osoaviakhim with light aircraft. The Society's aviation section took responsibility for supervising the development of a low horsepower motor and an aircraft designed for its own use. In order to expedite output, the aviation section of the Central Council devised a system of "cooperative production." Small plants, capable of producing subassemblies of the aircraft, received contracts from Osoaviakhim. These parts were assembled at plants operated by the Central Council. The first three such assembly plants were built in Leningrad, Moscow, and in the Ukraine. L. Raskin reported on this program in considerable detail but with unwarranted optimism to the III Plenum of the Central Council in 1932.[77] Four years later the scheme was called a failure owing to incompetent management.[78]

A similar venture, ostensibly more fruitful, was the manufacture of gliders. A model costing 300 rubles was designed as the standard type for all glider training. In 1932 plans were made to build plant capacity for 5,000 gliders annually.[79] In that year Osoaviakhim actually built the first glider factory in the USSR and manufactured about 1,000 gliders.[80]

In conclusion it may be noted that Osoaviakhim inputs came from a wide variety of sources and that the policy of making the local organizations pay their own way was vigorously, if not always successfully, pursued. To the degree that it was successful, it forced the population as well as the enterprises and other institutions to grant direct support for defense activities. Whether or not this policy secured defense inputs more efficiently than the al-

[77] *Samolet*, 7 (1932), 9-19.
[78] *Samolet*, 8 (1936), 14-15.
[79] *Samolet*, 1 (1932), 3.
[80] Leont'ev, *op. cit.*, p. 22.

ternative way, through the state budget, cannot be answered; but it does seem fair to conclude that resources were channelled into defense work which the official tax system might not have been able to tap.

Dangers to the center's authority were inherent in allowing local organizations to collect funds and to utilize labor and equipment. A cell or raion council that mobilized its own labor and capital might concurrently exercise a modicum of independence from the center in using this income. Although such organizations could hardly develop the autonomy necessary for challenging the center's policy, that is, for acting as a local interest group, they might well find passive ways to ignore the center's dictates while spending their funds for purposes of their own choosing. More often than not such "localism" took the form of corruption and misappropriation. There is no dearth of evidence in the Osoaviakhim journals to show that corruption was rampant.[81] But there were also legitimate ways to resist the center's policies. Extra persons could be put on the apparatus payroll. Funds could be allocated for construction projects according to local preferences rather than the center's preferences.[82]

It is also important to observe that the amount of resources rose exponentially during the First Five Year Plan. The Central Council's budget was reported as 29,340,000 rubles in 1928-1929; 65,620,000 rubles in 1931; and 120,000,000 rubles in 1932.[83] To be sure, these figures reflect only a small part of the funds actually used in the organization. A total figure would require summing all the local budgets. The trend, nevertheless, is valid for the Society as a whole. Gains in membership and installation construction also amounted to parallel sharp increases between 1928 and 1935.

Whatever the level of inputs, resources alone were not

[81] *Osoaviakhim*, 30 (1931), 10-11. This cites a typical case.

[82] *Osoaviakhim*, 17-18 (1930), 25-26. The Ural organization, for example, chose to build one large defense house rather than several smaller ones.

[83] *Pervoe vsesoiuznoe*, p. 7; *Osoaviakhim*, 21 (1931), 13.

sufficient to insure the kind of outputs desired by the central leadership. That depended entirely on what organizations were able to do with the means at their disposal and the center's capacity to dictate and measure what was done. The ubiquitous "plan" in Soviet society had its place in Osoaviakhim as the device for central control. We must, therefore, examine its special character and role in the defense society.

Chapter XI

The Organizational Process

It was one thing to mobilize resources for Osoaviakhim but quite another to convert them to desired outputs—attainments of organizational goals. The conceptual problems involved in planning and plan execution within the context of an organization can be both vast and complex. Among socialists, some traditionally have assumed that planning in the name of the public interest or for any set of organizational goals is largely an unambiguous task that can be accomplished by all persons who are literate and have mastered arithmetic. Engels brushed the whole matter aside with the phrase, "administration of things," and Lenin initially insisted that the capitalists had worked out all the genuine difficulties and had reduced organizational management to simple accounting procedures. To be sure, a great deal of planning experience has been gained in the Soviet Union since 1917, but the efficiency of Soviet planning is a very uncertain matter. At the same time, the political leadership has repeated a dubious claim to scientific advances in planning methods. Western students of Soviet planning have in turn made cogent arguments for dismissing a great deal of what is implied by these claims, and, more recently, Soviet planners themselves have admitted the need for improved criteria for decision making about programs and allocations.

In order to have a point of reference for describing Osoaviakhim planning and a background against which we can perceive the significance of its description, it is necessary to elucidate a perennial issue that plagues students of economic and political decision-making and that also lies at the root of the ideological distinctions between socialist and capitalist methods of planning and allocation.

The most rigorous development of organizational decision making is found in Western micro-economic theory. The applicability of micro-economic concepts, however, depends in large part on the possibility of finding scarcity prices for all inputs and outputs. Furthermore, the major focus in the development of these concepts has been on finding the *best* or optimum solution for achieving a goal. Soviet rejection of a market pricing mechanism (except in some sectors, the labor market for example) and the concept of scarcity prices in general makes micro-economic theory of limited value for Soviet planners.[1]

The kinds of problems arising in planning for goals whose achievement cannot be tested by the demands of the market place are hardly unique to the Soviet Union. Most institutions of Western governments and many private organizations do not sell their services in a competitive market and therefore face many of the same ambiguities plaguing Soviet planners. It might be argued that, because Western organizations operate within a market economy, they can at least find scarcity prices for most of their inputs, whereas the same is not true in the USSR. In any case, the application of micro-economic theory to public administration has not been widespread even in the West.[2]

If Soviet planners have not employed the most advanced

[1] For excellent studies of the way Soviet firm managers make decisions see Berliner, *Factory and Manager in the USSR*, and David Granick, *Management of the Industrial Firm in the USSR*. For discussion of theoretical and practical problems in macro-planning in the Soviet economy, see Abram Bergson, *The Economics of Soviet Planning* (New Haven: Yale University Press, 1964) and P. J. D. Wiles, *The Political Economy of Communism* (Oxford: Basil Blackwell, 1964).

[2] The so-called McNamara revolution in the U.S. Department of Defense was an effort to introduce such methods.

methods for finding optimum programs, they insist all the more that they have found the *best* programs. This is implicit in the party's claim that its decisions are the scientific results of applied Marxism-Leninism. An examination of Osoaviakhim planning reveals that this is not at all true— perhaps a point that one could surmise without the trouble of research. There is little to be learned from belaboring an obvious conclusion, but a study of Osoaviakhim planning and management has far more instructive possibilities. If the best programs were not necessarily selected, what kind of programs were chosen? Did they have a rational relation to the organizational goals? If so, how was this relation achieved? Were effective methods used for discriminating among acceptable alternative programs? These questions are equally appropriate if asked of public organizations in most political systems because few such organizations can evaluate their outputs in scarcity prices. Thus it makes sense to place the analysis of Osoaviakhim planning and program execution in the context of a general theory of organizational decision-making in order to discover more about the comparative rationality of Osoaviakhim methods and their potential efficiency. March and Simon offer a convenient theory for use here, especially because of the way they treat the problem of optimality in planning.[3]

March and Simon take as a starting point the distinction between the kind of criteria necessary to find an *optimum* solution and the kind needed for a *satisficing* (satisfactory and sufficient) solution. Satisficing solutions require that there be a set of criteria that describes satisfactory and sufficient alternatives; optimum solutions require a set of criteria by which all alternatives may be compared and which insure that the selected solution is actually preferred to all others. In most real situations, the latter kind of criteria is not available; therefore most planning and decision making has to be about finding satisfactory solutions. One only has to recall the debates over the military question in the early 1920's in the USSR

3 *Organizations*, pp. 137-71.

to conclude that no set of criteria was advanced that could have led to an unambiguous *best* or optimum military posture.

From whence, then, came the criteria by which policy makers chose Osoaviakhim and its goals as part of a satisfactory solution? March and Simon would say that they derived them from the chooser's definition and perception of his real world situation. The definition is not "given" but ". . . is the outcome of psychological and sociological processes, including the chooser's own activities and the activities of others in his environment."[4] When stimuli from the environment prompt the planners to make choices, search begins for alternatives that satisfy minimum standards explicit in the planners' definition of their situation. This description is entirely compatible with what occurred in the Soviet policy process concerning the military question. Osoaviakhim satisfied a complex set of criteria which were tied up in the ideological lore of the party, the perceptions of Russian cultural realities, the perceptions of technology, budgetary limitations, and the personal ambitions of individual Bolshevik leaders.

But how did planners move from the party decisions about establishing Osoaviakhim to the operational pursuit of its goals? Presumably, "assistance to defense and aviation and chemical construction" were the goals, but they were vague and could hardly make obvious what ought to be done to realize them. If one follows March and Simon, when an organization's task is complex, the limits of human rationality constrain planners to break the task down into a sequence of subgoals. "The principal way to factor a problem is to construct a means-end analysis. The means that are specified in this way become subgoals which can be assigned to individual organizational units."[5] The first factorization into subgoals may still leave the individual units with the need to factor them further into smaller or more discrete subgoals to a point where it is clear that a criterion exists for testing the achievement of

[4] *Ibid.*, p. 139.   [5] *Ibid.*, p. 152.

the subgoal. Such a test may be called an operational criterion. The criteria by which the general Osoaviakhim goals were chosen, on the contrary, were non-operational. For example, the need to militarize the whole population was not a discriminating measuring rod with respect to expected results. It was far from clear to the party elite exactly what such a population would look like. The same operational and non-operational distinction may be made with respect to goals. A non-operational goal "does not provide a measuring rod for comparing alternative policies, but can only be related to specific actions through the intervention of subgoals."[6]

Another conceptual distinction can also be useful for analyzing Osoaviakhim planning. March and Simon provide the caveat that it is not always possible to maintain the analytical boundary between the operational and non-operational goals. This is apparent in many Osoaviakhim programs where the subgoals served by a program did not supply an entirely clear measuring rod. In such cases, program output was difficult to test. Yet the program was made operational by specifying activities that it was presumed would beget the desired end if they were pursued. In other words, program content can be analyzed as a mix of output specification and activity specification. Where output is difficult to relate to inputs or merely difficult to observe, one can expect to find greater activity specification. The reverse should be true if there are no intervening variables. March and Simon suggest that program content is the function of three variables: (1) the ease of observing activities; (2) the ease of observing output; and (3) the ease of relating activities to output.[7] In looking at Osoaviakhim programs, therefore, we want to notice whether the operationality of the goal is related inversely to activity specification. In other words, when it was difficult to find operational criteria for subgoals, did actual programs include a greater elaboration of activity? At a far simpler level of examination, it is interesting to see if Osoaviakhim

[6] *Ibid.*, p. 156.   [7] *Ibid.*, p. 145.

plans did in fact involve a means-end analysis, a factorization of the non-operational goals into operational subgoals.

What follows is a description of the Osoaviakhim planning and program execution process. Four topics are treated: planning, accounting and reporting methods, information channels among all levels of the hierarchy, and finally methods for measuring results. These topics have been selected as the outline for the description because they are the categories used at various times by Osoaviakhim leaders for describing and prescribing organizational procedures. This emphatic endeavor should allow us to grasp something of the Osoaviakhim leaders' own perspective on planning and program execution and thereby to judge the extent to which it fits the general analysis advanced by March and Simon.

The Work Plan

Like all other sectors of "socialist construction," Osoaviakhim was called on to develop a five year plan of its own, one that both directed the work of the Society and insured integration of that work with all aspects of the state's Five Year Plan. P. Levin, a member of the Central Council's secretariat, admitted in 1929 that the development of Osoaviakhim until a short time beforehand had been largely spontaneous rather than planned growth.[8] After "tides of toilers poured into the ranks of the Society," he went on to mix the metaphor, "entire layers of our puffed up organism dropped off. Why? Because we were not able to interest those who flowed into the Society with definite forms of practical work." Developing a five year plan for Osoaviakhim, Levin insisted, was the essential first step toward a remedy for this situation.

Certain experience, he continued, had already been gained in providing rough quantitative guides to local organizations on growth and social composition of the membership. In 1928, precise quantitative figures for military programs had been issued along with time schedules for

[8] *Osoaviakhim*, 16 (1929), 5.

fulfillment. The response at local levels proved satisfactory enough to justify more ambitious planning—a five year plan that Levin proceeded to adumbrate. It was to be broken down functionally:[9]

1. Membership growth
2. All types of military training
3. Aviation work and assistance to aviation industry
4. Agricultural activities
5. Agitprop
6. Finance
7. Supply

In 1930, Osoaviakhim reported to the XVI Party Congress that its *piatiletka* was coordinated with the state Five Year Plan, especially with those aspects concerning defense.[10] Thereafter Osoaviakhim continued the practice of coordinating its planning in five year increments with the state plan.

For implementation the *piatiletka* had to be broken into shorter term plans, a series of one year plans, which in turn were broken down into quarterly plans. Because a copy of the 1928 annual work plan of the presidiums of the Union and the RSFSR Osoaviakhim is available, it is possible to make some specific observations about it. The twenty-two page document is divided into nineteen short subsections, each concerning a functional branch of the Society's programs.[11] The subsections are:

1. Organization
2. Agitation-propaganda
3. Mass campaigns
4. Questions of the press
5. Program-methods work
6. Military training of toilers
7. Marksmanship affairs

[9] *Ibid.*
[10] *Osoaviakhim,* 17-18 (1930), 4-5.
[11] *Plan raboty prezidiumov soiuza Osoaviakhim SSSR i Osoaviakhim RSFSR na 1928 god* (Moscow: 1928).

8. Air-chemical defense
9. Scientific research work
10. Work among women
11. Aviation
12. Gliding
13. Model airplanes
14. Aviation law
15. Naval work
16. Assistance to chemical industry
17. Assistance to agriculture and forestry
18. Application of aviation in agriculture
19. Dog training and carrier pigeons

Each subsection contains a list of projects to be accomplished in the course of the year. Some examples of projects allow us to see how the planners linked these broad goals to subgoals that were sufficiently specific to suggest purposeful activity. In other words, they show the planners' progression from non-operational to operational goals. The ten projects in the area of aviation were:

1. Organization and conduct of long distance flights.
2. Organization of aid to industrial and scientific-theoretical aviation and aeronautics.
3. Organization of an all-union congress of workers in aviation affairs during the fall of 1928.
4. Construction of light motors, 60 horse power, of two standard types.
5. Build ten Pal'men motors, 20 horse power.
6. Conduct experiments in rebuilding large motors into small ones.
7. Organization of construction of light weight low horse power airplanes in the provinces.
8. Prepare local construction for building two-seater light aircraft, using only the most reliable designs, including in this plan:
   a. local designs and local construction.
   b. purchase of seven motors from abroad.
9. Further development of experimental construction including:

  a. construction of a trainer aircraft, 100 hp.
  b. construction of experimental 20 hp. aircraft.
10. Conduct experiments in re-building motors and test the quality of aircraft in practical use.

The subsection on military training listed eight projects:

1. Report to the Revvoensovet SSSR (through the GURKKA) for receiving clear guidance on the task of Osoaviakhim:
   a. in the general system of the Red Army training.
   b. in the training of toilers not having ever served in the Red Army; and from the Political Administration the number of persons in need of military training, broken down by age and category with the aim of distributing them among Osoaviakhim organizations.
2. Organization of military games for senior reserve officers working in economic institutions.
3. Organization of a conference of former responsible [party] workers in the Red Army who now work in civil institutions.
4. Work out instructions for *uchet* of all Osoaviakhim military training.
5. Work out statutes for military training.
6. Review the experience of courses for re-training reserve officers.
7. Work out a system of correspondence study for reserve officers.
8. Develop the question of work with junior commanders of the reserve [NCO's].

Other sections were longer. Agriculture and forestry included twenty-three projects; thirty-five were listed in connection with the chemical industry. The program-methods section included projects primarily concerned with publishing textbooks and standardizing courses. The striking feature of the plan is not that it is the result of rigorous analytical techniques for finding optimum solutions, but rather that it strives to set up *programs, procedures,* and *standard patterns* for organizational activity. Some common sense priorities are followed in the process. For example, the military programs could not be prescribed effectively until the requirements of the Red Army were known. Design, production, and distribution of cheap reliable aircraft were the preconditions for a mass aviation program. Finally, there is an implicit division between activities needed primarily to maintain the organization and activities directly relating to general goals. The former group includes organization, agitprop, mass campaigns, matters of the press, and program-methods work. The latter group includes the military, chemical, and aviation activities.

The local organizations were expected to complete their own general and special plans. Perspective on their planning system can best be gained by examining practices in the primary organizations. Cells were expected to use three types of plans: a general plan, a calendar plan, and a plan for the conduct of separate campaigns.[12] The general plan enumerated basic tasks and objectives for a period of three to six months, along with measures to be taken in their execution and achievement. The calendar plan was composed monthly on the basis of the general plan in that actions and programs of the general plan were assigned precise dates for execution. The calendar plans also indicated locations for activities, material, persons in charge, and the series of practical matters essential for such programs. The plan for separate campaigns, like the calendar plan, included considerable detail on the practical measures necessary for a campaign. Lottery campaigns, defense holidays, and fund-raising efforts fell into this category.

At every level, beginning with the cell, there was a strong effort to plan activities, to organize them in quantifiable terms. If the guidance on planning in 1931 had stressed quantity indicators, by 1934 it had become more

[12] *Spravochnik aktivista,* pp. 117-19.

specific and elaborate. The prescribed format for the cell plan included a column for "control figures" for every project on the plan. All itemized activities, therefore, had to be connected to some unit of measure. Quarterly breakdowns were expected as well as indication of the responsible supervisor of the work and the raion instructor responsible for checking the execution.[13] In its most developed form, the plan assigned tasks, resources, and personnel in a more or less orderly fashion and required deadlines for completion, reports of results in quantitative terms, and a check on the results by the next higher organization.

There seems to have been no requirement for an organization to submit its general work plan for approval. Certain functional divisions of the plan did, however, need review and approval from above. The financial estimates of income and expenses and the military programs are the most important examples.

Financial planning started each year in the Central Council. Guidance figures and instructions reached the cell, according to regulation, by October 25. The cell drew up its own income-expenditure estimate (which was not allowed to show a deficit) and returned it to the raion council by November 15. The rules required that it be returned approved or altered to meet approval within one month.[14]

The finance plan is interesting in particular because it reveals some attempt to relate specific inputs to specific outputs and thereby to allow a planner to have some idea of the monetary costs involved in various kinds of goal-satisfying activity. Take, for example, the Zamoskvoretskii Raion Council's financial planning for 1927-1928. (See Charts V and VI.) First of all, planned expenses were kept within planned income. Second, the listing of expenditures shows that expenses were meant to be calculated according to functional categories, i.e. budgeting for

[13] *Osoaviakhim v kolkhose*, pp. 17-20. A sample format is shown in this book.

[14] *Sputnik Osoaviakhima*, pp. 85-89.

specific activities. The general listing follows a typical
line-item budget approach, the very opposite of budgeting
for activities and goals. The motivation for budgeting by
activity seems not always to have been inspired by planners who wanted the advantages of comparing costs of
alternative programs but rather by the center's desire to
prevent misappropriation, treachery, and the use of grants
from the Central Council for other than specified activities.[15]

In the particular case of the Zamoskvoretskii Raion, it is
interesting to observe that only one functional category
was planned for, marksmanship. All items under general
expenses, in contrast, were planned for. It might be assumed from this case that planning by activity was more
difficult and therefore neglected. The year 1927-1928,
however, was the first of Osoaviakhim's existence. The
actual expenses for that year perhaps offered a basis for
future budgeting by activity. In any event, to the degree
that the characteristics of the Zamoskvoretskii Raion
budget were general among Osoaviakhim organizations,
we have some notion of the role of the budget in providing
planning connections between financial outlays and desired organizational outputs. Budgeting by activity might
achieve planning consistency, but there is no evidence that
it led to cost-effective comparisons among programs and
activities.

The special planning and reporting procedures for
military training are not so well documented. As mentioned
in the 1928 Work Plan, quoted above from the section on
military training, development of a special system of as-
sessing and reporting was among the tasks for the year.
The obligatory military training, particularly, required coordination and accurate information flow between the Red
Army and Osoaviakhim.

---

[15] *Khimiia i oborona*, 3-4 (1932), 33. Loktev, the financial
expert, implies as much. There was much complaint of misuse
and redirection of earmarked funds. See *Itogi VI Plenuma*,
p. 59.

What has been said here about the planning process not only was true for the hierarchical structure but also came to apply to the larger practical organizations such as gliding schools, aeroclubs, training points, and camps. As the organization shifted the center of gravity of its training into fixed installations, that is, into training points, camps, and schools, it seems that planning tended to be done on an installation as well as on the cell and raion level.[16]

Production Accounting (uchet)

Planning and directing activities were certain to come to naught unless results could be checked and measured. Since the cell and the practical organizations were the organizational elements where the production process largely took place, accounting and measuring had to begin at that level. A brief review of the cell's accounting procedures is thus the quickest way to discover the essential nature of uchet.

Every cell was required to follow a standard recording procedure in four categories. Special forms and instructions had been worked out and distributed by 1931.[17] First, membership uchet: A standard card was to be kept on each member. Personal data, record of participation, reports of achievements and other such information supposedly were recorded regularly on this card. Second, uchet of practical organizations: Circles, teams, courses, and most other activities connected with training were recorded under this category. The results of their work were maintained in the "Journal for Activities of Practical Organizations." Third, uchet on marksmanship: This branch of training was kept separately from other practical organizational activity. The "Marksmanship Book"

[16] Boris Leont'ev, Vooruzhennyi narod (Moscow: 1936), p. 80.

[17] Spravochnik aktivista, pp. 230-42. This source explains the uchet technique in greater detail than the summary treatment here.

provided a recording format. Fourth, *uchet* of the cell buro and mass measures: The "Cell Buro Work Diary" served as the record of all general management work to include agitation and mass propaganda. A rather strong warning was issued against treating "mass work" as part of training activity.

For the most part, *uchet* amounted to gathering statistics. Anything that could be counted tended to be. Figures, of course, can be highly ambiguous indicators of organizational activity, a point that certainly did not escape the Soviet leadership, but this caused no reluctance to search out and record all sorts of statistics.

Production Reporting (otchet)

Reporting consisted foremost of rendering counts to the higher levels of the organization. A special form for *otchet*, containing 79 columns into which quantitative data were entered, was required for use by the cells.[18] These data can be grouped into three general areas. First, information on the social composition, nationality, and liability for military service was considerable. Next, information on military training was given special attention, and a distinction was maintained between obligatory and voluntary training. Finally, numbers of persons in all other kinds of activities to include the precise number entering, the number dropping out, and the number completing cycles or courses in each activity were reported. Implicitly *otchet* revealed the type and number of practical organizations.

It was recognized that reporting might usefully include information on the quality of activities. A written section on quality, therefore, was required as an appendage to the *otchet* form. It included subjective assessment of practical work, organizational and propaganda work and also dealt with the nature of relations with the party, Komsomol, and trade unions. By no means the only source of information available to the center, the *otchet* system did re-

[18] *Ibid.*, pp. 239-42.

main the basic source. Until 1930, semi-annual reports were submitted to the center, but the volume of information created a glut during the reporting months, October and April. The system was then revised to spread reporting throughout the year. Twenty-three kinds of reports, some submitted annually, some twice a year, fell under four major groupings.[19]

Operation reports, the first group, included information on reorganization progress, campaigns, instructional visits to lower level organizations, and corrective measures for ineffective management. Propaganda and agitation reports made up the second group. All training activity, the work of practical organizations, came under "special work" reporting. The fourth group was a catch-all: work in transportation, among women, and in schools among students.

Information Channels

The center took the occasion of the reorganization of the *otchet* system to emphasize all of the channels of information flow on which operations were dependent.[20] Specifically the upward flow channels were enumerated:

1. Results of investigations
2. Statistics from *otchet*
3. Periodic reports on local successes and failures in practical work
4. Materials from conferences, congresses, and meetings
5. Protocols from oblast, krai, and republican presidium meetings
6. Talks with local workers visiting the center
7. Letters and voluntary reports by individuals
8. Data from experimental indicators in local organizations

[19] *Osoaviakhim*, 23-24 (1930), 17.
[20] *Ibid.*, pp. 16-17.

Downward flow channels included:

1. The press, primarily Osoaviakhim publications
2. Instructions delivered during personal visits
3. Information summaries and reviews
4. Directives, orders, and circulars
5. Publication of investigation results, of generalizations about operations, common problems, and conclusions
6. Congresses, conferences, and meetings

The revision commissions also provided the center with information about irregularities and corruption. In addition to quarterly scheduled checks of organizational records, the revision personnel were expected to carry out special investigations and to maintain special liaison with the editors of Osoaviakhim journals.[21]

The press held a special place in the information system. Not only was it considered the most important daily source of guidance to local organization,[22] but it was also expected to scrutinize and reveal local problems, deficiencies, and corruption. Village and army correspondents could write about anything they observed. Individual members also were encouraged to write letters to the editors of journals when they felt they could expose poor leadership and illegal practices. To give impetus to this kind of prowling for information, a period of several months was occasionally designated during which surprise checks on all cells were to be carried out by *aktiv*, Komsomolites, correspondents, and the normal leadership hierarchy. In the fall of 1932, the Central Council allocated 25,000 rubles in prize money for "best cells" during a three month campaign of surprise inspections.[23]

Osoaviakhim and *Na strazhe* were the organizational

[21] *Osoaviakhim*, 28-29 (1931), 25; *Pervoe vsesoiuznoe*, pp. 70-72.
[22] *Osoaviakhim*, 23-24 (1930), 16.
[23] *Samolet*, 10-11 (1932), 6.

journals most concerned with management and policy. *Samolet* catered to aviation and provided a wide range of technical information. *Khimiia i oborona* did the same for chemistry, but they both also devoted significant attention to organizational problems.

Measuring

The primary method of measuring Osoaviakhim outputs was statistical counting. It is less obvious what sense was made of the figures flowing into the center. Which figures were viewed as end products? How were figures commensurated? Although no total or general reports summing up the whole of Osoaviakhim's activity are available, some published partial summaries do exist that offer insight into the measuring style.

In the mid-1930's, stock was taken of progress in Osoaviakhim's five year plan, and projections for 1933 were calculated. Training was the only aspect of goal attainment dealt with in this report, but the categories are interesting:[24]

Local cadre trained in schools or courses	165,000
Agitation workers	23,000
Pilots and glider pilots	2,700
Aviation technicians	5,900
Other aviation specialists	900
Instructors for pest control (one month course)	20,000
Instructors for pest control (four month course)	1,000
Tractor drivers	40,000
Mechanics	10,000
Chemical technicians	7,000
Air defense instructors	"thousands"
Military circles (KVZ)	5,000,000
Chemical circles	6,000,000
Agricultural-chemical circles	1,600,000

[24] *Osoaviakhim*, 17-18 (1930), 31.

Marksmen trained	2,000,000
Dog and pigeon handlers	85,000

The total number of persons embraced by all these programs was said to be 16,000,000. In 1936 another partial summary of organizational results was reported. It was not a projection but a record of completed training.[25]

Pilots trained (without break from place of employment)	8,000
Persons having made jumps from parachute training towers	1,406,000
Glider pilots (trained in 2,000 gliders at 240 glider stations)	20,000
Holders of the badge, "Prepared for Air and Chemical Defense"	5,000,000
Self-defense groups (air defense) trained	4,670
Air and chemical defense instructors	70,000

Many of these figures are not very discriminating. How many jumps each person made from a parachute tower is not specified. In the 1933 projections, no effort is made to distinguish between pilots and glider pilots. The types of courses completed in military circles are omitted. Perhaps even more important, there is no attempt to distinguish between intermediate and final products. Airplane pilots are end products, but glider pilots are intermediate products. Although these data do not necessarily reflect the most sophisticated analysis that Osoaviakhim officials achieved in striving to measure accomplishments, the publication and interpretation of such figures were bound to have an educative effect on the lower level Osoaviakhim *apparatchiki*.

There were other kinds of reported results. The funds raised in campaigns for direct aid to aviation procurement abroad, for dirigibles, and for other uses outside Osoaviakhim could be viewed as final products. Hours of free labor time contributed by Osoaviakhim work brigades to plants

[25] *Khimiia i oborona*, 8 (1936), 2.

and factories also could be considered outputs, as well as hectares of crops under pest control by Osoaviakhim detachments.

Another approach to measuring results amounted to a check of the work "form," or method, rather than a direct measure of the consequences of using the method. For example, it was apparently believed that the application of "socialist competition" and "shock work" (*udarnichestvo*) would well nigh guarantee satisfactory results. The center, therefore, took interest in simply counting the number of organizations which used these methods. The center expressed sharp displeasure when it was discovered that only 30 percent of the cells in the Nizhegorodskii oblast and none in the Ivanovo industrial region and in the Bashkirskii Krai actually employed these techniques for stimulation of organizational activity.[26]

Still another example of a measuring technique was the establishment of standardization norms. The well-known GTO badge (Prepared for Labor and Defense) provides a ready example of the norms required in elementary military and physical training in circles at the cell level. Course content and achievement norms were spelled out even in the early days of the organization but not in the detail that was achieved by 1936.[27] The badges for "Voroshilov Shooters" and "Prepared for Air and Chemical Defense" appeared in the 1930's.[28]

[26] *Osoaviakhim*, 17-18 (1930), 13. The Western Siberian Krai, on the contrary, appeared to use such methods. At least the report of a krai congress underscored the efforts to do so. See *Sbornik reshenii I(III) kraevogo s"ezda Osoaviakhima Zapadnoi Sibiri*, p. 65.

[27] See *Sputnik Osoaviakhima*, pp. 111-238. This handbook outlines the norms and test procedures for every aspect of Osoaviakhim's work. V. N. Strutsa, *Krepite oboronu SSSR* (Moscow: 1927), offers an example of a handbook in the early period. Course content was extensively spelled out, but norms and tests were very few at that time.

[28] Standardization, to be sure, is also necessary simply to

In summary it can be observed that Osoaviakhim measurement of organizational results amounted to insuring that a wide range of fairly specific programs was being implemented. Measurement of program performance began with statistical accounting and was augmented by standardized norms and achievement tests. There was no way to commensurate all of the organizational results in a common unit such as the ruble. The goods and services Osoaviakhim tried to render were extraordinarily diverse. Even in a particular branch of work such as aviation the subactivities remained diverse and thus had to be measured in an incremental fashion, not by a set of operational criteria for end products.

Where programs were interrelated, poor results in one caused difficulties in others. As military training was structured more and more in a hierarchical or progressive fashion, advanced courses and training could proceed smoothly only if elementary courses had imparted acceptable skill levels. Not all programs were interrelated, however. Stables and riding schools were independent endeavors. Osoaviakhim shock brigades in factories served no direct supplemental role in other programs. The same was somewhat true of mass propaganda endeavors; at least fairly wide latitudes of effective results could be tolerated when such propaganda was for other purposes than recruiting people for Osoaviakhim membership and training programs.

It should be noted that the Osoaviakhim leaders expressed a continuing skepticism with respect to statistical data even when the units counted were ambiguous. It will be remembered that Eideman, himself, depreciated the membership figures by almost 50 percent. Revision commission endeavors, although entirely absent in some organizations, did on occasion submit the reported data to critical scrutiny. The variety of information channels seems to have allowed the center to be accurately informed when it desired to be.

---

coordinate activities and programs, not only to facilitate measuring.

To return now to the analysis advanced by March and Simon, its conceptual appropriateness for the Osoaviakhim case should be clear. The annual work plan for 1928 certainly demonstrates a means-end analysis, a factorization of non-operational goals into operational subgoals. Moreover, the lower levels of the organization were given fairly precise guidance on further factorization of tasks assigned to them. Beyond that, the relationship between product specification and activity specification is apparent. Measuring output was difficult if not impossible for most programs. Activity specification, therefore, was more often characteristic of the plan. In the subsection on aviation, seven of the ten subgoals specified activity. All eight of the subgoals in the military program specified activity, although two of them could possibly be classified as output specification.

If we take "program" to mean the set of administrative procedures prescribed for managing Osoaviakhim (as opposed to aviation, chemical, and military programs), and consider, as March and Simon do, that program content is the function of (1) ease of observing activities, (2) ease of observing outputs, and (3) ease of relating inputs to outputs, it is obvious that none of the three was easy in Osoaviakhim. The sensitivity of the leadership to this reality is vividly indicated by the administrative program content, the elaborate specification of planning, accounting, and reporting procedures. The emphasis placed on a multiplicity of information channels reflects the same sensitivity. The administrative response to the difficulty level in each of the three variables suggests that the leadership was behaving quite rationally. On the whole the scheme for dealing with the observation difficulties (information) are more impressive than the technique of relating inputs to outputs (making sense of reporting information for corrections in further planning).

If the planning methods can be described as rational in that they permitted satisficing programs to be developed, what can be said about discrimination among alternative satisficing programs? In other words, was there a method for knowing which of several acceptable programs was most efficient? There is no evidence in Osoaviakhim practice of rigorous methods for making this kind of choice as far as initial programs were concerned. The manner in which successive programs were designed and modified did have an implicit rationale for increasing efficiency. Once a program was implemented and found to be satisfactory, it might be changed by retaining the same goals while lowering the resource inputs. If the modified program succeeded, it is fair to say that it was more efficient because a greater level of satisfaction was realized for each unit of resource inputs.

To what extent was this searching procedure used in seeking efficient programs? The data on any single program are too incomplete to allow a thorough answer to this question, but it is quite clear from what we know about the setting of goals in the five year plan for Osoaviakhim that they were raised at a rate that exceeded the organization's capacity to meet them. Program goals were simply pushed up until programs failed in part or entirely. It must be remembered, of course, that inputs were not always held constant during the first five years and were frequently increased by large amounts. By the mid-1930's the inputs were sharply curtailed in some categories, especially personnel. But the range of programs was also reduced at the same time; therefore, it is difficult to say with certainty, in the absence of detailed planning figures, how explicitly these techniques were employed. It does seem fair to observe, however, that the leadership at the center realized that most local organizations were operating far below the theoretical production possibility curve. Raising output targets, which the center consistently did, was a simple and logical way to force the local organizations to move closer to the production possibility curve. Certainly other consequences, some of them most undesirable, were bound to result from such a policy. They will be treated later on. Here it is enough to learn that Osoaviakhim planners could manipulate their programs to increase efficiency. The methods were gross and rough at best, but they theoretically permitted rational modifications in programs.

Our perspective so far has been largely a static one, viewing the character of the organization on a general and more or less timeless level. In the following part, the dynamic character becomes the central topic. The formal features of the organization must be held in mind as a background, but our main interest will be the realities of organizational structure and programs during Osoaviakhim's first decade.

Part IV

Osoaviakhim as a Bureaucracy

Chapter XII

A Brief Historical Sketch

An analysis of the dynamic character of the organization can be facilitated by a short historical account of the time from its foundation in 1927 to the late 1930's. This procedure will allow us a better understanding of Osoaviakhim's environment, of the variety of external stimuli to which it was subjected, and it will permit us to come to the dynamic problems with the advantage of an overall perspective.

First, to review the changing context of Osoaviakhim's external environment. The Union Osoaviakhim was created on the eve of the First Five Year Plan, that is, in step with Stalin's programs for rapid industrialization. The following ten years, the period that saw the major changes in Osoaviakhim before World War II, were marked by a broad and painful transformation of Soviet society. The legend of Soviet industrial growth is commonly known. The peasantry, having escaped the confines of the village commune of Imperial Russia only two decades earlier and still euphoric over the privileges of private endeavor, were physically driven back into a communal system, the collective farms. Urbanization was taking place at an increasing rate. Career mobility was great for many who acquired almost any kind of modern skill. The technical intelligentsia that came over to the Soviet side after the revolution was suffering displacement by the first generation of Red technicians, which emerged from schools and responded to Stalin's beckon for assistance from below in intensifying the class struggle.

A counter theme, organizational development, was woven into the social and economic changes. The state bureaucracies expanded rapidly. A system of educational institutions was being built.[1] Along several fronts, the masses were being mobilized into public organizations, Osoaviakhim being only one example, where they could be transformed "from an unorganized citizenry into a reliable instrument for the achievement of administrative goals. . . ."[2] The party itself was experiencing internal change from alternative waves of recruitment and purges as well as from sharp modifications in the departmentalization of its apparatus. Reorganizations occurred in 1930, 1934, and 1939.[3] This sequence should be kept in mind, because two major reorganizations of Osoaviakhim took place in step with the party reorganizations.

The Red armed forces experienced a striking transformation in the same period. As Soviet industry could provide it, motor transport and modern weaponry were introduced. The organization of all branches of the military underwent modification during the process of integrating the new technology.[4] These changes were bound to have a direct impact on Osoaviakhim's military training programs, if those programs were to provide a "powerful reserve" for the Red Army.

The official view of a warmongering, irreconcilably hostile outer world was never allowed to wane as the central

[1] Universal elementary education was one of the targets of the First Five Year Plan. See A. S. Bubnov, *Vseobuch i politekhnizatsiia massovoi shkoly* (Moscow: 1930), pp. 76-83. Bubnov displays sensitivity to foreign charges that Soviet elementary schools not only were inadequate in number but were being used primarily for militarization of the youth instead of education.

[2] This phraseology is taken from Selznick, *TVA and the Grass Roots*, p. 220. Selznick was discussing the use of voluntary associations in the TVA, but he noticed similarity in their role in both democratic and totalitarian political systems.

[3] Fainsod, *How Russia is Ruled*, pp. 166-74.

[4] Erickson, *op. cit.*, pp. 325ff.

raison d'etre for this rapid transformation. Every handbook, every journal, almost every Osoaviakhim publication of any sort, even technical brochures, repeated the liturgy on the nature of the foreign threat. The leadership felt it necessary to chide even those who, although they agreed fully about the nature of the external threat, wondered if the implications for the priority of internal programs might not usefully be re-examined.

Although it is impossible to know precisely the nature of the impact of these environmental factors on the organizational development of Osoaviakhim, a general awareness of them is essential to an understanding of that development. The goals the party prescribed for Osoaviakhim make sense only as part of the party's attempts to control and manage the Society in a total way. If the party goal was the "construction of socialism" in the USSR, the Osoaviakhim tasks, assistance to defense and aid in aviation and chemical construction, were subgoals factored from the all-embracing (and non-operational) goal of socialism. Osoaviakhim's success depended upon finding programs that were satisfactory with respect to the general party policy aims and that could also thrive concurrently with all the other programs in the society competing for terribly scarce resources.

The historical evolution of the voluntary defense society can be broken into three periods. The first three years, 1927-1930, were marked by membership expansion, efforts to regularize organizational structure and procedures, and significant program development only in the military area. In other words, the organization allocated most of its energy to enlargement of its capacity for achieving its goals; relatively little energy went to contemporary goal achievement. The consequences did not entirely please the center. The Society tended to flourish in and around the large cities, Moscow, Leningrad, and Kiev. Osoaviakhim societies in the Ural industrial region and in the industrial centers of the South also showed some vitality, but the rural regions and the provincial towns remained largely untouched except in that they had "paper" organizations, no active membership and no programs. The second period in Osoaviakhim's development, therefore, was characterized by remedial measures both in organizational structure and in program implementation.

The Second All-Union Congress of Osoaviakhim, in February 1930, proclaimed the need for fundamental organizational change. Not only did past failures make this necessary, but the collectivization program, as it was successfully forced on the village, provided an increasing "socialist sector" of the population, which required militarization. Shortly thereafter, Osoaviakhim spokesmen at the XVI Party Congress confessed to shortcomings and promised to put the organization in step with the general struggle to achieve the aims of the Five Year Plan. The real work on reorganization took place at the conference of the Osoaviakhim *apparatchiki*, August 18-20, 1930. The general policy directives enunciated at this conference remained basically unchanged for the next five years.

These directives had two broad aims. First, it was deemed necessary to continue the development of the organizational structure, to fill it out and activate it where it was non-existent or weak. The second aim concerned programs. Additional aviation and chemistry programs were to be created while existing ones were expanded. The military program had to be kept in step with the changing Red Army, both in quantity and quality of activity.

The last period of Osoaviakhim's development began in 1935. The push outward from the center was not strong enough to affect the cells significantly although it did stir many of the raion councils to action. The next impulse, in 1935 and 1936, reached the cells, manifesting itself in two ways. First, the cell organization was renamed the "primary organization." A new statute, prescribing the primary organization's structure, tasks, and forms of work, was published in 1936.[5] Second, a review of membership documents was ordered for the purpose of eliminating "paper members," class aliens, and all other undesirables.

[5] *Sputnik Osoaviakhima*, pp. 69-79.

This period saw the realization of the goal expressed by Voroshilov in 1927: Osoaviakhim was to become the reserve of the Red Army. The territorial militia had originally served this purpose, but between 1934 and 1938, militia units had been either converted to regular Red Army units or disbanded.[6]

[6] *KPSS i stroitel'stvo vooruzhennykh sil SSSR*, p. 337.

Chapter XIII

Goals and Program Development

The evolution of goals and programs in an organization should not be thought of entirely apart from or independent of other dimensions of change. On the contrary, most of the dimensions of change are the consequence of interrelated variables, to be explained, if at all, by the character of their interaction. Insight into the interaction, nevertheless, requires first that the variables, in their individual dimensions, be identified.

Here we shall deal with the changes in Osoaviakhim goals and programs. There were some twenty branches of Osoaviakhim work in the beginning, far too many to treat individually. A better perspective on the evolution of programs is to be had by tracing out only the trends and constraints in each of the major areas of work, defense, aviation, and chemistry.

When one is beginning with no programs, as is frequently the case in countries where the political leadership is trying to accelerate the modernization process, one is apt to choose goals before programs. To the degree that this is true, program design is a function of goal choice. Once programs are designed and implemented, it becomes less clear which is a function of the other, and in reality programs may at times determine new or modified goals as much as the reverse is true at other times. Because of this interaction, let us first try to gain a perspective on the change that took place in Osoaviakhim goals roughly in the period we are studying, 1927 to the late 1930's. This can be done by comparing the officially stated goals at the beginning with later versions.

The 1927 version of the rules for the Union Osoaviakhim devotes its first paragraph to a statement of the broad purpose of Osoaviakhim. The second paragraph, a very lengthy one, articulates a series of subgoals that were more amenable to use as guides for operational programs. All of the subgoals can be sorted into three groups—defense, aviation, and chemistry. Within each group a further division can be made according to the following categories: mass education; specialist education; innovation work; direct support to industry, agriculture, and the military. It should be noticed that the civil-military boundary is straddled by this set of categories.

The same set of analytical distinctions cannot be made among Osoaviakhim goals later on. Stalin's secret decree on Osoaviakhim work in 1935 began with a reclarification of goals. Explicitly they were:[1]

1. Training pre-inductees and *vnevoiskoviki* for the Red Army.
2. Assistance in the retraining of reserve officers and NCO's without taking them from their place of employment in the civil economy.
3. Mass aviation training (pilots, technicians, parachutists, etc.) "without break from production," that is, from civil employment.
4. Mass marksmanship and elementary military training.
5. Mass air defense training (preparation of the populace for air defense, building bomb shelters, and organizing teams for damage repair and clearing).
6. Mass chemical training and organization of the populace for defense against chemical attack.
7. Horsemanship training for military purposes.

[1] WKP-186, p. 211. This is a paraphrase, not verbatim translation.

8. Naval training (naval clubs and training points).
9. Amateur radio training.
10. Training of dog and pigeon handlers.
11. Scientific research and innovation work for all of the above categories.

Noticeably missing in this list are tasks in support of agriculture, work in industry, and some of the more ambitious schemes for innovative endeavors found in the 1927 version of the rules. The secret decree was emphatically explicit in eliminating all activities but those directly contributing to the enumerated tasks. The defense role was thereby given priority over aviation and chemistry insofar as the latter two had previously included programs with a primarily civil orientation. Where once Osoaviakhim had dabbled in a broad spectrum of activities, it later had been directed into narrower confines and highly routine programs concerned entirely with adapting civilian skills and resources for both actual and potential military use. The new statement of goals was by no means the consequence of Stalin's whim. It reflected the emerging realities of program development. From this perspective, therefore, we shall examine the general outlines of that development.

Military Programs

The origins of the military programs are to be found in the conversion of the VNO to a mass voluntary organization, the OSO. The efforts of the OSO were meager, but a systematic program of "discussions," or lectures, was worked out for use by military training circles.[2] Marksmanship circles also flourished to some degree in the early years and enjoyed a popularity that contributed to successful recruiting. None of these endeavors, however, sufficed to prepare members for immediate induction into regular Red Army units without further basic training.

[2] S. E. Belitskii, *Besedy o voennom dele i Krasnoi Armii* (Moscow: 1928). This text is a summary of OSO work republished for Osoaviakhim.

Upon the formation of Osoaviakhim, pre-inductee training (formerly *vseobuch*) and programs for *vnevoiskoviki* were shifted as much as possible from territorial militia and *voenkomaty* responsibility to Osoaviakhim. Naturally this prompted new and expanded Osoaviakhim programs. By 1932, a four-stage progressive system of military training had crystallized.[3] The first-level programs retained the wide use of military circle courses for the purpose of liquidating "military illiteracy" on a mass scale. The courses took place in factories, plants, collective farms, and other institutions during work breaks, between shifts, and at other odd hours of the work day. No special installations were necessary, only literature and a few graphic training aids.

The second level also retained the military circle as its primary "work form," but courses were devoted to military specialist training (e.g., radio operator, machine gunner, artillery crewman, and the like—still rather elementary). The courses were 10-20 hours long, taught over a two-month period. The marksmanship circles also belonged to this level. They required small-bore ranges. Otherwise, no installations of a special nature were essential for the second-level courses.

The third-level program included all work in training points. The pre-inductee training, work with *vnevoiskoviki*, retraining of reserve officers, all these activities were scheduled in 120-hour courses, taught in repetitive two-month cycles. The facilities of the training point were presumed essential for the more advanced character of these courses.

The fourth and final level involved military formations organized from personnel engaged in the second and third levels. Reserve officers in the Osoaviakhim membership staffed these units. To the extent possible, platoons were formed by work shifts in factories so that the free time of all members coincided. In the summer, these formations

[3] Belitskii, "Boevaia podgotovka Osoaviakhima," *Voina i revoliutsiia*, 8-9 (1932), pp. 144-48.

went to the camps run by the oblast councils. These formations usually participated in the Red Army fall maneuvers, but they should not be confused with the Osoaviakhim shock brigades, which provided free labor in some factories and plants. Plant managers, nevertheless, did try to appropriate them for such purposes on occasions.[4]

The marksmanship program, although closely allied with the military program, developed a distinct pattern. There was always a separate staff section on the councils for marksmanship. Committees were set up at the oblast and republican levels for managing special endeavors in marksmanship, special teams, training of cadre for the lower levels, and training snipers. The centralization of the higher quality marksmanship training, which this program encouraged, also permitted the committees to lose interest in the lower level organizations and the task of mass instruction. In 1938, the committees were re-named "clubs" and presumably cleansed of "alien elements." To break the "closed character" of the former committees, sport rifle councils were set up at every level from the primary organization to the oblast and republic. They served to coordinate the programs of teams, clubs, circles, and schools involved in marksmanship work, but the operational responsibility was placed directly on the hierarchy of councils.[5]

By 1933, a system of cadre training centers was supplying the skeletal cadre for the net of training points.[6] In other words, at a few places, concentrated courses were being used to produce very quickly a supply of military instructors for the training points. Actually this effort to break the cadre bottleneck was remarkably similar to the assistance given Osoaviakhim military instructor cadres in 1928 and 1929 by the Red Army. Only now, in 1933,

[4] *Ibid.*, p. 146.

[5] *Dvadtsatiletie Krasnoi Armii i zadachi Osoaviakhim* (Moscow: 1938), p. 40. Hereafter cited as *Dvadtsatiletie.*

[6] *Itogi IV Plenuma*, p. 14.

Osoaviakhim could operate its own cadre training centers, rather than rely on the Red Army.

The military program was not entirely voluntary. The *vnevoiskoviki* and the pre-inductees were bound by law to complete certain minimum training standards. They could choose to do this in Osoaviakhim.[7] The second and third stages in the military program, therefore, embraced both obligated and voluntary participants.

Although the implementation of this program was uneven, non-existent in many regions, the progress of the construction program during the first Osoaviakhim five-year plan allowed some degree of success.

A number of consequences followed the military program development. First, increased specialization in the program content required more sophisticated cadres. The third level of training was supposed to yield such cadres, but shortages were perennial. The cadre problem could be alleviated by supplying a larger number of *apparatchiki*, full-time salaried military specialists, a practice increasingly resorted to.[8] In fact, a special status was given to many of the military instructors, which put them on the same material living standard enjoyed by regular officers in the Red Army.[9]

The shift of training into permanent installations tended to build a second structure parallel to the cell-raion-oblast council line.[10] Planning and budgeting, as it has already been noted, were also done at the training point, independent of the cell.

These practices by no means reinforced the pretense of voluntarism about Osoaviakhim activities. The *apparatchiki* tended to ignore the volunteer character of the organ-

[7] *Spravochnik aktivista*, pp. 257-59.

[8] *Osoaviakhim*, 23-24 (1930), 13.

[9] WKP-186, p. 215. These privileges were granted to a maximum of 10,000 persons by the secret decree of 1935.

[10] *Osoaviakhim na novom etape*, pp. 20, 26. The discussion at the II Plenum of the Central Council acknowledged an inter-cell organizational role for training points.

ization while the unpaid *aktiv* and the mass membership
were inclined to slacken their own efforts. The IV Plenum
of the Central Council, not surprisingly, included strictures
against this behavior in its resolutions.[11] In all likelihood
the continuing resentful relations that the trade unions
maintained with Osoaviakhim were in part due to the
growing visibility of paid workers and installations under
Osoaviakhim's supervision. The original concept of "extra-
barracks" military training of the proletariat was being
adhered to in a strange way: the barracks were being
moved to the proletariat rather than following the capitalist fashion of moving the proletariat to the barracks. If any
of them remembered the original doctrines, they were
bound to ask questions that could make the leadership
uncomfortable.

The Aviation Program

Although it was the oldest of Osoaviakhim's mass programs, originating in the ODVF in 1923, aviation work
made no spectacular progress in its first decade. The ODVF
had collected funds for purchase of aircraft, mobilized
free construction labor for building and equipping Dobrolet (the state civil airlines organization) airfields, and
was formally identified with some of the early Soviet
record-setting flying expeditions. Crop dusting, too, was an
aviation program of some consequence before collectivization was complete. On the whole, programs for training
pilots and technical personnel received serious attention
only after 1930.

To collect funds and shout propaganda to peasants and
workers about the immense future of aviation was much
easier than to implement a training program. Unlike many
of the military activities, aviation training beyond the
model airplane level could not be executed in "circles"
with brochures as the primary training aid. The lack of
installations and equipment constrained the aviation programs from the start.

[11] *Itogi IV Plenuma,* p. 45.

Aviation programs thus developed no faster than the building of aviation schools, some eight of which were extant by 1930, about 150 by 1936. Once this network began to unfold, there was an effort to back it up with glider clubs and stations at lower levels in the Osoaviakhim hierarchy.[12] Shortages of gliders prevented an effective proliferation of these stations until after the mid-1930's. In any case, the main effort in aviation work remained with the aviation school system.

Like the military program, aviation training followed a four-stage sequence, beginning with very elementary courses in circles, progressing in the second stage to ground training on instruments, and finally to flying in gliders during the third stage.[13] The fourth stage, learning to fly propeller-driven aircraft, was reserved for those few who successfully completed the first stages, normally about three percent of those who entered the second stage.[14]

The aviation school system at first worked on the principle of taking prospective pilots on a full-time basis, that is, removing them from their employment in industry for several months in the summer. Later this policy was reversed, and, by 1935, the pilot program, stage four, depended almost wholly on students who could arrive for a few hours, before and after their work day, and on holidays. Some 3,500 pilots were trained this way, "without break from production," in 1935.[15]

Pilot training certainly was not the whole of the aviation program. Mass propaganda of the kind practiced by ODVF remained a continuing activity. Neither gliding nor flying programs could advance without a growing supply of technicians and mechanics. Equally as important was the need for instructors to staff newly established aviation

[12] *Samolet*, 5 (1936), 7.

[13] Eideman's order in 1936 spelled out the structure for the aviation program as it had matured by that time. See *Samolet*, 5 (1936), 2.

[14] *Samolet*, 1 (1936), 3.

[15] Leont'ev, *Vooruzhennyi narod*, p. 26.

schools. To increase the already immense burdens of expansion, parachuting was introduced in 1934 and 1935.[16] After the successful operational air drop of more than a regiment during maneuvers in the fall of 1934, it was probably considered worthwhile to develop sport parachuting on a public mass scale. Obviously such a task was appropriate for Osoaviakhim. At least the timing suggests such a hypothesis.

Beginning sometime in 1935, a reorganization of the aviation program was begun. It started with the appointment of a deputy chairman for aviation in the Central Council who was instructed to build his own separate branch in the Osoaviakhim secretariat.[17] Increased central control was the declared leitmotiv for the change. Upon the model of the Central Aeroclub (which belonged directly to the Central Council) and with the cadre it could supply, the new aviation apparatus gradually converted the aviation schools to aeroclubs. The aeroclub concept differed from the aviation school in that it combined under one management and in one place all the aviation programs from mass work to pilot training. The first and second stages of the progressive training, rather than being left to cell supervision, were taught wherever possible at an aeroclub. Parachuting and gliding, of course, remained major activities at the aeroclubs.

The reorganization took more than three years to complete. By 1938, the system amounted to a net of aeroclubs attached directly to the republican, krai, and oblast councils. Supervision of the programs, nevertheless, was entrusted to the Central Aeroclub USSR. No longer were these clubs to look after their own finance and supply. Rather a central system of planning and finance was implemented by the aviation apparatus at the level of the Central Council's secretariat, and the aeroclubs were left

[16] *Samolet*, 9 (1936), 1. Tukhachevskii pioneered military parachuting in the Red Army beginning in 1929. See Erickson, *op. cit.*, p. 327.

[17] WKP-186, p. 215.

primarily with the administrative and operational responsibility of the training programs.[18]

The apparatus and staff responsibility at the raion level had also been removed from the raion councils and granted to the aeroclubs. Thus the original series of aviation programs, which had been dispersed for operational purposes among the Osoaviakhim local councils and cells, had in the end been almost entirely removed from the hands of the local administration and placed in a separate apparatus with its own installations and its finances guaranteed by the center. This evolution can be explained by two constraints somewhat beyond the arbitrary control of the leadership. The first was equipment availability and the second was the rising requirement for skilled personnel to implement programs.

The chapter on Osoaviakhim resource procurement has described how schemes for cooperative production of light aircraft had come to naught. A pilot training program dispersed widely within the Osoaviakhim structure depended on the increasing availability of gliders and airplanes as well as all the accessory equipment for airfields and ground training. In the chapter on Osoaviakhim planning methods, it was pointed out by way of an example from the 1928 annual plan that many of the aviation projects were concerned with developing cheap aircraft models that could be produced in abundance. These plans, in the event, supplied no panaceas. By 1936, it was admitted that all endeavors to provide Osoaviakhim with an organic aircraft production capacity had failed.[19] Glider production was no exception. The glider program itself was a scheme to lower the essential capital outlays for aviation. If airplanes had been abundant, gliding could have been omitted. The Osoaviakhim glider production, begun in 1932, did not meet expectations. As for receiving a portion of Soviet aviation industry's increasing output,

[18] The description of the aviation program as it stood in 1938 can be found in *Dvadtsatiletie* and also in *Samolet*, 2 (1938), 19.

[19] *Samolet*, 8 (1936), 14-15.

the satisfaction of the military's and the state airlines' demands left little for Osoaviakhim. Only in 1936 and afterward did Osoaviakhim apparently begin to receive a significant number of light aircraft.[20]

Until the supply bottleneck was broken, no amount of organization could yield an effective pilot training program. Even when aircraft did become more plentiful, they were not dispersed throughout Osoaviakhim local organizations. The maintenance and care of the material of the aviation program made centralization in well-managed installations imperative. The aviation schools of the early 1930's hardly met these managerial requirements. Notorious for waste and dissipation of resources, such installations did not promise the center the kind of training results it desired.[21] At this point, therefore, the leadership was face to face with the second constraining factor, cadre skill requirements.

Developing a competent cadre proved a no less formidable task than coping with supply and equipment problems. A great deal of the early aviation propaganda evoked an image of masses of youth flowing, more or less unassisted, through the model airplane program, into the glider program, from whence an elite, a fairly large one, would drift effortlessly but abundantly into the flying program of the aviation schools. The image encouraged a faith in the creative spontaneity of the masses that experience unkindly erased. Thus, by the 1930's, when Osoaviakhim became earnest about aviation, a cadre program had to be drawn up. The Red Air Fleet rendered limited instructor assistance in a few central schools in order to break the cadre bottleneck. For example, in 1931, the Central School for Glider Pilots was founded in the Crimea.[22] The Central Aeroclub USSR appeared a year or so

[20] Samolet, 5 (1936), 3.

[21] For examples of the wretched standards of the aviation schools, see Samolet, 1 (1932), 10; 2 (1932), 3; 7 (1932), 2; and 2 (1936), 7-8.

[22] Samolet, 4 (1932), 6.

later. The first moves toward centralization in the aviation program thus began as temporary measures to alleviate the constraint of cadre shortages.

Starting with a few programs at the center, the Osoaviakhim leaders of aviation work did not stop or were not allowed to stop until the program in its entirety had been drawn into the limited net of aeroclubs. A series of policy choices combined with material constraints to give the centralization process an inexorable logic. In the first place, the plan to train pilots "without break from production" meant that schools had to be located near industrial and metropolitan centers where trucks could shuttle students to and fro daily. This policy automatically excluded candidates from rural areas. Mass work and elementary training, to the extent it was carried out, was linked to the aviation schools. An Osoaviakhim *apparatchik* noted in 1932 that since aviation schools already had equipment, literature, and buildings, the mass work should be conducted there also because it would be cheaper to take the rank and file membership and even the mass public to the aviation schools occasionally than to equip organizations for aviation mass work. Such a policy, however, had the unintended consequence of bringing mass work to a state of increasing neglect. At best the aviation schools gave it last priority, which in their poor condition usually meant no attention at all.[23] And this was not even to consider that the number and location of the schools would greatly restrict the size of the public accessible for mass work.

Some vain efforts were made to prevent the total centralization. A program to back up the aviation schools with glider stations and gliding circles (circles for study, but without gliders) in the provinces was initiated by Eideman in 1936, but what came of it is uncertain.[24] It

[23] *Samolet*, 5 (1936), 2-4. The aviation schools, in particular the Central Aeroclub, were accused of a "closed life cycle" that ruled out proper attention to the mass membership and the public.

[24] *Samolet*, 5 (1936), 7.

would be wrong to represent the victory of the centralization trend in aviation programs as signaling the abandon-
ment of the goal of taking aviation to the masses. To do
that would have been to leave no difference between Osoaviakhim aeroclubs and the training programs of the Red
Air Fleet and Dobrolet.

It was made clear in 1938 that a net of new aeroclubs
would be expanded until a truly mass program was possible, but the Central Council denied all local organizations
the right to begin an aeroclub without the center's permission. In paraphrase, the Central Council's justification for
the restrictive permission went like this. Many aeroclubs
are started without sufficient resources and cadres . . . a
sign with "Aeroclub" painted on it is simply put up . . .
improper people are accepted into it who waste money
and time on improved techniques . . . this does not mean
to stop expanding the net of aeroclubs, but it is to insist
that tight financial and supply control must be retained
as the expansion takes place.[25]

Implicitly such an argument was an admission that the
earlier policy of a grass roots approach to aviation, one
that would tap the spontaneity of the toiling masses and
thrive on local resources, had utterly failed to achieve
more than wasteful *kustarnichestvo* and not a little local
corruption. Responding to these unintended consequences,
the Osoaviakhim leadership acknowledged more fully the
two technical constraints, equipment and skill scarcities,
and abandoned temporarily the goal of mass training for
goals defined by criteria of quality. The centralization
process was the logical consequence of the change in priorities of goals.

The aviation program development had its parallels in
the military program maturation. The technical imperatives of more sophisticated training endeavors led to the
organization of fewer and larger unitary structures under
tighter central control, structures that could execute a complex cluster of interrelated tasks. In the case of aviation,

[25] *Dvadtsatiletie*, p. 34.

this behavior was more pronounced. The system of aeroclubs was not only a separate set of installations but also
had its distinct apparatus line from the center downward.
Although the aeroclubs formally belonged to oblast and,
in some cases, raion councils, the secretariats in those
councils were not permitted to have aviation departments.[26] The councils were left with the supporting role
of making the masses administratively accessible to the
aeroclubs.

Chemical Programs

Chemistry remained the weak member of the Osoaviakhim trio (perhaps appropriately for its position as the last
syllable of the acronym!). Dobrokhim, founded in 1924,
never captured the public imagination and lasted only
one year, it will be remembered, before being joined with
the ODVF to form Aviakhim: In the first years of Osoaviakhim's existence, several eye-catching programs were pursued—pest control, experimental plots, fertilizer application—not least because they could have mass agitational
and propaganda effects. But these programs, as it has already been explained, brought interorganizational quarrels
with the Commissariat of Agriculture. A state Committee
for Chemicalization was created, which soon took away
many of the Osoaviakhim civil programs in chemistry,
with respect both to agriculture and industry. Osoaviakhim was left with latitude only in chemistry as it related
to defense. In practice this meant mass gas mask drills;
certainly that was not the only reason, but chemical defense programs quickly gained notoriety as the weakest
link in all of Osoaviakhim's work.[27] The center made its
desires for improvement increasingly felt in 1932 and
1933, and by 1936, a pattern of response was clear.

Some progress was achieved in building training points
that specialized in chemical defense work. Courses for
military chemical circles were standardized, and a four-

[26] *Ibid.*, p. 33.   [27] *Khimiia i oborona*, 13 (1932), 15.

stage program (the Osoaviakhim program designers seemed to have a predilection for the symmetry of "four stages") was formulated. The first stage involved mass propaganda to eliminate public illiteracy in military chemical matters. The second stage amounted to a fifty-hour course for young people aimed at making them an instructor force. The third stage included all programs in training points, and the fourth was designed to train permanent instructor teams.

This program was implemented with success in the formation of an air raid warden system, clearing and degassing teams and detachments, self-defense groups, and first aid programs. Gas mask training, construction of shelters, and the development of an air warning system (networks of observation posts) also fell to the chemical defense programs. Although it is possible to elaborate the structure of these programs down to the duties of a first aid team and an air raid warden, that need not detain us here.[28] It is enough to realize that the nature of the programs did not require the kind of concentrated installation development found in the aviation program, nor could success be claimed unless these programs touched a large number of people. A few persons trained in air and chemical defense were as good as none. An effective passive civil defense system was impossible without public knowledge of the rules and shelter facilities for the event of an attack. The chemical defense programs could not be confined to installations for concentrated development as aviation programs had been. Where this approach was tried with chemical programs, it failed. When a few chemical training points became operative, Kirillov, a high ranking *apparatchik* in the military chemical department of the Central Council secretariat, complained that the lack

[28] For such detail see *Posobie po degazatsii v puntakh i na ob"ektakh protivovozdushnoi oborony* (Moscow: 1935); P. Borisenko and V. Kletsov, *K protivovozdushnoi i protivokhimicheskoi oborone bud' gotov!* (Kiev: 1936); E. Burche, *op. cit.*

of coordination between cell work and training point work caused no end of difficulty.[29]

Like all Osoaviakhim programs, chemical defense work suffered from cadre shortages.[30] The chairman of the Ural oblast council put it plainly before the III Plenum of the Central Council. "As long as you send us no leader from the center for the chemical department, there will be no work done."[31] The tendency to retreat from using the *aktiv* in leadership and instructor roles in favor of *apparatchiki* and to resort to central school systems for instructor training was less prevalent in military chemical work than in most other branches of Osoaviakhim activities. The center, in dealing with military chemical programs, chose the tactic of trying to activate the military chemical staff sections at all levels in the hierarchy rather than build a new and separate apparatus.

Before the center used the III Plenum of the Central Council to emphasize chemical programs, only six local councils had military chemical departments. By 1933 the number reached 42.[32] The total advanced to 70 in the course of the year. These departments, it must be remembered, were part of the secretariat apparatus, not sectors on the council staff organization. Such sectors did begin to grow in number in response to the apparatus expansion, totaling 140 by the end of 1933.

The policy of activating chemical sectors ran into difficulty because air defense and chemical defense programs tended to become one. In practice, many organizations had amalgamated these ostensibly discrete lines of work.[33] Apparently the purpose was to conceal the absence of chemical defense work. The campaign by the center against the amalgamation may have prompted more interest in chemical defense, but the secretariat departmen-

---

[29] *Khimiia i oborona*, 1 (1933), 3.

[30] *Ibid.*

[31] *Khimiia i oborona*, 13 (1932), 15.

[32] *Khimiia i oborona*, 1 (1933), 25.

[33] *Khimiia i oborona*, 15-16 (1932), 1-2.

talization scheme combined the two in 1930 and left the combination intact through the reorganization in 1935.[34] Nor is there evidence that a distinction was made between air and chemical defense in the system of teams, self-defense groups, detachments, and air observation points.

By mid-1936, claims of success in the new programs were being uttered. Over 5,000,000 persons had qualified for the badge, "Prepared for Air and Chemical Defense"; 4,670 self-defense groups had been organized; 70,000 instructors in air and chemical defense had been trained.[35] Chemistry, in the Osoaviakhim triad, followed a course of program development that had little in common with the defense and aviation patterns. Instead of taking the path toward increasing complexity, it remained on a fairly elementary level. Its center of gravity, therefore, like some of the military programs, was nearer to the cell organization and thus to the mass public. This characteristic allowed it to evolve primarily within the original organizational hierarchy and to avoid the building of a separate structure that tended to obstruct low-level participation.

At the same time, program content suffered a metamorphosis. First of all, the subprograms in support of the initial Dobrokhim goals—assistance in chemical construction and application of chemistry in agriculture and other civil endeavors—all but vanished. Once the non-defense areas were removed, the remaining military chemical work tended to be subsumed by the air defense programs. Although the "chemical" feature was retained in part, the outcome of the transformation was an extensive program for passive civil defense against air attack with either chemical or explosive munitions. In the West, Osoaviakhim perhaps has been most widely perceived as little more than a civil defense organization, although that was only a part of its work.[36]

---

[34] *Osoaviakhim*, 23-24 (1930), 13; WKP-186, pp. 215-16.

[35] *Khimiia i oborona*, 8 (1936), 2.

[36] For an example of a study that unintentionally encourages this view of Osoaviakhim and its successor organization

Scientific Research Programs

Perhaps it is appropriate at this point to make brief mention of the translation into programs of Osoaviakhim's original responsibility for scientific research work. Obviously Osoaviakhim volunteers did not, except in the rare cases of recruitment of trained scientists, have personnel capable of serious research in chemistry, aviation, or military technology. Programs in purely scientific research were simply not a possibility. Osoaviakhim, of course, might contribute funds and unskilled labor to laboratories, which seems to have been done in the days of the ODVF and Dobrokhim. The VNO had claimed the name of science in its very title, but in practice its efforts amounted only to historical works on the civil war, working out tactical and staff doctrines, and designing organizational routines.

Insistence on scientific research work, nonetheless, remained a specific Osoaviakhim task. To understand what took place in the name of this work, the Western notion of scientific research must be abandoned. "Practical application of technology" is a more appropriate concept. Simple technical innovations, improved procedures in the use of equipment, equipment modifications made by the user, these were the kinds of things done by Osoaviakhim in the name of scientific research. For example, using a cable drum bolted to the rear axle of a truck as a winch for pulling gliders into the air: such was the product of scientific research.

On a more sophisticated level, the use of gliders to reduce the costs of pilot training is an example of innovation. The search for cheap light aircraft designs and improvised production means are other examples. Commonality (or standardization), a concept advanced by Trotsky,

---

after WWII, DOSAAF, see Leon Gouré, *Civil Defense in the Soviet Union* (Berkeley: University of California Press, 1962), pp. 7-61. Gouré briefly and accurately outlines the full range of programs, but only the civil defense work done by DOSAAF is relevant to his study.

meaning the selection of a single item of equipment for several unrelated roles in order to simplify supply and to reduce costs, is one more case in point.

Osoaviakhim publications, especially *Samolet* and *Khimiia i oborona*, provide numerous examples of such efforts in innovation. Enough has been said to reveal that Osoaviakhim's scientific research work was wholly devoted to applying technology and to exploiting whatever insights "Taylorism" might provide in matters of organizational design,[37] not to scientific research in the sense of advancing theoretical knowledge.

The Interaction of Goals and Programs

Treating changes in goals and programs separately, it has already been suggested, can be useful in gaining insight into the more important problem of understanding the interaction between goals and programs. The major observable changes in goals were first a narrowing of the variety of operational tasks for Osoaviakhim and, second, a diminution of programs that had no immediate military character.

In the development of programs, two patterns were apparent. Aviation followed the first pattern. It was most pronounced in the pilot training program, which took a restrictive and centralized form alien to the ostensible mass character of the defense society. Chemistry followed the second pattern. Once the chemical program was reduced to chemical defense work and combined with air defense programs for the population at large, it was able to assume a more genuine mass character. The military programs ranged between these extremes. Those of greater sophistication, often requiring expensive and scarce equipment and therefore following the aviation pattern, were restricted to appropriately outfitted training points. Marksmanship and elementary military training retained the mass style in the manner of the chemical programs.

[37] Frederick W. Taylor was an American student of scientific management at the beginning of the twentieth century.

The variations in the development patterns were explained as functions of the technical requirements of the programs, specifically, (1) scarce and complex equipment and (2) the prerequisite skill levels for cadres implementing the programs.

What, then, was the nature of the interaction between program development and Osoaviakhim goals? Although they do not wholly account for the narrowing of goals and the disappearance of many civil programs, the technical requirements placed acute constraints on the choice of goals. They became grounds for Osoaviakhim's conflict with the chemical and aviation industries as well as with agricultural organizations. Osoaviakhim did not compete successfully for the resources and skills necessary to operate its own aircraft industry. It ran into conflict with both the chemical industry and the Commissariat of Agriculture over the use of chemicals, a quarrel about spheres of administrative jurisdiction that was resolved against Osoaviakhim by means of the Committee for Chemicalization. As the Five Year Plans brought success in industrialization, chemical and aviation industries had less need for the sort of improvised shock programs Osoaviakhim could readily engage in with its relatively abundant sources of unskilled labor. Consequently, Osoaviakhim's capability to assist aviation and chemical construction (both by collecting funds and contributing its organized manpower as labor) diminished in a relative and in a technical sense. The industrial assistance programs became insignificant if not also a nuisance. The redefinition of goals in 1935 took cognizance of this change by broadening the emphasis on military programs at the expense of civil programs. From this point of view technical factors can be said to have had a determining role in the alteration of goals. When the policy maker resisted goal changes, the causal role was reversed.

To the extent that Osoaviakhim goals of the non-operational kind were kept constant, it became imperative to alter operational subgoals and programs. For example, because Osoaviakhim retained the broad goal of assistance to defense, programs had to be changed in step with the technical modernization of the Red armed forces. Marksmanship, drill, and aviation propaganda were not enough. Military specialty training and pilot training had to be implemented and constantly improved. Even mass propaganda had to be altered to take notice of changing military technology. Goals, therefore, had their role in determining programs as well as vice versa. The interaction was certainly more complex than the examples provided can illustrate, but the general conceptualization of the two-way causation is sufficient to demonstrate the kind of answer that must be given to the question about the nature of the goal and program interaction.

One might complain that such an answer rests too much on material determinants. Because men rule organizations and choose their policies, and especially because the Soviet environment was the scene of an extraordinary concentration of power in the hands of Stalin, the arbitrary preferences of the dictator must be taken into account and may in some events be in themselves a sufficient explanation for policy and goal choice. If, as David Apter says, politics is a matter of "choice,"[38] the policies of organizations designed to expedite political and economic modernization are revealed choices. That Stalin personally expressed his preferences about Osoaviakhim policy goals in 1935 is important. But what has been observed about the interaction of goals and programs remains essential for perceiving the sense in which the dictator's options were physically and technically limited. To be sure, the problem of political choices cannot be dodged, and not only the choices made by the dictator and his agents at the top of Osoaviakhim, but also the choices made by a great portion of the membership must be examined before fuller explanations of the organizational dynamics can be offered.

[38] *The Politics of Modernization* (Chicago: The University of Chicago Press, 1965). See especially the introduction.

Chapter XIV

Development of the Formal Hierarchy

The description of Osoaviakhim's formal structure presented in Part II was intentionally kept as much as possible to a static point of view, but it included occasional digressions on the topic of growth. Changes in names, new kinds of practical organizations appearing at various times, and disappearances of some structures were briefly treated because a description of the Osoaviakhim structure at any point in time would have been incomplete. In this chapter we shall return to the question of hierarchical structure and examine more fully its dynamic features.

Osoaviakhim's structure and operating procedures almost always appeared to be in a state of transition. Upon reading the Osoaviakhim journals, one gains the impression that the single unchanging factor was the center's fondness for the term *perestroika* (reorganization). Thoroughgoing policy review and fundamental structural alterations, however, were not everyday, or even annual, occurrences. To grasp the logic and the unintended illogic of the dynamic behavior of the organization, it is necessary to identify and study, first of all, those less frequent but fundamental attempts to modify Osoaviakhim's structure. We shall then be able to understand the nature of change, and we can also isolate some determining factors which will help us to explain the change.

Explanation, to be sure, will also depend on what has already been said about program development, and the factors emphasized in that context must be kept in mind here. But it is necessary to continue the procedure of isolating certain phenomena, presenting the dynamic trends, by describing them separately before we try to understand their interrelationships. Specifically, we shall examine major changes in the hierarchical structure and in staff departmentalization, significant shifts in leadership and task responsibility, modifications in control and operating procedures, and particularly changes in the size of the membership, both its volunteer component and its salaried bureaucracy.

At three junctures the Osoaviakhim leadership prescribed major structural and operational changes. The first was the unification of the ODVF, Dobrokhim, and the VNO (OSO) in 1927. The second reorganization was initiated in 1930, and the last began in August 1935.

The Reorganization of 1927

The first case, the Osoaviakhim unification, has already been treated in detail in Part I. It is necessary here only to recount the consequences of the unification for structural change and to review the reasons advanced for unification.

The policy of unification was evident in 1925 when the ODVF and Dobrokhim were combined to form Aviakhim. The VNO had been forced to imitate the hierarchical pattern of Aviakhim, to form cells, raion councils, and so on up to a central council for the USSR level. In the case of all three of the predecessor societies, the formal structure, that is, congresses, councils, presidiums, chairmen, secretaries, and the secretariat apparatus, was generally of the same design found in Osoaviakhim. Only the practical organizations had not been as fully developed.

The predecessor societies were initiated and effectively managed by salaried apparatuses (the OSO apparatus was in fact supplied by the military-political administration of the Red Army and the territorial militia). From the volunteers, an *aktiv* was recruited to assist the apparatus, although, according to the rules, the volunteers were to manage all affairs assisted by the apparatus. The initial predominance of the apparatus was never overcome, notwithstanding the rapid growth of the volunteer membership. This was as true of local organizations as it was of the central councils in Moscow.[1]

The major structural change in 1927, therefore, was simply the replacement of two organizations with one. To restate the reasons for the unification, the first was the need to reduce conflict and competition between such similar voluntary societies as well as conflict with the several other voluntary associations in the USSR. Second, parallelism in decision making, planning, and general administration made the party and state supervision of the two organizations more difficult. Third, the resulting weakness in central administration had been accompanied by "localism," that is, resistance in local organizations against central policy. Finally, local party committees, trade unions, and Soviet organs had become hostile to voluntary defense societies that demanded their time and resources. Reducing the number of societies was a concession to the hostility. Two more reasons were implied by Osoaviakhim spokesmen in 1927. First, administrative consolidation was appropriate as part of the overall state bureaucratic coordination on the eve of the First Five Year Plan in an effort to prepare for the vast undertakings the plan involved. The second, less certain reason, pertains to Stalin's consolidation of control over the military establishment, control that Frunze's Red Commanders had helped him wrest from Trotsky with the apparent intention of making it their own. Osoaviakhim might enhance mobilization capacity without allowing control over that capacity to belong to the Red Army.

[1] See *Pervyi oblastnoi s"ezd ODVF Tatrespubliki*, pp. 21, 36, 39-41. Discussion at this provincial congress made it clear that salaried "instructors" and "specialists" were the prerequisites for local organizational vitality, although no assurance of it.

Upon the creation of Osoaviakhim, the central leadership promulgated a program of standardization, of establishing norms and statutes for every level of the hierarchy and every type of practical work, and for reducing the number of the heretofore proliferating apparatuses in Moscow. The combined membership amounted to about 3,000,000, not a figure that could insure the militarization of the whole population, yet a number so large that the inadequately developed hierarchy could not manage it. If size had exceeded organizational capacity, why reduce the number of apparatuses and independent hierarchies? Whatever causes may have derived from the party elite factional struggles, the explicit reasons advanced to answer this question by Rykov, Unshlikht, and Voroshilov at the unification congress in 1927 have a cogency of their own.

They argued that the central organs and the apparatuses had become congested. At the same time, effective councils and secretariat staffs were rare at the republican, krai, and oblast levels, not to mention the deplorable inadequacies at the okrug, raion, and cell levels. The available records of provincial organizations wholly vindicate the complaints registered from the floor of the unification congress concerning the rising costs of the apparatus (12.6 percent of the Aviakhim income compared with 5.4 percent in the case of ODVF) and the simultaneous absence of an apparatus in the provinces.[2] At the ODVF oblast congress in Kazan in 1924, the local leaders made it plain that cells and raion councils had achieved existence only on paper in most places.[3] Judging from the instructions published by the military section of the Nizhegorodskii council in 1929, conditions had not greatly improved five years later.[4] It was admitted that almost no work in other sections had begun due to the absence of qualified apparatus workers. If there was neither staff nor program at the

[2] *Pravda*, January 20, 1927.

[3] *Pervyi oblastnoi s"ezd ODVF Tatrespubliki*, pp. 36-41.

[4] *Osnovnye tekushchie zadachi*, p. 1.

oblast level, productive activity could hardly be expected at the raion level.

For the first three years (1927-1930), then, reorganization meant trying to create the hierarchy of councils and secretariat apparatus that was formally prescribed by the 1927 rules. In no respect was membership expansion allowed to slacken in order to permit the councils a breathing spell for consolidating their own staff sections. Ambitious targets were set, and recruiting was pressed forward relentlessly. The consequences of this policy were not surprising. Success in recruiting could be represented in apparently unambiguous figures. Programs and activities were more difficult to measure. Norms and indices for judging their results were still being formulated. Membership, therefore, grew. An effective council staff and an apparatus that could implement programs did not. The local leadership responded quite rationally to the incentive structure created by the center.

The Second All-Union Congress of Osoaviakhim (February 1930) acknowledged these outcomes and solemnly promised to put substance into the local organizations, but intentions alone were not sufficient to deal with some of the realities. In the summer of 1930, the central leadership provided several examples of the disorder below the okrug level.[5] Secretaries of raion councils and cell buros changed three to five times annually in many places. The Crimean and Siberian organizations left raions without secretaries for three months at a time. Where secretaries were present, councils not infrequently remained inoperative for most of the year. In rural areas raion councils hardly existed at all. Even when local organizations were vital, the spirit of corruption often lurked within. At Luna in the Ukraine, three secretaries were removed because they were spendthrifts. In Poltava, several were expelled for "private business" activities. The Tver okrug presidium had not met for more than four months—and so on the story of misfortune continued.

[5] *Osoaviakhim*, 17-18 (1930), 6-7.

The Reorganization of 1930

In August a conference of the Osoaviakhim *apparatchiki* was convened to deal with the provincial problems. On this occasion, the second major reorganization plan was unveiled, one that was to occupy the Society for the next five years.

What, precisely, had all the organizational stir since 1927 achieved? In the matter of size and structure, two trends were clear. Membership had more than doubled and would increase to 9,000,000 by 1931. Although rules and statutes had been composed for virtually every aspect of the Society's activity, either they were not being followed or they were provoking undesired behavior. The most disturbing inadequacy of the rules seems to have been the ambiguity about where the responsibility for task execution lay. The choice of "collegial" instead of "individual" responsibility may have facilitated recruitment, but it also permitted pernicious behavior by leaders at all levels and more than a little corruption. The resulting weakness in the organizational structure and programs left thousands of members uncontrolled and allowed them to drift out of Osoaviakhim as swiftly as they came in.

The growth of the secretariat staff followed an unmistakable pattern. If the glut of *apparatchiki* stood lodged at the center in 1927, by 1930 the imposed exodus had led only a short way into the provinces. Actually the secretariat apparatus had become active down to the okrug level. In other words, provincial towns, where offices, telephones, and typewriters were accessible, could attract and hold *apparatchiki*, but few wanted to go farther into the depraved localities.

For those who could find jobs near the center, there were strong reasons for avoiding the raion. The salary for a raion secretary, 70 to 80 rubles a month, depended on the capacity of the raion organization to pay. In 1929, the Red Army newspaper published a story on the raion secretary's distressing circumstances and pleaded for a guarantee of his income by the center as well as proper material and supervisory support from the okrug councils, the local party committees, and the trade unions.[6] Being on the last rung in the apparatus ladder, the raion secretary could be blamed for many program failures. Yet if his post was not envied by the *apparatchiki* at the higher levels, less fortunate persons valued it. There is some evidence that the Red Army treated many of the low-level salaried jobs controlled by Osoaviakhim as patronage for reserve officers, many of them veterans of the civil war and victims of demobilization in 1921. Complaining about a particular case of Osoaviakhim staffing the security guard force for the railroads, spokesmen for the Red Army claimed that "local scoundrels" habitually edged reserve officers out of salaried posts and then intimidated them from positions of authority.[7] The "local scoundrels" in Osoaviakhim were helped by "bureaucrats" in the Commissariat of Transportation. A rather infamous group of such cases of discrimination against reservists had occurred in Georgia.[8] Clearly the lower posts in the Osoaviakhim apparatus were not attracting the kinds of individuals who would resolve conflicts of interests in the center's favor when local or personal interests clashed with those of the hierarchy. Nor did the secretariat seem to have the power, when it could employ a local secretary, to force him to submit to central policy and desist from deceptive and self-interested practices. When central authority made itself felt, low-level *apparatchiki* simply ran away to avoid retribution.

At the conference on reorganization in August 1930, the failures at the local levels were explained as the conse-

[6] *Krasnaia zvezda*, September 19, 1929.

[7] *Krasnaia zvezda*, September 7, 1929. Incomplete serials of the Red Army newspaper make it impossible to trace the full implications of these complaints, but a proposal was advanced for an all-union commission that would supervise placement of all demobilized officers and guard their rights to jobs not only in Osoaviakhim but elsewhere.

[8] *Krasnaia zvezda*, September 10, 1929.

quence of a weak or non-existent apparatus.[9] The raion council was said to be overburdened and the few available *aktiv* were overworked. About 80 percent of raions reportedly had no full-time workers from local party committees. Material resources were least abundant at the raion level. The vast turnover of secretaries and instructors, party neglect, and party misappropriation of the services of the raion council *apparatchiki* and *aktiv* combined to make operations unsatisfactory, if possible at all.

The conference approved a resolution that committed Osoaviakhim to great improvements at the raion and cell level.[10] To insure that the necessary resources were available for building an effective raion staff, the okrug level, the council, its staff, and the secretariat were all to be abolished completely by October 31, 1930 (see Chart X). Ninety percent of the okrug *apparatchiki* were ordered to move to raion councils. Half the physical property of the okrug went to the raion, the remainder to the oblast level.[11] The oblast, krai, and republican organizations had to support the campaign for vitalizing the raion and cell structures. They organized temporary cadre training courses and took direct responsibility for supervising the dismantling of the okrug councils.[12]

The spirit of the reform nourished itself greatly on the center's recognition of the need, and hence the justification, for more salaried workers. Provincial workers had always asked for more apparatus posts. Now the Central Council agreed fully that the raion apparatus had to be enlarged. The source of new *apparatchiki*, nonetheless, remained a problem. The okrugs alone could not furnish enough people to staff the raion councils. Hastily improvised courses for secretaries and instructors might formally produce the required numbers, but quality could not be assured. The raion secretary of an Osoaviakhim council potentially had access to considerable local resources; in

[9] *Osoaviakhim*, 23-24 (1930), 14.

[10] *Ibid.*, pp. 14-17. This source elaborates the reform in considerable detail.

[11] *Ibid.*   [12] *Ibid.*

CHART X

Reorganization of the Osoaviakhim Hierarchy, 1930

Source: *Osoaviakhim*, 23-24 (1930), 12.

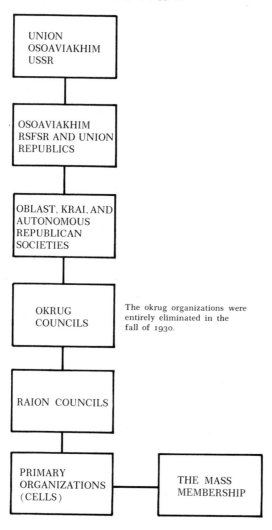

UNION
OSOAVIAKHIM
USSR

OSOAVIAKHIM
RSFSR AND UNION
REPUBLICS

OBLAST, KRAI, AND
AUTONOMOUS
REPUBLICAN
SOCIETIES

OKRUG
COUNCILS

The okrug organizations were
entirely eliminated in the
fall of 1930.

RAION COUNCILS

PRIMARY
ORGANIZATIONS
(CELLS)

THE MASS
MEMBERSHIP

fact he had authority for taxation through collection of dues and public fund raising, authority that the center would unavoidably have to leave largely to his discretion in a new sprawling organization like Osoaviakhim. Eideman revealed to the III Plenum how many secretaries exercised local discretion:[13]

> I do not think that the Moscow oblast organization is worse than any of our other organizations, but what do these facts reveal? Here is a list—I use materials from investigations—in 18 raions [the oblast had about 130 raions] the secretaries were either removed and tried by a court or they simply disappeared because financial losses were discovered. Here are some examples: the Kovrovskii secretary stole money; the Lotoshinskii secretary was removed for wasting funds and hooliganism; the Malinskii secretary stole two revolvers; the Pobedinskii secretary took 600 rubles and a bicycle to boot! (Laughter)

As a matter of fact the Moscow organization was one of the best. If these examples characterized Moscow's difficulties, it is fair to assume that many other organizations suffered more numerous and complicated scandals. Although Eideman declared he could not understand why personnel turnover in the lower reaches of the hierarchy was consistently a serious problem, his own testimony suggested a cogent explanation.

A variety of concomitant modifications in both structure and rules accompanied the elimination of the okrug organization. The statutes for the cell and raion were rewritten as well as the rules for Osoaviakhim RSFSR.[14] The class criterion for recruitment and the political propaganda justifying both domestic and foreign policy received added attention. The staff system of sections (*sektsii*) in the councils were renamed "sectors" (*sektory*), and the widespread practice of collegial responsibility in staff sectors and else-

[13] *Osoaviakhim*, 7-8 (1932), 7.
[14] *Spravochnik aktivista*, pp. 8-11, 19-23, 35-100.

where was pronounced as vicious as individual staff and managerial responsibility was virtuous.[15]

The staff reorganization involved more than a change of labels. In substance, three aims were pursued simultaneously. Standardizing the local council staff as much as possible (the policy since 1927 but apparently blatantly disregarded) promised two improvements if it were achieved. First, it would defeat the local practice of merging the organization sector with the finance or agitation sector. The purpose of such combinations was to conceal the fact that only one kind of work was being done—finance, for example, taking up all the sector's time while organizational matters were thoroughly neglected. Agitation work also could be mixed with organizational work to create a similar misimpression. (See Charts XI and XII for the required departmentalization of the council staffs and the apparatus in 1930.)

Second, standardization also applied to the staff departments (otdely) of the secretariat apparatus. The reorganization was meant to insure congruence between the council sectors and the secretariat departments.[16] Congruence, of course, might make the grip of the secretariat fit more tightly over the "public" sectors. At the same time, it presumably facilitated the intermingling of volunteer aktiv and apparatchiki in the departments of the apparatus. The hope was expressed not only that some sectors should have apparatchik leaders, but that aktiv should head some of the secretariat departments as well.[17] There is no evidence, however, that such hope was justified.

The third aim was connected with program evolution. Treating women as a special category, to be handled by one staff section, did not work out. This section, therefore, was dropped. The same was true of the section for aviation law. An agricultural section was added in 1930 but dropped a short time later. Unfortunately, information on the secretariat staff in 1927 is not available, but the

---

[15] Ibid., pp. 24-26.
[16] Osoaviakhim, 23-24 (1930), 12-13.
[17] Ibid., p. 13.

CHART XI

Public Staff Organization of
Osoaviakhim Councils—1930

Source: *Osoaviakhim*, 23-24 (1930), 13.

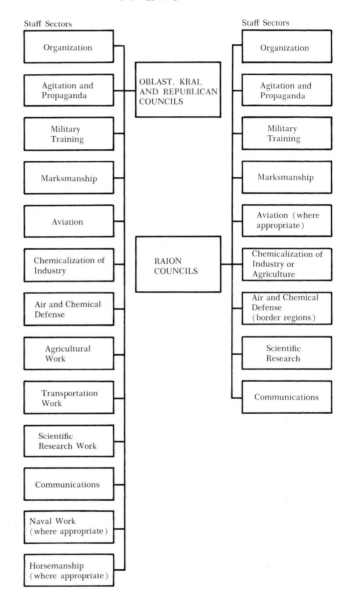

Staff Sectors   Staff Sectors

Organization		Organization
Agitation and Propaganda		Agitation and Propaganda
Military Training	OBLAST, KRAI, AND REPUBLICAN COUNCILS	Military Training
Marksmanship		Marksmanship
Aviation		Aviation (where appropriate)
Chemicalization of Industry	RAION COUNCILS	Chemicalization of Industry or Agriculture
Air and Chemical Defense		Air and Chemical Defense (border regions)
Agricultural Work		Scientific Research
Transportation Work		Communications
Scientific Research Work		
Communications		
Naval Work (where appropriate)		
Horsemanship (where appropriate)		

CHART XII

Organization of the Apparatus at the Oblast, Krai, and Republic Levels in 1930

Source: *Osoaviakhim*, 23-24 (1930), 13-14.

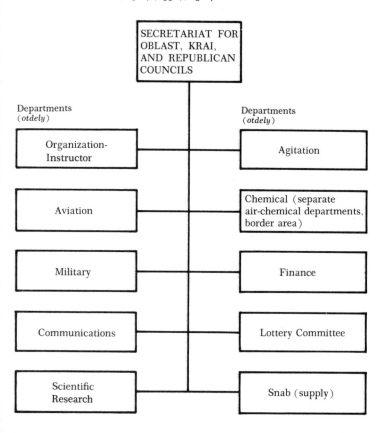

SECRETARIAT FOR OBLAST, KRAI, AND REPUBLICAN COUNCILS

Departments (*otdely*)

Departments (*otdely*)

Organization-Instructor

Agitation

Aviation

Chemical (separate air-chemical departments, border area)

Military

Finance

Communications

Lottery Committee

Scientific Research

Snab (supply)

departments prescribed in 1930 are shown on Chart XII. The impression is gained from the discussion about the new departmentalization that previously there had been fewer departments. In any event, some enlargement and modifications of the council staffs and the secretariat can be attributed to changes in training programs.

Staff functions were also increasingly differentiated in the secretariat (see Chart XIII). At the II Plenum of the Central Council, a resolution was taken to create cadre departments at all levels.[18] The raion cadre departments were to maintain records of non-apparatus volunteers, primarily the *aktiv*. A planning, accounting, and checking department was established at the same time.[19] These new departments persisted through the reshuffling of the secretariat in 1935.

The staff reforms brought significant standardization of reports rendered by the cells and raion councils. Financial records, local leaders had always complained, were too complex for the average cell secretary and treasurer to master. The same was true of forms for *uchet* and *otchet*.[20] Now all kinds of forms were being redesigned with these problems in mind. The supply organ, Snabosoaviakhim, also experienced changes. Okrug supply points were expected to proliferate in order to provide the new raion councils and the growing network of training points with essential materiel.[21]

The center's determination to pursue the reorganization in all its interrelated phases was evident from the set of progress indices that had to be reported to the Central Council every 15 days until the okrug councils were fully dismantled.[22] The center was not all thunder and fury, demanding response in an arbitrary fashion, but showed a willingness to bear part of the burden. The republican, krai, and oblast councils received together a grant of

[18] *Osoaviakhim na novom etape*, p. 19.
[19] *Ibid.*, p. 33.   [20] *Spravochnik aktivista*, p. 23.
[21] *Osoaviakhim*, 23-24 (1930), 12.
[22] *Ibid.*, p. 16.

CHART XIII

*Organization of the Secretariat Staff of
the Central Council—1931*

Source: *Osoaviakhim*, 22 (1931), 13.

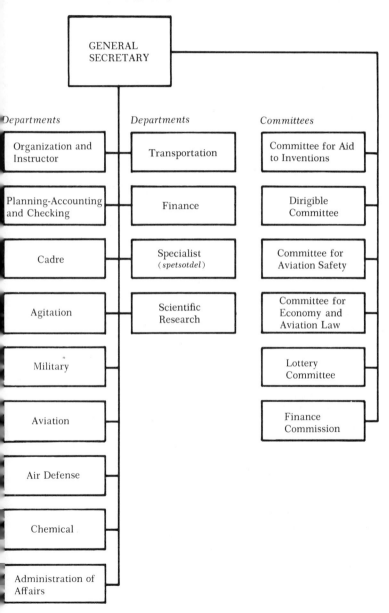

GENERAL SECRETARY

Departments

Organization and Instructor

Planning-Accounting and Checking

Cadre

Agitation

Military

Aviation

Air Defense

Chemical

Administration of Affairs

Departments

Transportation

Finance

Specialist (*spetsotdel*)

Scientific Research

Committees

Committee for Aid to Inventions

Dirigible Committee

Committee for Aviation Safety

Committee for Economy and Aviation Law

Lottery Committee

Finance Commission

CHART XIV

The Public Staff (Volunteer) Organization for the Union Osoaviakhim, 1927

Source: *Ustavnoi sbornik* and *Spravochnik aktivista Osoaviakhima.*

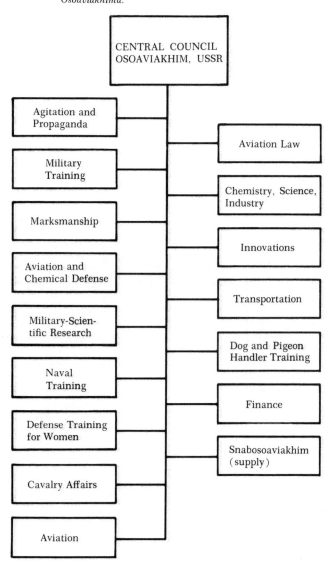

221,000 rubles from the Central Council for use in the reorganization in 1930 and another 5,000,000 rubles the following year for expenditure in strengthening raion councils.[23]

Finally, the reorganization included plans for improving information flow within the hierarchy. The center was determined to have multiple channels from below in order to prevent collusion and "drifting leadership." For a time, staff members specializing in "information reporting" were meant to be trained and employed on council staffs.[24] "Informers" among the *aktiv* and general membership were also to be trained to search out and report information on program breakdowns and mismanagement. They could report by mail directly to the Central Council as well as through the informer instructors on the council staffs. Apparently this practice never materialized as a lasting and regular alternative to the normal command lines. Formally, the revision commissions were supposed to provide an impartial accounting and to make the informer system unnecessary, but their absence in many places and their perfidy in others promised the Central Council anything but reliable revision reports. The first all-union conference of revision commissions, held in 1931, was meant to regularize and improve revision work.[25] The consequences of this endeavor, however, fell short of expectations.

The Reorganization of 1935

The push downward toward the local levels, the cell and the raion council, was only partially successful. In the densely populated regions, the response to reforming efforts was much greater than in the rural areas. Some progress in building a local apparatus unquestionably had been achieved, but, to borrow Bolshevik parlance, that progress had been quantitative; qualitative change proved a more elusive goal. The same result was more pronounced

[23] *Ibid.*   [24] *Ibid.*
[25] *Pervoe vsesoiuznoe.*

in membership growth. The quality of cell leadership had not stayed abreast of growth.

Something of the quantitative change can be grasped from the membership figures. A target of 17,000,000 by 1935 had been set, but only 13,000,000 had been reached. Even that number exceeded Osoaviakhim's organizational capacity at the cell level. Eideman chided the III Plenum of the Central Council in 1933 about the falsity of the reported 11,000,000 members in that year. Only six or seven million were effectively controlled by cell leadership. Stalin made the same charge about the 1935 figure, only with more acerbity.[26] Although the membership swelled faster on paper than in reality, the same was not true of the apparatus. It grew both in reality and on paper! It had become "puffed up" with persons who only superficially addressed the tasks of leadership while they deceived the Central Council with "eye wash" and "paper" reports of progress that had not in fact been achieved.

These unhappy circumstances were directly attributable to the policies of 1930. The membership recruitment was not slackened to permit hierarchical consolidation. It progressed at a regular rate, between one and two million each year. There are no available figures that allow an estimation of the rate of the apparatus's growth, but we know that in 1935 Stalin put a limit of 25,000 on the number of salaried workers, a limit requiring a reduction in the actual number.[27] At the II Plenum in 1931, the policy of expanding the apparatus was still in favor at the top. A petition for more low-level salaried posts was presented to the state authorities, and cadre departments were added to the secretariat at all levels including the raion.[28] Thereafter the apparatus expansion needed no encouragement from the top.

In 1932 a limit of 197 was placed on the secretariat staff of the Central Council.[29] Both the size and the qual-

[26] WKP-186, p. 210.   [27] Ibid., p. 215.
[28] Osoaviakhim na novom etape, p. 19.
[29] Khimiia i oborona, 9-10 (1932), 37.

ity of the apparatus was beginning to disturb the center. The III Plenum of the Central Council passed a resolution requiring all councils to review the work of all *apparatchiki* as well as volunteers in leadership posts for the purpose of eliminating class aliens and incompetent persons.[30] A year later at the IV Plenum, Eideman complained that the councils increasingly depended on an inflated apparatus rather than the *aktiv* and the mass membership.[31] Activating the raion council and strengthening its staff had been the aims of the reorganization in 1930. That policy succeeded in a way that was becoming not only undesirable but also dysfunctional for mass participation.

An abrupt halt to several features of the expansion policy was ordered in the secret decree of August 8, 1935. The VI Plenum of the Central Council convened at the end of the month and passed a series of resolutions for implementing the decree.[32] The plenum, therefore, publicly signalled a new course for Osoaviakhim, one followed until the eve of the coming war.

Many references have already been made to particular features of the secret decree, but here we shall describe its broad purpose and some of the practical measures it prescribed.[33] It was intended to raise the quality of Osoaviakhim work and to stop, or at least to limit, the widespread corruption in the apparatus, that is, the advantage individuals were taking within the limits of their own bureaucratic discretion to advance their personal interests and welfare at the expense of the organization. The tactics for pursuing this motive were comprehensive.

[30] *Osoaviakhim*, 7-8 (1932), 23.
[31] *Itogi IV Plenuma*, p. 7.   [32] *Itogi VI Plenuma*.
[33] The document from the Smolensk party archive is a comprehensive eleven-page typed communication to the oblast committee. The language is concise, even cryptic, but the scope of the decree reveals by implication that prodigious investigative staff work went into its preparation. And the acuteness of the decree leaves no doubt that the center was displeased with provincial realities in Osoaviakhim work.

In the first place, the decree narrowed the tasks of the organization. In doing so, it also reorganized the Central Council apparatus in a manner that facilitated central supervision (see Chart XV), and it directed that staffs at lower levels conform to the center's pattern more closely than they had previously. At the same time, setting a numerical limit on the apparatus size (25,000) provided leverage for bringing the provincial staffs into line with the new structure.

Second, supply procedures, financing, and fund raising were subjected to limits and new regulations. In particular, commercial activities not directly supporting a specific Osoaviakhim activity were flatly forbidden. Financial accounting, in addition to being simplified, was subjected to closer scrutiny by the Commissariat of Finance. In order to prevent dilatory adoption of the new policies, investigations were to be initiated by party committees, assisted by deputies of party and state control, to seek out *apparatchiki* engaged in thievery, embezzlement, and other illegal practices.

Third, the investigations were also intended to put some integrity and vigor into the revision commissions. Another ramification of the investigations was the creation of formal linkages between the party committees and the Osoaviakhim hierarchy. Second secretaries of the raion and oblast party committees thereafter were held personally accountable for Osoaviakhim activities. At the same time, all Osoaviakhim council chairmen were made members of the corresponding level party committees. Where the party had effectively ignored Osoaviakhim or had misappropriated its cadre for party work having nothing to do with Osoaviakhim programs, the new arrangements made such malpractices more difficult.

A fourth feature of the decree, in contrast to all the restrictive measures, was the loosening of controls on weapons and equipment. The NKVD was instructed to tolerate greater access to small arms for Osoaviakhim military programs in the rural areas. Some of the recent fruits of

CHART XV

Organization of the Secretariat Staff of the
Central Council—1935

Source: Smolensk Party Archive, WKP-186, pp. 215-216.

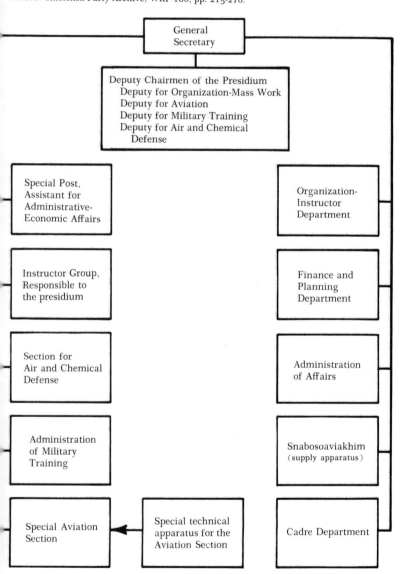

industrialization were also to be allocated, even if sparing-
ly, to Osoaviakhim. In the last half of 1935, 90 trucks, 35
light motor vehicles, 15 buses, 10 tank trucks, 10 ambu-
lances, and 30 tractors were authorized for delivery to the
Central Council at the expense of the state reserve fund,
that is, at no cost to Osoaviakhim. The Commissariat of
Light Industry was also ordered to take immediate measures to improve supplies for aviation programs.

The final gambit in the cluster of directives was a purge
of the entire membership. All membership documents had
to be exchanged for new ones. The exchange was to be
used primarily to strengthen the cell organization. Persons
not directly participating in Osoaviakhim programs, those
failing to pay dues on schedule, and class aliens were to
be eliminated from the Society. Furthermore, leaders of the
cells and raion councils, the chairmen and secretaries, had
to be elected, and the practice of appointing them was cate-
gorically forbidden. The purge and the new elections were
to be carried out by April 1, 1936. All this was to lead toward an all-union congress later in 1936.

The timing of the purge coincided with the beginning
of the Great Purges that engulfed all institutions of Soviet
society, but it would be a mistake to explain the purge in
Osoaviakhim as merely a spilling over of the Great Purges
into the defense society. Certainly there were connections,
just as the unification in 1927 was related to the general
plan for a vast social and economic transformation of
Soviet society. But a rationale for the purge, unique to the
organizational development, can be discerned from a review of the successive reorganization policies.

In the first period of Osoaviakhim's growth, the apparatus and the staff at the center had been consolidated and
regularized even if it was not allowed to become firmly
ensconced and resistant to further change. A similar development did not follow in the local organizations. The
policies promulgated in 1930 were prompted by the
wretched circumstances in provincial organizations; the
response to those policies had been effective mainly in
building the apparatus at the raion level. More than 3,000

raion councils were reported to be active by 1936.[34] Even
there, the quality of the cadre remained poor, the level of
deceit and corruption high, and the success of the program
for installation construction not always what was desired.
A large bureaucratic structure had been created, but it
was hardly embracing the bulk of the membership with
its programs. The cell, therefore, where the voluntary
membership prevailed, became the next logical target for
organizational development. The purge was part of the
scheme to reach that target. The political criterion was
certainly applied in the conduct of the purge, but it did
not occupy first place. Stalin's decree mentioned first of
all the Osoaviakhim rules that declared that "members can
only be those who belong to one of the primary organizations of Osoaviakhim, participate in its work, and pay
dues promptly."[35] Previously, formulas for Osoaviakhim
policy included a demand for simultaneous attention to
quantitative growth and qualitative improvements. That
kind of unrealistic clamor was missing from Stalin's decree.
The emphasis was clearly placed on quality—on consolidating gains. The document exchange was a very sensible
way to respond to discomfort over an exaggerated membership figure and a desire to put substance into cell activities.
The purge marked the third organizational push downward,
one that reached the individual member.

The insistence on elections is also an interesting aspect
of the tactics for invigorating the cell organization. Although it might be interpreted simply as part of the democratic or participatory facade characterizing many sides
of Soviet life, there was more to it than that. In order to
hold elections, cells and councils had to convene meetings.
Many cells never held meetings. If a raion council forced
all of its cells, many of which were likely to be existent
only on paper, to carry out elections, there would be a better chance to remove some of them from the "paper"
category. Elections also could have the effect of making

[34] Leont'ev, *Vooruzhennyi narod*, p. 69.
[35] WKP-186, p. 212.

the local leadership uncertain of election results unless it
exerted authority and took a positive role in the meetings
and activities. Far from being perfunctory affairs, elections
could increase the center's influence by initiating action,
raising questions about the local chairman's continued oc-
cupancy of his salaried post, and generally unsettling the
local *apparatchiki*'s sense of personal security.

Finally, it should be observed that the construction program for training installations and the training programs
themselves were maturing by 1936. At last Osoaviakhim
was gaining the capability to handle a large portion of the
mass membership in moderately effective programs. A few
years earlier it had no such capability. A purge of the rank
and file membership in 1936 could be used to increase
program participation in a large way, whereas the effect
of a purge at an earlier date would likely have been simply
to reduce the membership, an outcome many members no
doubt would have welcomed.

The full consequences of the purge are not easy to discover. No other plenum of the Central Council took place
after 1935, and the Third All-Union Congress never convened, although it was scheduled for 1936. The available
Osoaviakhim journals, *Samolet* and *Khimiia i oborona*, for
1937 and 1938 do not contain the plethora of criticisms
and commentary on organizational matters that were so
common in the years before. Eulogies to Stalin and Voroshilov are interspersed only with technical articles. A small
book on the tasks of Osoaviakhim published in 1938, however, does report that "because of the recent destruction
of the Eidemanites the majority of the Osoaviakhim cadre
is new in the councils, and includes people from all parts
of the Soviet society."[36] Apparently the turnover among
the *apparatchiki* and the *aktiv* had been high.

Although Eideman was executed in the spring of 1937,
he had remained at the head of Osoaviakhim for a year
and a half after the reorganization of 1935 was begun.
The apparatus was not idle under Eideman's direction.

[36] *Dvadtsatiletie*, p. 29.

Evidence of some of its work is to be found in the rewriting of many of the Osoaviakhim statutes and the detailed formulation of standard achievement norms for every training activity managed by the organization.[37] The organization handbook, published in 1936, integrated the changes dictated in the 1935 reorganization and contained the most complete instructions for the new primary organizations (cells) that Osoaviakhim members had yet seen.[38]

The structure of the new primary organization is shown on Chart XVI. The major change was an increase in the number of managers or assistant leaders. The old cell buro disappeared, making way for the "council," a staff of three to nine persons, depending on the size of the primary organization's membership. The practice of subdividing cell membership by work shift, by shop, section, or brigade, the so-called production principle, was introduced in 1929-1930 as part of a change to facilitate training. The 1936 statute formalized this practice and added official posts for the leaders of these groups within the cell. In large factories and other institutions, when there were several primary organizations, an *ad hoc* Osoaviakhim factory council could be organized to coordinate all Osoaviakhim work. These councils, where they existed, were subordinate to the raion councils.[39]

The standardization of organization, procedures, and achievement norms facilitated central control and reduced the discretion left to local leadership. What the primary organization and the raion councils now needed was not so much aggressive and imaginative leadership as persons who could and would adhere to well-developed routines and who would agitate against mass apathy. Admittedly, more sophisticated technical skills were also required to conduct some of the training, but it will be remembered that programs had become centralized in training points, special schools, aeroclubs, and other composite installations.

[37] *Sputnik Osoaviakhima.*   [38] *Ibid.*
[39] Leont'ev, *Vooruzhennyi narod,* pp. 59-68.

CHART XVI

Cell Organization before Changes in 1936

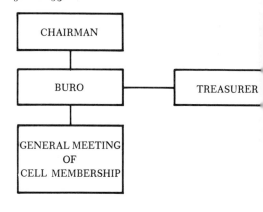

Primary Organization in 1936
(Replaced the Cell)

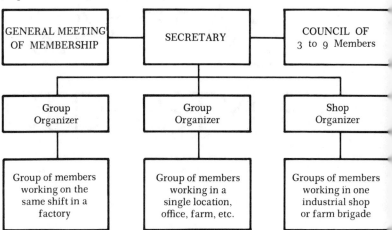

Note: The number of groups varied according to the size of
the primary organization and the nature of the institution by which most of its members were employed.
Source: *Sputnik Osoaviakhima*, pp. 51-57.

Precisely these consequences, however, facilitated the purge. Routinization made large personnel turnover possible without a breakdown of the programs. It is difficult to imagine that Osoaviakhim could have survived a purge in the early 1930's. The raions lacked the administrative capacity to conduct it among the mass membership.

In summing up, it is useful to review changes according to the separate variables mentioned in the beginning of this section.

1. *Structure of the hierarchy.*   One entire level, the okrug council and its staff, was abolished in 1930. The cell structure was elaborated and its leadership shored up by the creation of new posts in 1936. In principle, however, the formal structure of the hierarchy remained essentially unaltered.

2. *Departmentalization of staff functions.*   Three kinds of change are observable. First, there was a continuing and modestly successful trend toward uniformity among all staffs. In the beginning, local adaptations caused wide variances in staff departmentalization. By 1936, staff uniformity was more often the case from place to place and from level to level. Second, symmetry between the secretariat departments and the public sectors of the council staff was increasingly achieved after 1930. Symmetry, of course, facilitated atrophy in the council sectors because the apparatus tended to substitute itself for the volunteer and *aktiv* membership. Third, some staff sectors were dropped and others added. These changes reflected both program developments and the problems in maintaining the hierarchy and support functions.

3. *Operational procedures.*   The statutes for the cell and raion organizations were re-written twice after the initial versions in 1927. Forms for reporting were repeatedly changed, ostensibly to achieve greater simplicity and to

facilitate compliance. In reality the changes also brought increased refinement and detail in operating instructions. Both achievement norms and activity prescription proliferated and thereby diminished the latitude for local discretion in a formal sense.

4. *Apparatus and volunteer membership.*   Membership growth continued steadily until 1936 when a serious change from the quantity criterion to the quality measure took place. The apparatus also grew but not quite in step with the remainder of the organization. Rapid expansion of the apparatus occurred mainly before the Osoaviakhim unification in 1927 and between 1930 and 1935.

5. *Shifts in goals, tasks, and reponsibility.*   Two striking trends are apparent in this respect. First, the apparatus found it easier to take leadership responsibility on itself than to inspire and oversee a large cadre of *aktiv*. The limit placed on the apparatus strength in 1935 obstructed and perhaps temporarily reversed this behavior. Second, the personnel in the hierarchy, the chairmen and the secretaries, devoted more time to Osoaviakhim's administration, or system maintenance, than they gave to the management of programs for training. The latter, it will be recalled, had developed its own hierarchy in the network of training installations. The persistence of commercialism in local council activities indicates not only the durability of self-interest and illegal practices but also that the tasks of administration and finance could easily displace some of the original purposes of the organization.

Finally, the links between the party and Osoaviakhim were formally prescribed, and personal responsibility for Osoaviakhim work was unambiguously placed on individuals in the party committees. Such formalities, however, had come after eight years of mixed relations between Osoaviakhim and the local party leaders.

In what sense can these changes be related to program developments? In the first place, they concern functional requirements of the organization that are distinct from the programs for training activity. They are the consequences of Osoaviakhim's response to organizational maintenance requirements. They are about management problems and securing organizational inputs. They are not primarily about Osoaviakhim end products—trained personnel and mass public enlightenment on technical matters of war and defense. Their rationale derives in part from the nature of these products however. As programs changed, the hierarchy, the managerial system, and the quantity and type of inputs had to change in a way that could provide an organizational support capacity. The expanded apparatus, new rules, and the enlarged membership were essential concomitant developments if programs for the practical organizations were to succeed.

Chapter XV

Bureaucracy: Rational Structure or Political Arena?

In the last two chapters, we have been describing several kinds of change that took place in Osoaviakhim over the course of a decade. An effort has been made to show the relationships and interactions among those dynamic trends. Changes in programs were discussed primarily as responses to technical constraints: equipment and skill scarcities. But it was also pointed out that program goals were a matter of choice even when physical factors severely limited the chooser's options. In the analysis of the series of reorganizations of the hierarchy and the operational procedures for organizational maintenance, dysfunctional consequences of organizational structure and operational patterns were identified as the stimuli for each successive reorganization. The conceptual approach in both of these chapters was largely paramechanistic. Our study, taking a set of goals and the Soviet environment as given, has focused on the paramechanistic interaction of structure, physical constraints, and goals. To the extent that this approach accounts for Osoaviakhim's development over a decade, explanation depends on discovering a rationale in the interaction.

Both Merton and Selznick have developed models of bureaucracy that provide such a rationale for organizations in general.[1] A great deal of what has been observed about

[1] For a concise and critical analysis of both models, see March and Simon, *Organizations*, pp. 34-44. See also Robert K. Merton, *Social Theory and Social Structure* (Enlarged

Osoaviakhim is entirely compatible with these models. Merton's well-known strictures to study "unanticipated consequences" of organizational policies lead him in his own model to emphasize that the demand for control at the top of the organization begets rigidity in the behavior of subordinates. Techniques used to secure central control, and thus reliability of subordinate behavior, tend (a) to reduce personalized relationships, (b) to encourage internalization of the rules, and (c) to limit the range of alternatives that will be examined in decision making.

The demand for control certainly characterized the behavior of Osoaviakhim's leadership. Numerous observable techniques were used to secure control over membership behavior. Rules, achievement norms, activity specification, all of these tended to narrow the scope of local decision making. But there were other control techniques, whose consequences are difficult to explain in the context of the model: ineffective revision commissions, surprise investigations, shifting responsibility, Osoaviakhim entanglements with other organizations, and a purge of the membership.

For example, the first of Merton's general unanticipated consequences, a reduction in personal relationships, was apparently valued by Osoaviakhim leaders, who sought to achieve it, although not always with success. Personal cliques and informal groups were perceived as a danger to be eradicated. Investigations, exposures in the press, reorganization, elections, and the purge were conscious endeavors to depersonalize local organizational relationships. It would be wrong, of course, to ignore the center's encouragement of a kind of personalized approach by cell leaders toward the members for purposes of securing their fuller cooperation. The "positive hero" role was commended to all, but that did little to mitigate the rigor with which the center consciously struggled to break up personalized relationships.

1968 edition; New York: The Free Press, 1968); and Selznick, *TVA and the Grass Roots*, pp. 249-66.

The second unanticipated consequence, internalization of the rules—that is, when rules, originally designed as means to ends, become ends in themselves for organization members—does not fit the Osoaviakhim experience a great deal better. The center, by prescribing activity routines in the greatest detail, hoped to profit from rule internalization by members. The dysfunctional consequence of a more serious nature was deceit and misinformation perpetrated by local Osoaviakhim leaders and staff workers. Perhaps one exception was the enduring enthusiasm for "commercial activities." Commercialism had apparently become an end in itself, although it was originally conceived as a means of support for local programs. In any event, it is fair to say that the center would have been pleased if most of its rules had been internalized to a much greater extent than they actually were.

The last of the consequences of rigidity deriving from central control, the increased use of standard categories for decision making and thereby the limited search for alternatives, offers no more help in explaining Osoaviakhim behavior than the first two. Localism, *kustarnichestvo*, and individual initiative outside the prescribed pattern for decision making disturbed the center greatly. Even when a surge of local initiative was inspired by genuine intentions to support overall Osoaviakhim goals, it frequently led to a waste of energy and resources. The example of local councils starting aeroclubs where resources and skills were inadequate for the clubs to operate successfully is a case in point. At least within the time period we have studied, when the organization was being built, limited latitude for local decision making was both a desired and a functional consequence from the center's viewpoint. At the same time, the center demanded creative initiative from local leaders. It called for unleashing the creativity of the masses within Osoaviakhim. Such was the ambivalence of Osoaviakhim policy, demanding at once spontaneity and control.

Selznick's model also has its starting point in the demand for control, but it takes delegation of authority as the rational response for securing that control. Delegating authority has, as an anticipated result, the effect of increasing specialized skills and competences. The scope of subunit tasks is narrowed to increase subunit control over task achievement, and special competences tend to develop in the subunits of the increasingly specialized nature of subunit goals. This consequence in turn leads to a repetition of the cycle, apparently because "delegation of authority" is deemed the only rational response by the top.[2]

The important unanticipated consequence of delegation of authority is a bifurcation of interests at the subunit level. To subunit specialists and managers, subunit goals become more important than organizational goals. In order to defend their preferences for subunit goals, the subunit members may develop ideologies of their own to justify their own policies at the expense of central policies. Subunit ideologies, too, may play a role in conflicts among subunits over the consequences of organizational decisions.

The resulting internalization of subunit goals, moreover, depends in part on the extent to which subunit goals are operational. The ability of subunits to influence organizational decisions is determined by the degree to which subunit goals provide measuring rods for testing achievement. Internalization of subunit goals is apt to occur more fully where unambiguous achievement is possible.

This skeletal presentation of Selznick's model is sufficient to suggest explanations for some of the developments we have observed in Osoaviakhim, but, like Merton's model, paradoxes arise in trying to achieve a conceptual fit of the model on the data.

Delegation of authority to subunits with a narrower range of tasks did occur in Osoaviakhim. It took place in two ways. First, the required physical dispersion of the lower levels of the hierarchy carried with it a specialization not so much in types of tasks as in the size and social

[2] March and Simon, *Organizations*, p. 43. This failure to consider alternatives to delegation of authority is underscored and elucidated by March and Simon as an unsatisfactory feature of Selznick's model.

composition of the population to be dealt with. Second, the staff divisions and formation of practical organizations reflected the factorization of organizational goals into subgoals, some more operational than others. Delegation of authority may not, however, characterize what the center intended for the subunits. The Osoaviakhim central leadership stressed the delegation of *responsibility* more than delegation of *authority*. For a number of years, of course, the Central Council's administrative capacity for exerting its authority at the raion and cell level was sorely restricted. When and wherever this was true, a *de facto* delegation of authority might be said to have existed.

Where subunits had a modicum of authority, they only occasionally used it to press for the primacy of subunit goals or to develop subunit ideologies. Nor did the center seek increased control by responding in every case with another delegation of authority to more specialized subunits. A few exceptions to these conclusions do appear.

The aviation program, when it finally developed a network of aviation schools, was accused of a closed cycle, of tending only to its narrow interests at the expense of broader organizational goals. The same problem remained after the change to the aeroclub system. This result certainly was not intended. The intended result was, as Selznick's model suggests, concentration of skill levels in smaller subunits in order to deal with a difficult and complex task. The concentration of able cadres in a few aeroclubs did seem to coincide with significant advances in the output of pilots by Osoaviakhim. The outcome, as late as 1938, is difficult to assess from our limited information. If delegation of authority, in the sense Selznick intends, includes functional differentiation, it may be observed that the aviation program had an independent apparatus even within the Central Council. Local organizations lost control over pilot training. Even the finances had become centralized and the requirement that aeroclubs generate a fraction of their own funds locally had been dropped.

That the aviation program held a special status is clear enough, but it is far from obvious that this status was the consequence of delegated authority and internalization of subunit goals. Nor is it clear to what extent aviation leaders fell into conflict with other subunit leaders as the Selznick model indicates will happen. Such conflict did arise. There was the occasion at the IV Plenum of the Central Council when "neutral departmentalism," an attitude emerging especially in connection with military programs, was soundly condemned.[3] What else can this label imply but that subunit members were giving subunit goals priority over Osoaviakhim's goals? In this respect Selznick's analysis is vindicated. But it fails to explain why the center was able to overcome subunit independence while encouraging greater differentiation of tasks. The center did not respond to dysfunctions by delegating authority so much as it took aviation programs from the lower hierarchy and concentrated them in a fewer number of subunits which were nearer the center and easier to subject to central authority.

Although the Merton and Selznick models highlight the relationship of several variables in organizational behavior, important phenomena are left unexplained and even appear in some instances as contradictions to the logic of the models. The check for conceptual relevance, however, has not been an idle endeavor because it draws attention to the exceptional behavior. Unique Russian cultural patterns offer cogent ways to account for the exceptions, but it must not go unnoticed that the rational character of the models may also supply clues about where to turn for explanations. Merton and Selznick treat organizations as systems with a rationale of their own. Individual behavior is implicitly treated as probabilistic. Occasional unique behavior by a few individuals is not considered sufficient to alter the system's rationale. Suppose we set this point of view aside and assume that Osoaviakhim had no logic as a system. Rather let us assume that its dynamic character is only symptomatic of the interaction of rational behavior by individuals and small groups. Beginning with this assump-

[3] *Itogi IV Plenuma*, p. 45.

tion, it may be more enlightening to give up modeling the organizational dynamic and instead, to analyze certain elements of the development. Where the Osoaviakhim experiences did not fit the theories of organization, it was usually because leaders and subordinates chose alternatives not deemed rational in the context of the theories.[4] As the analysis by March and Simon emphasizes, there is a rational and mechanistic quality to these models. At certain points they prescribe a machine-like and highly restrictive range of managerial choices.[5]

Michel Crozier, taking similar notice of these conceptual difficulties in the study of bureaucratic organization, devises an approach precisely for the purpose of emphasizing the variable of human choice.[6] The individual in an organization has ". . . a head, which means that he is free to decide and to play his own game."[7] The way to understand this reality, Crozier declares, is to take power relationships among individuals within an organization as the central problem for study. This suggestion alone is sufficient to cause us to remember the varieties of individual behavior observable in Osoaviakhim, to think about the kind of "game" various groups played and the countergames played at the center.

Furthermore, it takes us back to the realities that the party elite saw confronting their aspirations to build socialism in general (i.e. to modernize a backward country) and to resolve the military question in particular. The cultural level of the population and the concomitant mass values sharply differed from Bolshevik values. The very inception of mass voluntary societies was fundamentally related to the abyss separating party and mass values.

[4] Henry L. Roberts has stressed this point in a subtle but devastating comment on "systemic" approaches to the study of Soviet politics. See his "Succession to Khrushchev in Perspective," *Proceedings of the Academy of Political Science,* XXVIII (April, 1965), 2-12.

[5] *Organizations,* p. 45.

[6] *The Bureaucratic Phenomenon,* pp. 175-208.

[7] *Ibid.,* p. 149.

Osoaviakhim was conceived as an instrumentality for allocating party values on a mass scale, for destroying and replacing traditional values with modern ones. Osoaviakhim, therefore, was one of several organizational gambits the party played in the struggle to exercise public power and to dictate Soviet political development. But the game was also being played by the masses with a measure of success. Drawing up rules for Osoaviakhim and inviting mass participation did not inspire mass compliance. Stalin even doubted the organization's grip on 13,000,000 members twelve years after the ODVF had been founded, nine years after the birth of Osoaviakhim. For an adequate comprehension of Osoaviakhim's dynamic nature, therefore, we must conceive of it and study it as political development, change occurring as the result of struggle by all participants to acquire, to exert, to limit, and to obstruct the use of power; or in Lasswell's neo-Hobbesian language, "to get the most of what there is to get."

The change of focus does not render useless our discussion of the paramechanistic character of organizational development. Political choice is never unlimited for anyone, Stalin notwithstanding. Physical and mechanical constraints are real in every organization and in every political system. As much is implied by the conventional wisdom that politics is the art of the possible. The mechanistic and technical features of organization form the terrain and obstacles on the playing field. They broaden or narrow the options open to players. Failure to perceive them clearly will mislead us in endeavors to explain the players' behavior.

Giving up the search for a model that accounts for bureaucracy as a rational system in its own terms, Crozier defines bureaucracy as *"an organization that cannot correct its behavior by learning from its errors."*[8] This is true because the organization embraces a set of internal equilibria whose maintenance generates "vicious circles" rather than error correction in the organizational system. Rationality, then, is to be sought in each of the internal equi-

[8] *Ibid.*, p. 187. Italics are in the original.

libria. As Crozier identifies them, these equilibria are established by the power relations among strata within the organization. The shift in focus from concern with the organization as a rational system to interest in these equilibria leads one to ask what is the rationale in the behavior of particular groups of functionaries. The dynamic of the organizational system, accordingly, is the consequence of the interaction of these equilibria, and its striking characteristic turns out to be little or no system learning at the organizational level, a "bureaucratic vicious circle" in Crozier's words, until dysfunctions can hardly be ignored if the organization is to survive. In order to impute a rationale to the exercise of choice by strata within the organization, however, Crozier has to develop a concept of power and its exercise within an organization.

Taking Robert Dahl's definition, *"the power of a person A over a person B is the ability of A to obtain that B do something he would not have otherwise done,"*[9] Crozier introduces the notion of uncertainty into the definition. In the hierarchy of an organization, subordinates can derive power vis-à-vis superiors when there is uncertainty on the superior's part about the outcome of a task. If by rules, routines, and highly impersonalized procedures the superior can insure the task's accomplishment without a cooperative attitude by the subordinates, the subordinates have no power. But in reality that is seldom if ever the case. Program execution is more likely to be surrounded by uncertainties that can only be dealt with successfully by cooperative and skilled subordinates. Knowledge of outcomes is a sure sign of strength. Superiors and subordinates, rationally using their own limited knowledge and others' uncertainties, can play games with one another for stakes of power accretion. As Crozier reformulates Dahl's definition, "the power of A over B depends on A's ability to predict B's behavior and on the uncertainty of B about A's behavior."[10]

Uncertainty in an organization is of two types. First,

[9] As quoted in *ibid.*, p. 157.   [10] *Ibid.*, p. 158.

it surrounds the accomplishment of the task itself. Second, the rules that make tasks more predictable may or may not be applied. The manager's leeway with the rules is his source of power for bargaining with subordinates. "As long as uncertainty remains about carrying out a task, the most menial subordinate retains some slight discretion."[11] The subordinates seek to widen their discretion as a source of power; the manager seeks to reduce it by impersonal rules over which he has discretion in applying; hence his source of power. As long as humans are preferred to machines, Crozier insists, this game of power is inevitable in organizations.[12]

The foregoing and incomplete description hardly does justice to the subtleties of Crozier's arguments, and it entirely omits his analysis of the elements of the bureaucratic vicious circle. But it does provide two basic insights that are useful for explaining what can be observed in Osoaviakhim. First, power is always diffuse in an organization. Because an ordinary Osoaviakhim member or a raion *apparatchik* could not compel the Central Council to do a particular act it would not have otherwise done, it does not follow that the member and the *apparatchik* have no power. Second, uncertainty about program execution and rule implementation abounded in Osoaviakhim. Thus it is important to relate behavior at all levels to that uncertainty, to observe the ways in which uncertainty was exploited as a source of influence.

An eclectic application of Crozier's model is dictated by his own caveat. It was suggested in the critique of the Merton and Selznick models that cultural differences may account for the poor "fit" discovered when their models are used in an analysis of Osoaviakhim. Crozier demonstrates that ethnic social structure and cultural patterns in France go far in explaining what his analytical model

[11] *Ibid.*, p. 160.
[12] It should be observed that Crozier's view of organizational politics has something in common with Hobbes's characterization of a "perpetuall and restlesse desire of Power after power, that ceaseth onely in Death."

already presumed to account for in his two case studies. He acknowledges accordingly the implications for any claims of universality for his model and then goes on to examine the variations in cultural patterns in Russia, France, and America and their significance for individual behavior within organizations. For example, the phenomenon of strata isolation, peculiar to French organizations, has no cultural basis in the context of Russian traditions and values. Yet strata isolation is one of four elements Crozier identifies in the bureaucratic vicious circle.[13] Perhaps it should not surprise us, then, that Selznick's model fits well in many American cases but poorly in a Russian case. Similarly, the elements of Crozier's concept of the bureaucratic vicious circle have limited heuristic value for the study of Soviet bureaucracy, although the vicious circle might be redefined to achieve a uniquely Russian fit.

[13] The others are (a) impersonal rules; (b) centralization of decisions; and (c) development of parallel power relationships around areas of uncertainty. *Ibid.*, p. 187.

Chapter XVI

Power Relations in Osoaviakhim

In a formal sense Osoaviakhim's authority derived from the mass membership, which elected the all-union congress. At the same time, this apparent democracy was "counterweighted" by the central controls.[1] In spite of the controls, the novelty of many of Osoaviakhim's programs, the size and dispersion of the membership, and the somewhat limited communications system combined to create a plethora of uncertainties about program execution. In other words, power to control outcomes was diffused throughout the organization. The central controls might insure that certain outcomes *would not occur*, that alternative programs would never receive public articulation, but they could not insure that prescribed outcomes *would occur*. Because power was shared, however unequally, by many subunits, struggle over power by various groups and individuals in Osoaviakhim must be examined.

The available evidence for such a study may be more systematic and representative than at first meets the eye. Because it is taken from the Osoaviakhim press and reports at plenums and conferences, it is found in the context of correctional action taken by the center. The center was explicit about the pertinence of the press and published reports from organizational meetings as policy guidance. It made no sense to publish accounts of episodes

[1] This concept of "counterweights at the peril points" in the democratic form of Soviet government is John N. Hazard's. See his *Soviet System of Government*, pp. 240ff.

and morality stories in connection with unique or exceptional behavior. Critical guidance from above, to be effective, had to be based on widespread problems. Consequently, a few vignettes from the Osoaviakhim press or from a speech by a Central Council official cannot be dismissed easily as statistically irrelevant. It may be a biased sampling, but the source of that bias was the center's preference about program outcomes and is in itself a rational bias with respect to goal achievement. Not only does such evidence reveal a great deal about behavior at all levels, but it also expresses the values of the Central Council. From the reported behavior of individuals in various roles in the organization, more such "revealed preferences" can be identified.

Limitations plague the analysis in any event. Specifically, discrimination among subgroups must remain restricted because the evidence does not differentiate among subgroups in a rigorous way. For our purposes here, four groups of organization members will be used: (a) the volunteer membership, including *aktiv*; (b) the apparatus below the Central Council; (c) the oligarchy at Osoaviakhim's center; (d) the party elite, particularly Stalin and his agents at the Osoaviakhim center.

The Mass Voluntary Membership

The amorphous nature of the mass membership might be thought to leave the ordinary Osoaviakhim member utterly powerless in his relations with the organization. Certainly he could not suggest policy initiatives to the Central Council nor could he use the Osoaviakhim structure as a vehicle for pressing group demands on the party or anyone else. Yet he did have a latitude for obstructing central policy. He could delay and often avoid paying his dues. He could refuse to participate in programs or malinger when he was coerced into a training program. He could dodge voluntary labor contributions on holidays.

The success the individual member enjoyed in exercising these options is indicated by numerous counteractions and complaints by the *apparatchiki*. Eideman's critique of the membership figure in 1932 suggests that nearly half of the members were effectively remaining untouched by Osoaviakhim demands and programs even without losing formal membership status.[2] Unshlikht admitted in 1930 that the Society could not hold on to the membership it had recruited because of the lack of a firm program and cadre base.[3] Many departed its ranks as easily as they had come in. Migrations within the Soviet Union, itinerant workers in the construction industry,[4] and the random movement from country to city and from city to city made it difficult to keep track of individuals.

The incompetency of the low- and middle-level *apparatchiki* contributed more than a little to the individual member's leeway for avoiding entanglement in the practical work and general programs. The Shuiskii Okrug organization, for example, had recruited less than eight percent of the workers in the okrug by 1930. The okrug council did not meet for intervals of seven and eight months. The Tver organization had ostensibly raised its membership, but largely among school children. Workers actually declined in number in the okrug organization.[5]

Incompetency in the apparatus was not the whole story. Geographical location widened or limited the individual's latitude for personal choice. In the rural regions, the apparatus simply could not reach him, or, as was admitted by the Tatar Republican organization, one might as well recognize, in the historic phrase of Gogol, that most members were "dead souls."[6] In the urban and industrial areas, he was more accessible but by no means without devious ploys for minimizing his involvement. The Komsomolites ignored military training so blatantly at times that Oso-

[2] *Osoaviakhim*, 7-8 (1932), 5.

[3] *Pravda*, February 23, 1930.

[4] WKP-107, p. 94. This document from the Smolensk party archive describes how migration of construction workers virtually destroyed an Osoaviakhim raion organization.

[5] *Osoaviakhim*, 15 (1930), 10, 12.

[6] *Pervyi oblastnoi s"ezd ODVF Tatrespubliki*, p. 38.

aviakhim officials resorted to the police as a means of enforcing attendance at obligatory military training programs.[7]

Following Crozier's formulation, "the power of A over B depends on A's ability to predict B's behavior and on the uncertainty of B about A's behavior," in several respects, then, the rank and file of Osoaviakhim had A's position while the center found itself in B's position. The center, of course, was far from being ignorant of the residual power belonging to the masses. It was not for nothing that a local *apparatchik* worried about the need to show peasants some airplanes in order to maintain a spirit conducive to fund-raising for aviation.[8] And the Central Council was certainly serious when it demanded that local leaders explain fully the Osoaviakhim construction program in the 1930's.[9] To recognize the need to negotiate and persuade was to acknowledge the uncertainties about how the ordinary member would exercise his minute discretion.

The Center's Exercise of Power Over the Volunteers

A rough analytical distinction between persuasion and coercion is useful in distinguishing among the gambits the center played in the game of diminishing the individual member's power. Gambits based on persuasion amounted to promising benefits from participation. The benefits can also be subdivided into collective and non-collective benefits.[10]

The most widely proclaimed benefit Osoaviakim offered was state defense. Personal security from external threat

[7] *Osoaviakhim*, 15 (1930), 10.

[8] *Pervyi oblastnoi s"ezd ODVF Tatrespubliki*, p. 35.

[9] *Osoaviakhim na novom etape*, p. 12.

[10] For a novel critique of group theory and group participation, see Mancur Olson, Jr., *The Logic of Collective Action*. Non-collective benefits, he argues, inspire participation, not collective benefits or group interests.

has been noted as a powerful incentive for voluntary participation in organizations.[11] The threat from the capitalist encirclement, of course, was the cornerstone assumption in Stalin's policy of "socialism in one country," but because war loomed only in an indefinite future, repeated warnings about its imminence were, like the shepherd boy's false cries of "wolf," hardly sufficient to secure mass participation in Osoaviakhim. "Defense days," agitational campaigns, and "defense weeks," nevertheless, were consistently used for recruitment, playing on war fears, exploiting international crises and diplomatic incidents as agitational topics. Another collective benefit, also used to persuade the masses, was the attraction of modernity in contrast to the discomforts of traditional social and economic patterns. Postyshev of the Central Committee, KP(b)U, in telling the Komsomolites why they should join Osoaviakhim, used this appeal: "the people of Tsarist Russia stood on their knees for centuries . . . , but they have arisen from chains, tears, and groans and destroyed the past. . . ."[12] Undoubtedly, such images kindled a few youthful imaginations, but the daily demands of Soviet life were too great for such vague advantages to inspire masses of volunteers.

Non-collective benefits for individuals also had a place in the recruiting policies. Marksmanship especially appealed as a form of entertainment, and it was used specifically in many cases to draw attention and interest.[13] More

[11] Bernard Barber, "Mass Apathy and Voluntary Social Participation in the United States," unpublished Ph.D. dissertation, Harvard University, 1948, pp. 258-59. See also Lewis Coser, *The Functions of Social Conflict* (New York: The Free Press, 1956), pp. 122-49. Coser analyzes Georg Simmel's contributions to sociology. Both Coser and Barber conclude that external threats, particularly wars, minimize attention to value differences in a society and sharpen perception of shared values.

[12] Quoted from N. V. Popov, *Osoaviakhim Ukrainy na boevom postu* (Kiev: 1936), p. 7.

[13] V. N. Strutsa, *Krepite oboronu SSSR*, p. 196.

attractive yet were the exemptions from Red Army service to be gained from participation in Osoaviakhim's military programs. For a limited number there was hope of attaining a valuable skill, of advancing oneself in status and income. The pilot programs opened one such opportunity. Party membership also was advertised as possible through active work in Osoaviakhim.[14] For reserve officers and veterans of the Red Army in particular there was the chance to secure a salaried post in the apparatus. Or one might simply join to please one's superior in some other institution if it was perceived that the superior desired one to join. Badges and uniforms, too, were used to give members symbols invoking social approbation. Last, the program for children, "The Young Friends of Osoaviakhim," was meant to secure a voluntary flow of youth into the Society by catching children's imaginations, especially through the model airplane program.

When the gentler methods of inspiring volunteers failed, others were found. The pre-inductee training was obligatory for all youth of draft age. Where Osoaviakhim ran the program, membership in the Society was virtually enforceable by law if police assistance was available.

Recruitment by factory, by school, or by any other institution, took the character of mass joining, particularly during defense weeks and other campaigns. In such cases, individuals were simply herded into the organization without concern for their preferences. It will be recalled, in connection with Osoaviakhim's relations to the trade unions, the Komsomol, and the party, that coercive mass joining was common. In the case of the Komsomol, it was made concomitant with Komsomol membership.

All in all, the center brought together an impressive array of gambits for influencing the hesitant or recalcitrant; but such influence was not uniformly effective throughout the USSR. It depended on the administrative capacity of the apparatus and the control of all other institutions overlapping with Osoaviakhim. In the rural areas and in the regions of national minorities, this influence

[14] *Spravochnik aktivista*, p. 129.

largely remained ineffective. Thus the Society, while officially possessing 13,000,000 members in 1935 and 1936,
was virtually non-existent in many of the raions of the
Western Oblast (Smolensk) as late as 1936 and 1937. The
Far East, Western Siberia, parts of the Ukraine, parts of
the Urals, the North Caucasus, and Central Asia were
bulwarks of passive resistance to active participation, only
slightly less so to recruitment.[15] It would be wrong, however, to ignore the success Osoaviakhim realized in recruiting and training in other regions. The funds gathered,
the reports of training results, and the constructive programs all attest to that.

The Apparatus Versus the Center

The position of the apparatus in a political sense was
far more complex than that of the volunteers. The *apparatchik* had to depend on subordinates—the volunteers—
to carry out programs. At the same time, the center depended on the *apparatchiki* to perform supervision at each
level of the hierarchy. Also, because their primary income
came from Osoaviakhim, their interest was greater. Although a variety of roles existed in the apparatus, our
data are either too general or too incomplete to discrim-
inate rigorously according to subgroups and particular
roles. Some general observations, in any event, are de-
fendable and perhaps offer the most instructive insights
into the rationale of policies.

Crozier's analytical approach can provide a starting
point even if it loses relevance for particular developments.
"Planned cooperative action is possible," he says, only if
regularity in participant behavior can be relied upon,
and ". . . achievement of necessary conformity will be the
central problem of an organization's government."[16] His

[15] *Osoaviakhim na novom etape*, p. 16. Language and ethnic
barriers played a role in retarding work in Central Asia and the
North Caucasus.

[16] *The Bureaucratic Phenomenon*, pp. 183-84.

studies of long-established French organizations lead him to focus on the "basic strategy" of increasing one's own discretion and at the same time limiting others' discretion by means of impersonal rules that confine their behavior to predictable patterns.[17] When these conceptualizations are applied to Osoaviakhim, their relevance for the center's game is clear. The center wanted both increasing discretion for its own policy making and predictable behavior by all other participants, and it tried to achieve both by imposing detailed rules that reduced the uncertainties surrounding program execution without bargaining away central authority. The *apparatchiki*, in contrast, began with wide discretion in local affairs. Their game accordingly was exploitation of that discretion in local affairs. Regulation of behavior by rules could only harm them in all but a few instances. They could profit, however, by making a few rules apply to subordinates, especially payment of dues, and they wanted the trade unions, Komsomols, and local party committees to aid them according to rule prescription. Perhaps it is a matter of degree, but they essentially differed from any of the groups in Crozier's studies in having so little to gain from increased regularity through rules. They differed in another sense as well. Spread widely over the state, they did not develop as an isolated stratum with corporately perceived interests and tacit cooperative behavior patterns. Rather they took the Soviet pattern of isolated "family groups."[18] Another motive sometimes distinguished the *apparatchik*'s game. If he was ambitious, he might play his game for the center's advantage in order to be promoted to a better position. Although upward mobility in Osoavia-

[17] *Ibid.*, pp. 160-61.

[18] Raymond A. Bauer, *et al.*, *How the Soviet System Works* (New York: Vintage Books, 1956), pp. 88-89, 92-93, 166, 176. This study defines the pattern from data taken in interviews and questionnaires from Soviet emigrés. For discussion of the family circle in Soviet industrial organization, see Berliner, *Factory and Manager in the USSR*, pp. 259-63.

khim contributed to a wider choice of games for the individual, those who sought responsibility and promotion faced difficulties in meeting the extreme demands levied by the center when resources were acutely scarce. These ambitious ones could not simply apply the rules mechanically and hope to rise in the bureaucracy. Thus, they too needed discretion and were forced to engage in illegal behavior in order to advance their careers.

Now to identify some of the common ploys that *apparatchiki* used in advancing their personal and "family" interests. Many examples of irregular and self-interested behavior have been mentioned in the description of Osoaviakhim's structure, processes, and development. Here an example or two will be added to demonstrate particular practices of each of the common patterns.

Paper leadership (*bumazhnoe rukovodstvo*) and drift (*samotek*) were complained about at every plenum of the Central Council, at the congresses, and regularly in the press. They meant that *apparatchiki* simply passed on instructions from above, sent reports to the center, and did little more than occupy their office desks. At the III Plenum, Eideman discussed the grounds for these charges against the apparatus.[19] During a recent inspection of the Leningrad organization, none of the leaders there had been able to say which raion council was performing best or which was worst. One oblast secretary only sat in his office reproducing lists of deficiencies and resolutions. His response to reports by eight raion councils amounted to a one-sentence addition (refreshing brevity, Eideman noted, in view of the usual "watery" verbosity of such commentary), "resolve exactly as the resolution of such and such raion." "And one wonders," Eideman remonstrated, "why all of our decrees sound the same! . . . This, comrades, is an example of our leadership in general."[20]

In other words, when rules and instructions were sent down the command line, no one tried to make them applicable or appropriate to the particular situation. Nor was there a discriminating response to the information re-

[19] *Osoaviakhim*, 7-8 (1932), 8.   [20] *Ibid.*

ceived from below. A year later at the IV Plenum, Eideman said the Chernigov organization behaved this way intentionally to nullify the reorganization policy.[21]

Reporting (*otchet*) in a deceitful, incomplete, or quib-
bling manner was another way to resist the center's demands and control. The Nizhegorodskii Krai Council reported construction of nine training points, one naval
station, and eight defense houses in rural areas. A month
later it was discovered that none actually existed! The
Transcaucasus organization reported building 72 training
points when in fact only two were constructed.[22] Sometimes organizations simply refused to report. By February
1932, only four of 24 member societies of the Union
Osoaviakhim had rendered financial reports.[23] Nor did
apparatchiki easily surrender funds collected during campaigns and lotteries. Illegally holding back portions, mis-
appropriations by spending funds from one category for
other categories of activities, and thievery were common-
place violations.[24] The head of the finance department for
the Ukrainian organization made a 22,000,000-ruble mistake in funding, the discovery of which caused wringing
of hands and shouts of "How could it be?"[25] The VI
Plenum, in 1935, heard complaints that thievery and
waste had not abated in spite of repeated strictures, warnings, and arrests.[26]

Deceitful reporting was not always a matter of presenting false data. The misleading character of some of the
success indicators used by the center has already been
discussed in the section on measuring techniques. The
apparatchiki proved adept at presenting the most favorable image of their work with technically honest reports.
The Ivanovo organization, for example, gave an outstand-
ing appearance according to the formal indicators, but an
investigation revealed that affairs were not so happy in

[21] *Itogi IV Plenuma*, p. 16.
[22] *Osoaviakhim*, 7-8 (1932), 6.
[23] *Khimiia i oborona*, 3-4 (1932), 33.
[24] *Ibid.*   [25] *Itogi IV Plenuma*, p. 9.
[26] *Itogi VI Plenuma*, p. 57.

reality.[27] The ambiguities of success indicators provided the *apparatchiki* considerable latitude if they were clever enough to exploit it.

Commercialism and corruption flourished at least until the purge in 1936. The rules permitted the use of commercial activities for local fund raising, but the privilege was not always used for the intended purposes. For example, the collusion discovered in the Crimean organization in letting contracts to private construction agents reportedly cost the Society 70,000 rubles.[28] Such behavior thrived best where the local "family groups" could establish themselves. Another case, the scandal in the Pensa organization, suggests that the phenomenon was far from unique and that families could be rather large. There, the entire okrug apparatus, it seems, had been exploiting business activities under the guise of Osoaviakhim enterprises. The Pensa organization was distinguished for founding the first civil aviation school. Nonetheless, "embezzling, swindling, and profiteering" gripped even the aviation school. The secretary of the okrug apparatus was the patriarch of these familial deviants who included ten extsarist officers. How had they survived so long? By keeping up illusions at the center with false reports about the existence of local cells and raion councils. Upon investigation it was discovered that almost none of the reported practical work had been accomplished in fact.[29] If this episode was typical, perhaps it is surprising that Stalin waited so long before trying to deracinate commercialism on a sweeping scale.

Osoaviakhim's disposition made it very difficult to prevent such opportunities for local corruption. The very lack of trained and reliable personnel coupled with a policy of encouraging local acquisition of resources meant that discretion had to be delegated to provincial agents beyond the minute control of the center. Rare indeed was the in-

[27] *Osoaviakhim*, 15 (1930), 10.
[28] *Osoaviakhim*, 31-32 (1931), 11.
[29] *Osoaviakhim*, 15 (1930), 14.

dividual who would forebear in the desperate Soviet economic milieu.

The "exclusive circle" phenomenon (*zamknutyi krug*) appeared in certain subunits of the organization. This pejorative metaphor described the tendency to focus inward, to operate like a composite unit, evading interdependent relations with other subunits in the Society. The nature of aviation program development encouraged this behavior in aeroclubs, and it was not absent in training points. Snabosoaviakhim, the supply organization, also proved worthy of a reprimand for exclusiveness. It was said to be acting like "a state within a state." Eideman told the IV Plenum, "Look what kind of people sit in Snab departments. They often are not even members of the Society." What is more, he added, if cells of the apparatus members were the worst in the Society, Snab cells were the worst in the apparatus![30] They had evaded the spirit of the reorganization and indulged in "paper planning," which led to a complete breakdown of supply in many organizations.

Evasion of responsibility (*obezlichka*) and eye wash (*ochkovtiratel'stvo*) appeared frequently and effectively as defense mechanisms for the *apparatchik*. A speaker at the IV Plenum suggested that the very methods of the Society's management was the source of these pathological traits.[31]

> It would be naive to think that the eyewasher is an inveterate crook, an old fox, and a liar who comes out and consciously lies, reassures, soothes, and promises. The very pathos of the plenum can infect him. . . . He speaks, talks; they record him in the plenum stenogram; and after a time they present him a check, and he reaches for his head and begins to talk about whatever you wish. . . . Very often such assurances, accompanied by applause and music, hang in the air because people who give them do not feel responsible for them.

[30] *Itogi IV Plenuma*, p. 14.　　[31] *Ibid.*, pp. 9-10.

This behavior was natural for the aspiring *apparatchik*, but a less ambitious fellow could also find it profitable. He could learn to repeat self-criticism, to dodge responsibility, to emasculate the center's directives, and thereby to survive.

Another such example is found in the response to the III Plenum's resolution that *apparatchiki* spend one-third of their time visiting cells, observing and assisting their progress. The visits seemed only to increase travel expenses, because the *apparatchiki* performed them in a formal fashion, reminiscent of the tsarist bureaucracy, if one may judge from the Soviet critic's diction. "A little fellow will appear, like a Gogol rat, sniff about, collect information, and leave . . ." offering no advice, providing no assistance, bringing no experience from successful cells.[32]

Finally, the total effect of these ploys helped the *apparatchiki* make a case for increasing their own number. Eideman explained the argument clearly enough. Ask any *apparatchik*, he declared, and he will say he is for a larger paid staff. In this way he hopes to avoid the uncertainties of mobilizing *aktiv* and other volunteers and depending on them to execute programs. Moreover, the only interest such *apparatchiki* have in Osoaviakhim is that it provides them a job and a source of income. Many are entirely devoid of the proper attitude toward public work, of a selfless fervor to mobilize the mass membership in practical work.[33]

The Central Council Versus the Apparatus

In view of the *apparatchiki*'s behavior, the Central Council's policies take on a special rationale. They were conceived not only as solutions to analytical and technical problems, as scientific responses to mechanistic organizational disorders, but in large part as ploys and gambits in the game to limit local discretion, to reduce uncertainty about program outcomes, and very often simply to raise

[32] *Ibid.*, p. 7.　　　[33] *Ibid.*

the uncertainty level of the *apparatchiki* when a more direct and coercive means of influence over them was not immediately possible.

Reorganization was very important as one of the center's gambits. Reorganization not only permitted the center to place personal responsibility more definitively, but it also tended to increase the *apparatchiki's* uncertainty about the center's behavior. Abolishing the okrug level in the hierarchy in 1930 is a case in point. Setting up cadre departments and insisting on separate organization departments in the apparatus staff also increased the center's capacity for keeping touch with the local personnel resources. The proof lies in the local staffs' hesitancy to comply. Authorizing posts for "informer-instructors"—free agents on the staffs to browse about in others' business—quickened the sense of uncertainty in the local staffs and in practical organizations. Otherwise the whole system of informers as a differentiated staff function did not make much sense. It is difficult to believe that special staff workers, concerned only with reporting data to the center, were better able to do this than the persons directly supervising the projects of informational interest if those persons had no reason to conceal what was actually occurring.

Finally, when a ceiling was placed on the total number of *apparatchiki*, uncertainties mounted over who would retain his post and who would not. Following Crozier's analysis, one would expect the *apparatchiki* to demand the center's adherence to the rules as a means of preventing such arbitrary policies on personnel matters. Although this response is seldom found in the available evidence, there were cases of it. Eideman reported one instance when a group of *apparatchiki* serving the permanent military scientific conference (a body existing for a time on the Central Council staff) was reduced from 13 persons to two. "When we told those people good-bye, they raised a howl about the 'principle' of the matter. I recall as if it were today a conversation with the leader of that group who presented me ten questions on the point of 'principle.' "[34] The rarity of attempts by the apparatus to impose predictable behavior on the center by means of impersonal rules, "principle" in this case, is no doubt a reflection of the lack of stratum corporateness, of the failure of groups to emerge on a broader basis than the local "family circle."

The policy of forcing local organizations to generate much of their own financial and material support, although it was bound to have undesired consequences, prevented the squandering of the center's funds. In the milieu surrounding Osoaviakhim, it is difficult to imagine that larger financial grants to local organizations would have increased the level of goal attainment. If incompetency, cultural backwardness, and ignorance led to the degree of waste claimed by the center, at least the waste occurred in significant part at local expense rather than as a loss to the state budget. Continual demand for financial discipline, revision of reporting forms, budgeting for specific activities (disallowing local councils to shift funds from one purpose to another although the money was on hand), special control of lottery funds, all these were part of the game played by the center to hold the line against loss of resources.

The center, of course, tried to make use of party committees, the Red Army, the Komsomol, and the trade unions to improve local performance. Recalcitrance by these organizations was to be expected in every case but the party's. The thorough disinterest and neglect displayed by the local party committees, even the pirating of Osoaviakhim cadres, is somewhat at odds with the view of the all-embracing and smothering control of societal institutions usually attributed to the party.

The center's multiple-channel information system seems to have been a fundamental advantage in the game against the apparatus. Investigations, encouraging individual volunteers to send letters to the center, the formal statistical and qualitative reporting, bringing local workers to conferences at the center, publishing journalists' accounts of local deceit, incompetence, and irregular behavior, all of

[34] *Ibid.*, p. 8.

these sources of information must have revealed a valid picture when taken together. At no time did the center appear to be ignorant of local conditions. It was powerless to correct deviations quickly most of the time, but it was hardly deceived over the long term.

The *apparatchiki* did manage to neutralize almost entirely one information channel, the system of revision commissions. The Moscow oblast revision commission chairman in 1935 did not even know about the existence of 60 percent of the raion revision commissions in the oblast. Only 30 of over 130 raions in fact had revision commissions at the time.[35] Revision work was said to be no more effective in most other places.

Central influence reached its zenith when Stalin could effectively purge the mass membership and the apparatus without destroying the Society. Whether or not the purge was effective from an organizational point of view is another matter, but it surely demonstrated whose influence and discretion prevailed in the political struggle within the Society. From the point of view of the game, it also raises another and much more difficult question. If Stalin believed it necessary to carry out a purge of the entire apparatus, can it be inferred that the local *apparatchiki* were playing a dangerously successful game in defending their own interests? Did their success demand a response of such proportions and terror? Because the purge of Osoaviakhim occurred in the context of the more general purge of the party and other institutions in the Soviet Union, it is all the more difficult to find a satisfactory answer to this question. Perhaps within the restricted boundaries of Osoaviakhim more moderate policies would have secured an acceptable performance from the *apparatchiki*. If that is true, the cause of the purge must be sought in Stalin's personality or outside the limits of Osoaviakhim. In any event, the patterns of bureaucratic games appearing in the apparatus were not likely to be broken up easily; the rapid pace of expansion, the heavy demands of the programs, and the scarcity of resources had taught

[35] *Itogi VI Plenuma*, p. 50.

the *apparatchiki* strong defense mechanisms. Moderation at the center could have produced apathy and paralysis, which is really to say that the purge was far from being an irrational response by Stalin.

Stalin Versus the Central Council Leaders

Members of that small oligarchy at Osoaviakhim's center were hardly free agents. Their fortunes in many cases were not exclusively bound up with Osoaviakhim, because they also held posts in other organizations. It is, therefore, impossible to view the conflict between them and Stalin purely in the context of Osoaviakhim, but it is possible to make some observations about the consequences of those conflicts for the composition of the Osoaviakhim oligarchy.

The turnover at the top of the organization is striking. Of the presidium members in 1935, of whom there were 55 and 16 candidates, only eight had been members of the Central Council or its presidium in 1927:[36]

> Avinovitskii
> Bazilevich
> Belitskii
> Budennyi
> Eideman
> Kamenev, S. S.
> Kuibyshev
> Unshlikht

The presidium in 1932, numbering 47, had only nine members who had been on the Central Council in 1927. That

[36] The full membership of the presidium is available for 1932 and 1935. See *Khimiia i oborona*, 7 (1932), 20; *Rabotu Osoaviakhima—na rel'sy bol'shevitskoi organizovannosti* (Moscow: 1935), p. 64. Partial listings for ODVF, Dobrokhim, OSO, and the 1927 presidium of Osoaviakhim can be found in *Pravda*, September 13, 1923; June 5, 1924; January 20 and 25, 1927.

number included seven of the above and B. M. Fel'dman and Ia. M. Fishman. Both of the latter were associated with the Red Army, Fel'dman as head of the Administration of Commanding Personnel in the Defense Commissariat, Fishman as Chief of the Chemical Administration of the Red Army.[37] Fel'dman perished in the purge of the Red Army in 1937. The same fate probably befell Fishman, because he simply disappeared in the mid-1930's. Bazilevich, an obscure figure, was on the presidium of the Central Council in 1927 and in 1935 but not in 1932. No information has been found on his particular activities or responsibilities at the center.

Others in this small group were not closely involved in Osoaviakhim day-to-day management. Kuibyshev, who mysteriously died in 1935, was a Politburo member and head of Gosplan. Budennyi was unable to do more than speak occasionally about horses, a subject dear to his heart.[38] S. S. Kamenev, a former tsarist colonel, who had commanded a front for the Bolsheviks in the civil war, was consistently in the Osoaviakhim elite circles and came there as a leader in the OSO. His background was not a political asset in bureaucratic struggles, and he appears to have retained a neutral stance, rendering his services largely in the form of technical expertise combined with undeviating loyalty and personal sacrifice. Eideman singled him out at the IV Plenum for being the epitome of the selfless soldier and Osoaviakhim volunteer.[39] He died in 1936, apparently of natural causes. The remaining persons in this small group, Eideman, Unshlikht, Avinovitskii, and Belitskii, were very active in articulating and implementing the center's policy.

Eideman entered the tsarist army in 1916 as a recruit, joined the Bolsheviks in 1918, and rose to command an army during the civil war. Associated closely with Frunze's Red Commanders, he was appointed head of the Frunze

[37] Merle Fainsod, *How Russia is Ruled*, p. 369; *Khimiia i oborona*, 5 (1936), 3.
[38] *Itogi IV Plenuma*, pp. 36-37.   [39] *Ibid.*, p. 8.

Academy in 1925.[40] From the beginning, Eideman held
high posts in Osoaviakhim, as the general secretary in
1927 and 1928, and as deputy chairman from 1927 until
he became chairman in 1932. Apparently he held no important military post after relinquishing the command of
the Frunze Academy in 1932. Under his chairmanship, the
construction program and the training programs were
carried through after a stormy but uncertain start in 1930.
He presided over the consolidation of the membership
and the reorganization in 1936, and he took bows for the
Society in public, received eulogies, and symbolized the
central leadership to the masses. In carrying out the purge
of the membership and the reduction of the apparatus,
he certainly must have lost any special constituency that
he might have gained from patronage in the apparatus to
reserve officers or others. Whether or not there is substance in it, the charge was made in 1938 and 1939 that
Eideman had collected a large number of his personal
supporters in the Osoaviakhim apparatus.[41] To be sure,
he was not likely to employ his opponents! And the policy
of expansion meant that he and his staff would be responsible for personnel recruitment in the apparatus. Although it is doubtful that the charges of disloyalty and
subversion against Eideman had a basis when one considers the vital growth that was achieved in Osoaviakhim
under his leadership, it seems logical and probable that
he developed informal ties and loyalties in the apparatus
in his efforts to achieve organizational efficiency.

Unshlikht is the most curious figure among the Osoaviakhim elite. Trotsky called him "an ambitious but tal-

[40] Erickson, *op. cit.*, p. 838.

[41] *Dvadtsatiletie*, p. 29. This source reports that Eideman's
group had tentacles throughout the Society. See also Markovin,
Osoaviakhim—moguchii rezerv Krasnoi Armii, p. 26. In a brief
historical sketch of the Society, published in 1939, Markovin
declares that it took considerable time to search out and destroy
Eideman's supporters.

ented intriguer."[42] Born in Warsaw, he entered the revolutionary movement around 1900. In 1918, he became associated with the Cheka and served as a political commissar in the army. After the civil war, he was deputy chairman of the GPU and a member of the *Revvoensovet*.[43] Later he worked in Gosplan, where his duties were ostensibly so heavy that he requested relief from the post as chairman of Osoaviakhim. He disappeared in 1937.

Unshlikht's work in voluntary defense societies began in the ODVF in 1923. Of the persons associated with the initial ODVF presidium, only Unshlikht, S. S. Kamenev, and K. A. Mekhonoshin were on the Osoaviakhim presidium in 1932; in 1935 Unshlikht alone could claim that his seniority as a presidium member went back to the ODVF in 1923. He also held top posts in Dobrokhim (deputy chairman to Trotsky upon its founding), Aviakhim, and the OSO. For about one year, 1931-1932, he was chairman of the Central Council of the Union Osoaviakhim.[44]

Unshlikht's numerous articles and speeches were always of a policy nature and provide some of the most enlightening information available on the organization. Obviously he was well associated with Stalin's cliques in the party and the secret police. Although he did not gain the public identity with Osoaviakhim that accrued to Rykov and Eideman, he appears to have been the model Stalinist *apparatchik*, always on the scene, in a key post but not necessarily the top post, speaking authoritatively on policy but never castigating persons in public (as Eideman was wont to do), connected with the secret police, a shadowy but powerful figure insofar as he was willing to be an instrument of Stalin's dictates. Nonetheless, he did not survive the Great Purges.

Avinovitskii and Belitskii were a different sort from Unshlikht except that they were also reliable Stalinists. Avinovitskii appeared first in the presidium of Dobrokhim and remained associated with chemistry thereafter. He

[42] Erickson, *op. cit.*, p. 170.
[43] *Pravda*, February 7, 1925.
[44] *Osoaviakhim*, 7-8 (1932), 3-4.

was the responsible editor of the journal for chemical programs, *Khimiia i oborona*, until August 1937, after which no editorial staff was listed until 1938. He was associated with the Moscow Chemical Institute and headed the Osoaviakhim presidium section for air and chemical defense in 1935.[45] Apparently Avinovitskii's technical expertise made him of value as a senior *apparatchiki* in Osoaviakhim.

Belitskii brought military expertise to the apparatus. As one of the young Red Commanders, he fought in the civil war, attended the Frunze Academy, taught there, and edited some of the early materials for VNO, OSO, and Osoaviakhim military programs. Both he and Avinovitskii wrote authoritative articles on Osoaviakhim programs and the problems of implementing them. In the authoritative manner that Unshlikht spoke on organizational and political matters, they spoke on program affairs.

The persons with longevity in the presidium were not the only important individuals in the leadership at the center. Rykov, always on the scene in the ODVF, Aviakhim, and Osoaviakhim public meetings, was more figurative than involved. As head of the Council of People's Commissars, he represented the official blessings of the state for the voluntary societies, but he was too occupied with state affairs to lend Osoaviakhim more than occasional appearances and speeches. N. A. Semashko, who spoke with policy authority, made only a brief appearance in 1930 and 1931. L. P. Malinovskii, general secretary for almost a decade but never a presidium member, played a key role in running the Society. His articles confirm his involvement and authority. His background and connections remain obscure, but his longevity in such a key post suggests that, next to Unshlikht, Malinovskii was Stalin's most dependable agent in Osoaviakhim.

Beyond these few individuals, the center did not possess a firmly seated oligarchy. And even these perished in the purges. The new chairman in 1937, Gorshenin, first made

[45] *Itogi VI Plenuma*, p. 64; *Khimiia i oborona*, 7 (1932), 20.

a career in the Komsomols. Although he was a member of the presidium of the Central Council in 1932, there is no evidence of his regular involvement in Osoaviakhim affairs. His successor, Major General Kobelev, had no visible record with the Central Council. After Malinovskii vanished in 1937, it may be that his post in the secretariat was left vacant—at least no mention of his successor has been found.

The picture emerging from the scanty information we have on the center's *apparatchiki* and senior figures is one of a few individuals acting as key agents in announcing policy decisions and persevering in their implementation. Their successful endeavors in exercising the center's influence and in expanding it assured them neither longevity nor special acclaim.

In theory, the presidium and the Central Council were composed of volunteers. The membership changed regularly and remained conspicuous for its silence on organizational affairs. Beyond a doubt, it exercised no significant policy influence. If it had an effective role, it was in the tradition of the ancient *zemskii sobor*, to bind the masses morally to the arbitrary decisions of the central apparatus.

By controlling the few key posts, then, Stalin retained manipulative influence at the apex of the apparatus. But that was not enough. He also wanted to be able to destroy or withdraw the minimum discretion officials had to be granted in order to run the organization. Some cases in the aftermath of the reorganization in the early 1930's demonstrate how he preempted the use of discretion as a bargaining lever. He merely raised the "uncertainty" level of the central *apparatchiki*. D. E. Lipelis and P. N. Levin, deputy secretaries in Malinovskii's office, published a manual for Osoaviakhim leaders, especially at the cell and raion level.[46] In 1931, a scathing attack on the political errors in this handbook appeared in *Osoaviakhim*, the Society's main journal.[47] A short time later, a handbook

[46] *Spravochnik aktivista Osoaviakhim.*
[47] No. 30 (1931), 13.

for use in rural cells, edited by persons in the Commissariat of Defense, also came under attack.[48] Tsernes, an *apparatchik*, published the results of a conference of Osoaviakhim revision workers in 1931, for which he too was taken to task for "crude political errors."[49] The full significance of the alleged errors is obscure but unquestionably connected with failure to pursue the expansion of the Society with sufficient fervor. That need not detain us here. The point of interest lies in the uncertainty and personal insecurity these episodes must have provoked in the *apparatchiki* at the center. One might send harsh orders to the wretched local leaders from a warm Moscow office, but the amenities of the center were hardly guaranteed. Tsernes published his confession to the alleged errors, and Lipelis and Levin were called on to do so. Presumably they complied.

The nature of the game for influence and control seems to be transparent at the general level. Hearing the woes of the local organizations, the frequently unrealistic demands placed on them, and the close involvement in daily administration at the center could easily infect well-meaning *apparatchiki* with a sense of empathy, perhaps even sympathy, with local problems, a perception of the absurdities being perpetrated on the local leaders as a result of excessive demands from the center, excessive in the sense that resource scarcity and cultural backwardness made goal attainment physically impossible. If the pace of development and growth was to be sustained, not even the elite at the center could be permitted significant discretion with rules and policies for any length of time. They might become overly concerned with the gap between appearance and reality and take the local leaders' side on some matters.

The Soviet Bureaucratic Vicious Circle

In Crozier's own short analysis of the Russian bureaucratic system (he has in mind the tsarist administration

[48] *Osoaviakhim*, 34-36 (1931), 1.   [49] *Ibid.*, pp. 28-29.

but believes the Soviet experience has demonstrated the durability of the cultural patterns), he identifies the source of the vicious circle as the unrealistic goals set by the ruling elite.[50] Such goals cannot be achieved legally if at all. Subordinates, therefore, resort to illicit measures in an effort to satisfy the center's demands, making themselves feel morally guilty and more dependent on small "family groups" for protection. The center in turn feels justified and has the discretion to make even more stringent rules, but at the same time it cannot trust anyone to check performances against the established standards. Information, important to corrective feedback, is difficult if not impossible to secure. The center responds to the information problem by checks, counter-checks, and spy systems. These techniques frighten the subordinates, compel them to behave more deviously, and generally reinforce the cultural pattern of informal protective family groups. The vicious circle is joined when the center responds with even more repressive and arbitrary measures aimed at breaking up the protective groups and at securing accurate information about results.[51]

[50] *The Bureaucratic Phenomenon*, pp. 228-31. Crozier is following others who have emphasized the problem of unrealistic goals. For example, Berliner, *op. cit.*, pp. 23-24, says, "It is the combination of high targets with perpetual shortages that constitutes the most salient fact for the Soviet manager."

[51] For a corroborative analysis, see Fritz Morstein Marx, "Control and Responsibility in Administration: Comparative Aspects," *op. cit.*, pp. 145-71. Marx offers a view of Soviet administration in its unique historical and cultural setting that not only vindicates Crozier's focus on unrealistic goals as being of key importance but also emphasizes the two faces of power in Crozier's model, the power of the superior and of the subordinate in hierarchical relations. Interestingly, Marx turns to Russian literature, to characters in works by Griboedov, Gogol, and Goncharov for evidence. The opportunities for pursuing this kind of evidence farther are abundant. Semen, in Chekhov's *V ssylke*, an exile in Siberia, articulates the extreme tactic for obstructing hierarchical authority, that is, to remain so free of worldly goods and personal relations

To what extent does Osoaviakhim vindicate this analysis? In many respects the conceptual fit is well nigh perfect. The vicious circle built up until a thoroughgoing reorganization was deemed necessary in 1927, again in 1930, and once more in 1935. In each case the center's response was more extreme, more repressive, and exercised with a greater latitude of discretion. The ultimate source of the struggle lay in the stubborn adherence to goals that exceeded organizational capacity to attain them.

One is struck, however, by the apparently valid information the center could gather. Granted, it derived from multiple channels, from spying and informers. The advances in installation construction and program development indicate that corrective action by the center was not allowing a stalemate to set in, and goal achievement both in certain functional sectors and in particular geographi-

---

that one has nothing to lose, nothing the authorities can take away. In the Soviet period, Zoshchenko's electrician in a provincial theater, in the story *Monter*, indignant over what he believed to be mistreatment by the management, forced his terms on the manager by turning the lights off at the beginning of a performance. Many of Solzhenitsyn's characters reveal the latitudes of discretion, and thus bargaining power, that are open even to prisoners in Soviet concentration camps.

Historians also provide striking confirmation of the Russian bureaucratic vicious circle. V. I. Kliuchevskii's study of the reign of Peter I traces the upward spiral of gambit and countergambit as Peter copes with his bureaucracy and his subjects. By the time Sir Donald MacKenzie Wallace comes to observe Russian bureaucracy in the late 19th century, he sees and reports a highly institutionalized pattern of unrealistic demands from above being dealt with below by small group collusion, deception, and mixed feelings of guilt and helplessness. The image of unrealistic goals is conveyed in a story told to Sir Donald, picturing the Russian people as a growing boy who is forced to wear a tight jacket and tight boots. Better the boots and jacket burst, i.e., better that peculation and corruption continue to mitigate the burden from above, than for the boy to be held to the size of his clothes. *Russia* (New York: Vintage Books, 1961), pp. 3-26, especially pp. 6-7, 14.

cal areas—the urban centers—was apparently not unimpressive. Some of the planning and financing techniques cannot be written off as virtual tyranny by the Central Council, and the same is true for the establishment of achievement norms in some of the training programs. These factors undoubtedly contributed to organizational efficiency.

Here we come up against the static quality of Crozier's treatment of cultural variations within a single conceptualization of bureaucracy.[52] We also come back to the original Bolshevik goal of economic and cultural transformation. For all its energy and effort, did Osoaviakhim, in its narrow sector of the broader Bolshevik program, bring about fundamental advances? Modest and cautious answers to these questions take us to the conclusions of this study.

[52] *The Bureaucratic Phenomenon*, p. 295. Crozier admits this and essays briefly on the nature of change in a political and cultural system as a whole.

Conclusions

In order to tie together the diverse perspectives presented throughout this study, three general topics must be addressed. First, organizational consequences must be reckoned with. In this connection, the matters of goals and achievement will be discussed. What is concluded about organizational consequences forms the substantive basis for the second topic: modernization and change. Third, remarks will be offered concerning the conceptual approaches used in the study. Although each topic will be treated separately, analytical perspectives relevant to the third topic will unavoidably appear intermittently throughout.

Achievements and Consequences

Judgment of organizational success is a knotty problem, perhaps a quixotic one, for more reasons than the dearth of available information on program activity. Not only do institutional goals have a protean quality as yardsticks, but authorities are not of one mind about what constitutes organizational success.[1] Furthermore, "the unanticipated

[1] For a range of ideas, see Etzioni, "Two Approaches to Organizational Analysis: A Critique and a Suggestion," *The Sociology of Organizations: Basic Studies*, eds. Oscar Grusky and George A. Miller (New York: The Free Press, 1970), pp. 215-25; Theodore Caplow, *Principles of Organization* (New York: Harcourt, Brace and World, 1964), chapter 4; Philip Selznick, *Leadership in Administration* (New York: Harper and Row, 1957), pp. 1-4; Arthur L. Stinchcombe, *Constructing Social Theories* (New York: Harcourt, Brace and World, 1968), pp. 181-88, especially the footnote on p. 184. Etzioni declares

consequences" of organizational policy, Merton tells us, are as important and informative to study as the consequences intended by goal-setting. We approach our topic, therefore, with modest expectations and these caveats in mind.

In Part I of this study, the aims and conscious motives of Osoaviakhim's designers were explored in detail. It was concluded that the formal goals were a political tactic conceived to establish a value pattern, a set of norms, that would constrain, guide, and concert activity by the mass membership. Furthermore, the formal aims of Osoaviakhim were seen to reflect an entanglement of private and factional ends among the Bolshevik elite. Moreover, the goals were not synchronically established but rather worked out in a political struggle beginning several years before Osoaviakhim was founded and continuing through most of the period of the study. They also were altered occasionally due to organizational developments as well as changes in the economy and the structure of the military forces. Thus we are dealing with changing goals, confounded inextricably with factional interests, articulated within the value pattern of Bolshevik ideological sentiment in response to perceptions of domestic and foreign realities.

---

that the "goal model," measuring success against goals, leads always to judging organizations as failures because most organizations do not fully realize stated goals. His alternative, optimum resource allocation among all activities, goal activity being but one of several, is attractive in principle but difficult to make operational. Caplow offers a more explicit model for measuring efficiency as something more than commitment to goal activity; nonetheless, there can be problems in making the model operational. Selznick is definitely not satisfied with goal attainment alone as the standard for determining organizational success. He argues that there is more to success in organizational leadership than simply goal attainment. Stinchcombe makes an interesting argument that institutional goals and values are in fact more stable and explicit than most individuals' values and preferences.

Accordingly, it is important to be clear, when judging success, that we know what goals and whose goals are the reference criteria. At the end of Part I we distilled from all the discussion on Osoaviakhim's purposes a group of four broad and enduring goals for which there was an apparent consensus among the leadership. Additionally it was clear that two factional goals could be isolated. Not that there were only two, but these two became particularly apparent due to their political and objective significance for the role of the organization. In judging success against consciously chosen goals, therefore, these six shall be our criteria.

In addition to the intended outcomes, certain other objective consequences have been observed, which must be assessed. In making this distinction between the two kinds of outcomes, we are following, for heuristic purposes, Merton's distinction between "manifest and latent functions."[2]

A word on the logical status of our assertions about organizational success is necessary. We are "judging" success, not "measuring" it. The diction is important because of the non-operational character of the goals. We are not dealing with the operational subgoals such as recruiting targets, numbers of installations, and numbers of GTO badges awarded. They have been treated, insofar as the evidence permitted, in earlier chapters. Here we are dealing with goals that do not in themselves provide a measuring rod for achievement. In a strict sense, non-operationality makes it impossible to "measure" success with quantitative precision. Of course, the operational subgoal success forms some of the evidence on which to base a judgment about the overall goal achievement. It is possible in making judgments to specify whether there is evidence of either "some" or "no" success toward a goal's attainment. Beyond that, something may be added about the degree of attainment. It is also sometimes possible to see the implications of success in one sector for more or

[2] *Social Theory and Social Structure*, pp. 114-15.

less success in another. These are the kinds of statements that will compose our assessment.[3]

It might be argued that the more realistic way to judge Osoaviakhim's success would be to examine the contribution it made to defense mobilization in World War II. The drawbacks in using such a criterion are two. First, it would require another study focused on the Red Army and mobilization in the early months of the war. In other words, the scope of the present study is insufficient to make this criterion feasible. Second, and more important, many intervening factors shed doubt on its reliability. Osoaviakhim did not produce what could be called an "end product" for defense. Rather its product was intermediate or unfinished—manpower trained in elementary military skills. The Soviet military organizations that received this product as an input may or may not have used it effectively. The Osoaviakhim apparatus did not actually mobilize troop units in war time. That task was reserved to the *voenkomaty*. Thus it is possible that Osoaviakhim could have been producing an adequate manpower base that the military squandered in the early stages of the war.[4] For

[3] For those who consider this approach unduly imprecise, it can be pointed out that a decade of experience with PPBS (planning programming budgeting system) in the United States Government has failed to introduce the anticipated rigor into talk about goal attainment and program achievement. See James Q. Wilson, "The Bureaucracy Problem," *The Public Interest*, 6 (Winter, 1967), 3-9; and Aaron Wildavsky, *The Politics of the Budgetary Process* (Boston: Little, Brown and Company, 1964).

[4] There are scraps of evidence to suggest that this was the case. Western journalists in the Soviet Union were impressed by the rapidity with which the population made the shift to a war-time footing. See Ralph Parker, *The New York Times*, April 14, 1942; and Walter B. Kerr, *The New York Herald Tribune*, December 4, 1941. Other observers, German and Allied, attributed part of the large number of divisions the USSR was able to mobilize to Osoaviakhim endeavors. See Artur Just, *Die Sowjetunion* (Berlin: 1940), p. 118. Erickson, *op. cit.*, pp. 307-08, quotes von Blomberg as being impressed with Oso-

these reasons, therefore, we shall not resort to wartime experience as a criterion but rather adhere to the organizational goals.

Organizational goals. If we consider the consequences of Osoaviakhim's activity from the viewpoint of organizational goals, at least four kinds of achievements can be identified.

First, the organization had a striking capacity to provide direct access to local resources, meager and primitive though they were. It proved able to divert those resources directly into activities related to aviation and chemistry to a limited degree but more successfully to defense work. In the Western industrial states, where governments have highly developed administrative capacity to tax private incomes and transfer funds to specialized agencies for procuring defense inputs, the Osoaviakhim achievement seems pale. There appears to be no particular advantage in bypassing the formal budgetary process in allocating for defense, public works, and aid to industry. To the leadership in developing states, however, where the administrative infrastructure is weak and non-existent in some sectors, the extractive capacity of mass voluntary societies can be important. It can mean the difference between doing something and doing nothing in certain sectors. To be sure, as the administrative capacity in industry and government grows, the voluntary organizations may be displaced. We observed precisely this sequence in the case

---

aviakhim during his secret visit to the USSR in 1930. Michel Berchin and Eliahn Ben-Horin, *The Red Army* (New York: W. W. Norton, 1942), pp. 59-78, are praiseful. See Earl F. Ziemke, *The German Northern Theater of Operations, 1940-1945* (Department of the Army, No. 20-271, 1959), pp. 150-94, for accounts of impressive Soviet troop behavior in hastily mobilized units in the early months of the war. The Soviet military command structure may have faltered miserably in the first months of the war, but it may be wrong to infer from that conclusion that individuals and small units were also inept.

of Osoaviakhim's aviation and chemical programs. The military programs also had to be modified to remain relevant to the growing structure of the Red Army as it acquired new technology.

Second, Osoaviakhim helped the Soviet leadership mitigate the trade-off dilemma in manpower allocations between industry and the standing armed forces. By taking basic military training from concentrated installations such as military posts and camps and dispersing it to factories, schools, and collective farms, it permitted millions of workers and peasants to remain employed in the economy while receiving an introduction to military skills. The degree of achievement, of course, was not all that was desired. Osoaviakhim made little headway in penetrating the rural areas and the non-Slavic national minority regions with effective programs. Both recruitment and program success were limited largely to the urban and industrial regions. And if space and sparseness of population impeded organizational expansion in the early years, scarcity and cost of equipment were added obstacles as the programs became more technically ambitious. Language, as well, was a barrier obstructing expansion among the national minorities.

Third, insofar as the Bolsheviks correctly anticipated that they would be forced to fight the next war with quantity rather than quality of trained troops and civil defense cadres, Osoaviakhim's quantitative achievement was a positive contribution. It will be remembered that this tactic, compensating for quality with quantity, was very much in the minds of Trotsky, Frunze, Stalin, and Voroshilov when they explained the aims of the mass voluntary societies. They were part of a "shock tactic" for closing the cultural and technical gap. Poor quality of training, therefore, is not necessarily an index of Osoaviakhim's failure in goal-seeking activity. Mass exposure to elementary training was preferred over intensive exposure of a few. The consequences for the cultural gap, however, were mixed. Learning new technical skills was not accompanied by new participatory attitudes among the mass membership—even less by new participatory behavior in the apparatus.

Fourth, Osoaviakhim enjoyed considerable success in popularizing aviation and in developing a limited net of aviation schools. Numerous flying records and parachuting feats were achieved in the 1930's under Osoaviakhim's sponsorship in the Central Aeroclub. Aviation had come a long way in the Soviet Union between 1923 and the end of the 1930's. If Osoaviakhim's material contribution through airfield construction, fund raising, and training programs was mixed, its contribution to the public visibility of advances in aviation was quite real. The same is true for the spreading of awareness of the dangers of air and chemical attacks in the event of war. Whatever the failures in training programs, public awareness, a goal broadly proclaimed for ODVF and carried into Osoavia-khim, was realized.[5] Osoaviakhim's impact, in this respect, went far beyond the official membership.

Factional goals.   In the beginning, a cluster of not always discernible factional interests were entwined with the formal aims of ODVF, Dobrokhim, and the VNO. Frunze allowed his own interests and those of the Red Commanders to become rather transparent as his plans for the voluntary societies began to resemble a Trojan horse in which the military would pass through any walls defending state resources from military appropriations. As the development of Osoaviakhim worked out, the military programs gained the preponderant emphasis, but not due to Frunze's endeavors.

On the contrary, Stalin was able to make Osoaviakhim

---

[5] For evidence of the success in propagandizing aviation, see the reflections by A. S. Iakovlev in *Stalin and His Generals,* ed. Seweryn Bialer (New York: Pegasus, 1969), pp. 86-88. A member of the presidium of the 1935 Central Council, later a colonel general, and closely associated with the Central Aero-club, he says the public image of aviation was outstripping reality dangerously by 1939 although aviation had kept up earlier.

one among several organizational levers for holding the military in line. Stalin's interest in Osoaviakhim, insofar as we can infer it, not only coincided with most of the formal goals but included restricting the military's authority over certain resources. The Red Army effectively lost control over universal basic military training and the resources necessary to conduct it. At the same time, it was forced to render certain assistance to Osoaviakhim programs and to tolerate the existence of elective primary organizations of Osoaviakhim in its regiments. The militia too, organized by the Red Army in the aftermath of demobilization at the end of the civil war, was eventually replaced by Osoaviakhim. The training of reserve officers also became an Osoaviakhim task. As long as Osoaviakhim retained its formal voluntary and elective character, the use of military members within it was possible without allowing them to capture control. They could be routed through elections. They could be criticized and purged for not making the voluntary approach more effective: witness the fate of Eideman, the Red Commander, who was purged after his not ineffectual leadership of the rapid growth in the 1930's. Perhaps equally important, Osoaviakhim was used to support arguments against increasing the regular military force structure, particularly before and during the First Five Year Plan. Noisy and highly visible in the urban areas, Osoaviakhim was heralded by Voroshilov and others as evidence of Stalin's serious concern with state defense when he was accused of ignoring military readiness.

Organizational maintenance.   In organizational analysis, the question of success is sometimes treated not as a matter of degree, that is, as a question of efficiency, but rather as a matter of survival or failure.[6] Without resorting to

[6] See Etzioni, *A Comparative Analysis of Complex Organizations*, pp. 78-79, for an elaboration of this distinction and its implications.

"functionalism," in which this approach normally arises, we can answer an important question that it poses. How was Osoaviakhim able to survive? The party was able to make it survive by overlapping it with the trade unions, the militia, the Red Army, schools, factories, the Komsomol, and the local party organizations. The center denied charges that Osoaviakhim was a parasitic bureaucracy, but that is how it behaved. Favorable sentiment among the populace would have never sufficed for organizational maintenance. For cadres, facilities, members, and funds, an array of other institutions were called on, sometimes forced to contribute. The burden of supporting Osoaviakhim with local leadership could be passed around from institution to institution. The unions reluctantly, the Komsomol with dubious enthusiasm, and the military ambivalently took the burden from time to time. The local party secretaries more often than not put Osoaviakhim on the back burner in their busy kitchens. Industry and collectivization were peppery dishes of greater concern. The administrative option to shift Osoaviakhim to a front burner, nonetheless, was secured and exercised in 1935 when Stalin instructed the oblast party committees to give it first priority among mass public organizations.[7] This technique of administration gains comparative importance when we remember how often in studies of development administration the problem of cadre shortages arises. Although the technique may lead to periods of neglect and inefficiency in some institutions, it seems to insure their survival and the possibility for short-notice revitalization.

Unanticipated consequences.   If we follow the models of bureaucracy devised by Merton and Selznick, we would

[7] See Jerry Hough, *The Soviet Prefects*, chapters 4 and 5, on the role of the local party committees in coordinating the many activities of other institutions. Our findings here vindicate his thesis about the party's role in coordination. Hough, of course, is concerned with the post-war evolution of the party's role, while our study is restricted to the pre-war period.

look for "goal displacement" to be the most general unanticipated consequence in Osoaviakhim.[8] By goal displacement, they mean the tendency for "means" to become
"ends" in the eyes of members of subunits of the bureaucracy and for subunits to develop parochial ideologies to
justify subunit values even at the expense of the organizational goals. It is possible to identify behavior that could
be said to displace Osoaviakhim's goals. Localism and
the "exclusive circle" phenomena threatened the formal
goals. The factional interests of groups such as the Red
Commanders could be seen as displacing the formal goals
of the voluntary societies. More generally, the tendency
in the apparatus to ignore the voluntary character of the
society and to rely wholly on the salaried staff was dis-
tinctly and seriously a case of goal displacement. In some
respects, the center responded to goal displacement in the
way Merton and Selznick would anticipate: with more
specific rules and occasionally by the creation of more
specialized subunits.

Two other general responses by the center, however,
were hardly consistent with goal displacement models.
The first is the reckless persistency with which the center
fought and destroyed the conditions that would sustain
goal displacement. Not only were localism and other devi-
ant behavior systematically expurgated, but Stalin proved
quite willing to destroy large numbers of apparatchiki at
the zenith of program expansion when qualified cadres
were in greatest demand. Second, the center continued to
raise the operational subgoals such as recruitment, construction, and training figures even as smaller targets were
not being reached. Either Merton's or Selznick's model

[8] Merton explains goal displacement in Social Theory and
Social Structure, p. 253. Selznick describes it as the central
paradox of bureaucracy in "Foundations of Organization
Theory," op. cit., pp. 21-24. Sills, in The Volunteers, applies the
concept to the study of a mass voluntary organization. Peter
Blau, in Bureaucracy in Modern Society (New York: Random
House, 1956), pp. 91-95, modifies the concept to mean "suc-
cession of goals."

would lead us to conclude that the center's exercise of discretion was pathological, or at least surprising. Goal displacement, therefore, strikes us as important but not the most significant unanticipated consequence.

The apparently pathological attacks on the apparatus and the unrealistic goals, when looked at in the context of Crozier's model, became analytically very important. Demand from the center and response at the lower levels were followed by increasing counter-demands from the center and greater deception and evasion in the counter-responses. The upward spiral generated bureaucratic vicious circles, not a self-correcting social system. The most significant unanticipated consequence of the vicious circles was the failure to achieve one of Osoaviakhim's extremely important aims: inculcation of new cultural patterns and new attitudes toward organizational participation. Instead of teaching new behavior patterns on a mass scale, patterns that would reflect a metamorphosis of cultural values to forms more compatible with modern industrial and military organization, the effect of organizational policy was to reinforce and exaggerate traditional patterns of participatory behavior. The central importance of this finding is that it provides a key for analyzing Osoaviakhim in a comparative context of modernization and theories of organization.

Modernization and Change

In discussing the nature of change from tradition to modernity, Huntington argues that "the simple theories of modernization implied a zero-sum relation between the two: the rise of modernity in society was accompanied by the fading of tradition. In many ways, however, modernity supplements but does not supplant tradition."[9] This was certainly true in Osoaviakhim. Traditional patterns of participatory behavior were found thriving in a modern organization dedicated to changing traditional

[9] "The Change to Change: Modernization, Development and Politics," *Comparative Politics*, 3 (April, 1971), 295.

modes and attitudes. The relationship was even somewhat symbiotic. Thus, the most striking unanticipated consequence of policy and behavior in Osoaviakhim turns out to be a general phenomenon in modernization, not exceptional, although it retains its peculiarly Russian nature.

Studies of organizations in other societies have yielded similar findings. James Abegglen's study of a Japanese factory in the 1950's leads him to conclude ". . . that the development of industrial Japan has taken place with much less change from the kinds of social organization and social relations of pre-industrial . . . Japan than would be expected from the Western model of growth of an industrial society."[10] Morroe Berger found that traditional ways have amazing survival power in Egyptian bureaucracy.[11] Ernest Barker's essay on the historical development of public administration in England, France, and Germany also demonstrates the unique and lasting imprint that cultural and political circumstances plant on state bureaucracies.[12] Fred Riggs, in his study of the Thai bureaucracy, goes much farther in revealing the capacity of traditional culture to inhabit modern institutions and to baffle Westerners who take the institutions for what they appear to be.[13]

If much of tradition survived in Osoaviakhim, what can be said of change? To be sure, physical change in the form of installations and technology was enormous. The recruit coming into the Red Army with Osoaviakhim experience knew a great deal more of modern weaponry than had the recruit during the civil war. But with regard to organizational behavior there is a disturbing implication. The games peculiar to the Russian pattern of a bu-

[10] "Productivity in the Japanese Factory," *The Sociology of Organizations: Basic Studies*, p. 568.

[11] *Bureaucracy and Society in Modern Egypt* (Princeton, N.J.: Princeton University Press, 1957).

[12] *The Development of Public Services in Western Europe 1660-1930* (Hamden, Conn.: Archon Books, 1966).

[13] *Thailand: The Modernization of a Bureaucratic Society* (Honolulu: The East-West Center Press, 1966).

reaucratic vicious circle encourage players to avoid the internalization of rules and norms that could possibly increase the certainty level of all players and likely raise the organizational efficiency.[14] The question arises: can administrative rules and systems of organizational operation ever be stabilized in Soviet bureaucracy so that they are equally binding on both the apex of the leadership group and the lower level functionaries and members? To judge only by the Osoaviakhim case in the time frame of a decade, the answer is clearly no.

Two diverse trends were manifest simultaneously. Policies, rules, procedures, regulations, routines, and standard achievement criteria grew rapidly in number and complexity. By 1936, the apparatus had tentacles down at the lowest levels. Installations and facilities for programs existed in significant numbers. But this tendency was matched by a steady rise in the arbitrary and ruthless exercise of power by the center. Before 1930, the language of "self-criticism" and the tone of policy guidance gave the impression of a sense of responsibility and genuine concern for both the institutional goals and the membership. Starting at the II All-Union Congress of Osoaviakhim in 1930, the demands from the center became increasingly arbitrary in that they blatantly disregarded the limitations in resources. Senior members in the apparatus were forced to admit publicly their errors, which in some cases amounted to taking resource constraints into consideration when setting goals. The plenums of the Central Council from 1931 through 1936 mark the upward spiral of accusations, denunciations, and unrealistic demands being made by the center. The climax came with the sweeping purge in 1936 and 1937. Thus we find the paradoxical relationship where a rapid development of rules is accompanied by an increasing disregard for the advantages of

[14] S. P. Huntington, *Political Order in Changing Societies* (New Haven: Yale University Press, 1968), pp. 12-32. Huntington makes internalization of rules one of the most distinctive measures of success in institutionalization. It is for him the essence of "the public interest."

having those rules accepted as actual norms for behavior.

We have tried to account for this phenomenon with two explanations, a cultural determinacy argument on the one hand, and, on the other, a model of bureaucracy that emphasizes the individual's exercise of choice. But neither argument rules out the possibility for change. On the contrary, they both identify variable factors that must remain constant if change is not to occur. The technological and physical change that took place must not erode the administrative behavior patterns, and, at the same time, leaders must continue to choose unrealistic goals.

Change through choice.   There is nothing about the vicious circle of bureaucracy to preclude a reforming leader at the top from scaling down the center's demands to a level commensurate with resources and capabilities of the operational elements of bureaucracy. That is, the leadership has the choice to remove what Crozier sees as the source of the vicious circle: "the strong discrepancy between goals set by rulers and real possibilities of subordinates."[15] The consequences of such a choice in Osoaviakhim must remain a matter of speculation; and one might observe in rebuttal that Khrushchev's failure to retain power was due in part to the exercise of precisely this kind of choice, a conscious modification of the policy of extreme terror as a part of a broader plan to escape from the inefficient bureaucratic vicious circle of the past.[16] But the Khrushchev case (if we give such a rebuttal credence for demonstrating that one may have to pay the price of losing power for exercising the choice to reform) does not prove that change is impossible in this way. It only proves that the personal price can be very high for the leader who makes the choice. Nor does it rule out the

[15] *The Bureaucratic Phenomenon*, p. 230.

[16] For ideas on the rationale of Khrushchev's policies, see Carl A. Linden, *Khrushchev and the Soviet Leadership 1957-1964* (Baltimore: The Johns Hopkins Press, 1966) and Sidney Ploss, *Conflict and Decision-Making in Soviet Russia* (Princeton, N.J.: Princeton University Press, 1965).

possibility of a cautious reformer who is astute enough to initiate basic change without being tumbled from office. It could be equally expensive for successors to undo the change that Khrushchev achieved, although it is entirely possible if they too are willing to pay the price.

It must be admitted, of course, that the incentives for the top bureaucratic leadership to behave in this fashion are mixed, perhaps extremely forbidding. It is a dangerous gambit. The local functionaries could easily seize the opportunity to indulge in localism on a scale that would threaten the entire bureaucratic structure's existence. Persuading the *apparatchik* to see the advantages of some liberalizing compromises in calling off old deceitful and wasteful games would be difficult in view of past unscrupulous behavior at the center.[17]

Change through the impact of technology and information. Now to look at the other side of the question, what may change even if the top leadership does not choose the reform gambits? One of the inherent features of the Russian bureaucratic pattern is the rulers' fear that they do not know what is actually happening below. Uncertainties generated by distrust of all agencies for checking organizational achievements greatly encourage the rulers to arbitrary and despotic behavior, which presumably will increase the uncertainties for subordinates and thereby reduce their propensity for deceiving the center. Uncertainty at any level of the bureaucracy implies imperfect information. It is logical to assume, therefore, that increases in information fidelity would reduce uncertainty and

[17] See Andrei Amalrik, "Will the USSR Survive until 1984?" *Survey*, No. 73 (Autumn, 1969), 47-79. This young Soviet historian argues that the only possibility to avoid stagnation and collapse rests with the inchoate privileged group—a class of specialists, a middle class, to use Amalrik's categories—because it alone seeks and can understand the importance of legal norms. Yet he doubts that this class can achieve the corporateness and self-consciousness necessary for securing and defining such norms.

CONCLUSIONS

lessen the propensity of the rulers to behave in an arbitrary fashion. The central leadership of Osoaviakhim was very sensitive to the information problem. It showed itself able to maintain a rather clear view of the operational realities in the lower reaches of the Society. The documents from the Smolensk party archive corroborate the impression gained from the press and records of Central Council plenums that the center was accurately and extensively informed about activities at the raion and cell level. The more serious problem for the center was a lack of administrative capacity to act effectively on the information it possessed. The center's possession of credible information, nevertheless, was bound to have an effect on the way the local *apparatchiki* played their political games. The use of the press for exposure of local irregularities, frequent local and all-union conferences and plenums, regular visits by central *apparatchiki* to raions, interregional competitions in aviation and military sports, supervised educational excursions, and a host of other such activity caused both the local leaders and the central leadership to increase interpersonal exposure within the organization and to find utility in the common symbols, language, procedures, and rules that the center promoted. As Osoaviakhim built its administrative capacity from the center outward, more members were effectively mobilized in programs. Even if the programs themselves did not achieve a great deal, the mere fact that they could be executed means that the apparatus and the *aktiv* had learned new symbols and procedures. The point here has been made emphatically by Karl Deutsch in connection with cultural patterns and social communications within a national grouping.[18] When activities draw people together in new ways, new habits and new cultural symbols must be learned in order to form a cultural screen that facilitates perception and interpretation of information. Many of the standardized administrative procedures in Osoaviakhim

[18] *Nationalism and Social Communication* (New York: John Wiley and Sons, 1953).

were meant to be part of such an information screen. If a peasant who recently came to work at a factory found his way into Osoaviakhim and eventually became a cell secretary, it was probable that he also learned a series of new symbols. Keeping records, writing reports, and posting various forms of the work plan were tasks that could not be performed without acquiring modifications in one's cultural screen.[19] Increased physical mobility in the form of motor and air transport, coupled with broader use of radio and newsprint, occurred simultaneously and therefore increased the participant's need for adopting the organization's symbols.[20] All this, of course, is not to say what change took place. It is merely to point out a mechanism for change.

New cultural patterns do not emerge swiftly. In one decade, therefore, we should not expect to see significant change from this source in Osoaviakhim. Our model of bureaucratic vicious circles, nonetheless, gives us an idea about the way such change might become manifest. The old patterns have as a moral frame of reference a small group of friends and work colleagues. Trust is institutionalized at the level of this group, much in the sense of Banfield's concept, "amoral familism."[21] If the increased level of communications permits the expansion of the size of the moral reference group, the kinds of gambits and

[19] See Robert Denhart, "Bureaucratic Socialization and Organizational Accommodation," *Administrative Science Quarterly*, 13 (December, 1968), 441-50, for an empirical study of learning organizational symbols and norms by new members of an anti-poverty program in America's Appalachia region. The organization imparted new symbols and norms but conceded something to local attitudes and behavior patterns. The learning experience can be on both sides it seems.

[20] See Lucian W. Pye (ed.), *Communication and Political Development* (Princeton, N.J.: Princeton University Press, 1963), for a variety of essays concerned with communications and social change.

[21] *The Moral Basis of a Backward Society* (New York: The Free Press, 1958).

the amount of political power exercised by the group members would change. Especially if the top leadership is sluggish, yet reluctant to expand trust and alter the nature of the bureaucratic games, groups from below might increasingly insist on the universal binding nature of organizational rules to limit the power of the top. Increased information, as Crozier's model indicates, can increase the power of the subordinate as well as the superior. In the face of unimaginative leadership from above, leadership that repeats the old responses to localism but lacks the Stalinist sense of innovation, direction, and timing, reference groups larger than the local "family circle" and informal affiliations might gain initiative sufficient to force the top leadership to abide by the formal organizational norms. It is precisely this kind of development that has been anticipated by Western scholars who try to employ the "group theory" to Soviet politics.[22] But they have found it very difficult to verify the size and structure of the new reference groups if such groups are taking stable form.

Our analysis, although it cannot answer the question, can suggest caveats to those who try to answer it. The bureaucratic patterns do not tend to institutionalize the informal circles and cliques in the intermediate levels of the hierarchy. A group, built on mutual trust developed in a situation where the members survived crises through cooperative action, may ascend the hierarchy, spread out to other organizations, and create cross-institutional informal links in all-union politics.[23] But they never openly form an association that can formalize positions on issues, recruit mass support, and pass leadership to younger members who did not share the initial trust-building experience of the group.[24] At the intermediate levels they exercise

[22] See H. Gordon Skilling and Franklyn Griffiths, op. cit., for a collection of efforts in this direction and a discussion of the methodological problems.

[23] R. Conquest, Power and Policy in the USSR (New York: St. Martin's Press, 1961), offers some cases in point.

[24] See Etzioni, A Comparative Analysis of Complex Organizations, p. 245, for the logic of the "taboo against formalization of factions."

power within the formal administration. Theirs is not a "demand" or "input" orientation toward the policy process, as the group theory and systems theory assume. They are concerned with administrative politics, not parliamentary politics. They act in a collusive, insinuative, and constraining fashion, not in a demanding articulate fashion. Their incapacity to institutionalize makes a metamorphosis to a demanding posture unlikely. Except at the highest levels, they are likely to focus only on alternative ways to implement policy, not on fundamental policy issues. Questions of reorganization and task definition are the issues they tackle because such questions have great significance for who gets what in a bureaucracy.[25]

Interest group structure, therefore, may remain illusive and protean in Soviet politics. Comparative analysts might better look to the politics within the executive branch of government of the United States for conceptual analogies, but even there one can find interest group institutionalization. The Navy League, the National Guard Association, and the Association of the United States Army, for example, have constituency roots in the executive departments.[26] Analysts could also look to the concept of bureaucratic politics that Riggs developed in his study of modernization

[25] Roman Kolkowicz's study, *The Soviet Military and the Communist Party* (Princeton, N.J.: Princeton University Press, 1967), is more impressive not for his conclusion that the military behaves more and more like an interest group but that a clique of wartime colleagues, as its members spread beyond the military, seized the top command posts and edged out many competent senior officers through non-military loyalties. That feat hardly reinforced illusions of meritocracy in the military or a sense of institutional autonomy.

[26] See C. S. Hyneman, *Bureaucracy in a Democracy* (New York: Harper, 1950); Francis E. Rourke, *Bureaucracy, Politics, and Public Policy* (Boston: Little, Brown and Company, 1969); S. P. Huntington, *The Common Defense* (New York: Columbia University Press, 1961); Anthony Downs, *Inside Bureaucracy* (Boston: Little, Brown and Company, 1967); Alan Altshuler (ed.), *The Politics of the Federal Bureaucracy* (New York: Dodd, Mead, 1968), for studies of bureaucratic politics in America.

of Thailand. He offers a provocative comparative insight by distinguishing three types of polities according to their source of policy control.[27] In Western democratic polities, the people, through associations and political parties are largely the source of policy demand and the power that holds bureaucracy in government accountable. In totalitarian systems, a cadre party is the source of demand and control. It uses councils and the mobilized electorate to control public administration. In the third type, the bureaucratic polity, power is held by the public administrators. No other sector has the power to hold them to account. Thus effective policy demand comes from within the public bureaucracy. Private associations, parties, and the organizational structure of a democratic polity are usually present in all three types. The allocation of real power for policy demand and control, however, causes great differences in the roles of organizations in each type. The search for interest groups within the Soviet system, accordingly, must assume that the source of demand and control is shifting to organizations and hands outside the party and the public bureaucracy. If it is shifting in the other direction, from the party to the administrators (or if the party is becoming one and the same as the public administration), then Riggs's bureaucratic model is conceptually more appropriate than group theory. What does the case of Osoaviakhim suggest? After the NEP period and the initial phase of collectization, no significant concern or effort was given to preventing the private sector from gaining policy initiative or restricting the party's use of it. On the contrary, the struggle was against letting the power slip into the hands of the *apparatchiki* and the administrators. Stalin was able to insure that it did not. What has happened after Stalin is beyond our evidence, but the implications raise doubts about the group theory's usefulness.[28]

[27] *Op. cit.*, pp. 181ff.

[28] Hough's thesis, in *op. cit.*, that the local party organs play an integrative managerial and political role, is suggestive of Riggs's version of a bureaucratic model. Moreover, because

The military and modernization. The case of Osoavia-khim offers insights into another phenomenon that has drawn the attention of students of modernization: usurpation of civil power by the military in developing states. Uniquely, no communist regime in a developing state has experienced a seizure of power by its military elite. The communist record is usually explained by the set of

---

Hough finds the French prefecture system conceptually useful in describing the Soviet system, our attention is drawn to Mark Kesselman, "Overinstitutionalization and Political Constraint: The Case of France," *Comparative Politics,* 3 (October, 1970), 21-44. Horizontal relations between French mayors and prefects lead to local collusion directed against the national government. Neither the parliamentary parties to which the mayors belong nor the Ministry of Interior, which rules the prefects, can bring their subordinates into line when the local interests are opposed to a policy. Group theory, as it is being applied to Soviet politics, directs our attention to vertical fissures over issues, not this kind of stratarchy or horizontal alignment. And the Soviet concern, almost pathological, with "localism" makes the analogy with the French experience cogent. Furthermore, Brzezinski's characterization of Soviet politics since Stalin as increasingly bureaucratic and institutionalized, even degenerate as the result of entrenched *apparatchiki,* is highly compatible with Kesselman's concept of overinstitutionalization. See Z. K. Brzezinski, "The Soviet Political System: Transformation or Degeneration?" *Problems of Communism,* January-February 1966.

To be sure, exponents of the group theory can define "group" so loosely that the concept includes intra-organizational alliances and interbureaucratic coalitions. Such a broad definition, however, obscures an important distinction emphasized by Reinhard Bendix. "There is a significant difference between men who pursue their economic interests and officials who do their appointed task. . . . if officials are called upon to superintend the pursuit of practical interests by employers, then the organization of industry and the management of labor become subordinate to the maintenance and advancement of superordinated hierarchies." The latter case, Bendix contends, is typified in both Tsarist and Leninist Russia. See his "The Impact of Ideas on Organizational Structure," *The Sociology of Organizations: Basic Studies,* pp. 532ff.

complex checks and controls the communist parties place on their military establishments.[29] At the same time, the military's behavior in developing non-communist states is explained variously but is usually related to the lead the military takes in the modernization process.[30] When political institutions prove slow or ineffective in managing modernization, the technically more advanced military is wont to be impatient and to intervene in domestic politics, be it for radical or conservative purposes. All this is persuasive enough, but it does not account for communist systems. The usual explanation of the communist pattern, which is based on an array of organizational and police controls, begs the question of why the Soviet military has not outdistanced the remainder of the society in the modernization process. The assertion that it is due to party controls is tautological. Efficacy of the controls is merely symptomatic that the political institutions are developing more rapidly than the military. Moreover, the control mechanisms are applied not only to the military. In various forms they are found in all societal institutions in a communist regime.

A fuller explanation can be offered by recalling the perceptions of development tasks that were recorded in the early debates about the military question and the explicit desire to integrate military, educational, industrial, and resource procurement functions in mass voluntary associations. The Bolsheviks, and especially Stalin, were alert to the genetic question in modernization: what is an effective sequence for building institutions?[31] Stalin's par-

[29] See Kolkowicz, op. cit., pp. 11-35, for a recent example.

[30] For illustrative examples, see J. J. Johnson, op. cit.; Janowitz, op. cit.; Henry Bienen (ed.), The Military Intervenes (New York: Russell Sage, 1968); Eric Nordlinger, "Soldiers in Mufti: The Impact of Military Rule Upon Non-Western States," The American Political Science Review, 64 (December, 1970), 1131-48; Finer, op. cit.; and S. P. Huntington, Political Order in Changing Societies, pp. 192-244.

[31] "Genetic" here is used in contradistinction to the "requisite" question: what are the essential ingredients of a modern

rot, Voroshilov, summed up the matter succinctly when he told the visiting French communists in 1928 that the Red Army was a unique university but too expensive for the entire population to attend. Substitutes had to be devised—mass voluntary societies in which the individual could be induced to bear much of the cost of his own training. In other words, the Bolsheviks realized clearly that the military institutions could modernize more rapidly than others. But they wanted neither to permit the military to go ahead on a narrow front nor to surrender the advantages afforded by the military. Osoaviakhim, designed on the seemingly paradoxical principle that military training could be accomplished in a voluntary society with an electoral system, was one of the innovations that helped unite the horns of the dilemma. Non-communist states have more often accepted the dilemma as unalterable and have chosen between the horns.

Theory and Conceptual Approaches to Analysis

In the course of this study, a wide variety of conceptual viewpoints has been introduced, selected largely from the literature on modernization and organization theory. As a conclusion to the study it seems appropriate to review and elucidate the rationale in our eclecticism.

Any theory, model, or other heuristic device can manage for us only a limited number of variables. Social theories sufficiently broad to pretend to explain the whole of social action are so general that they tend to provide non-operational hypotheses, categories that are too broad for discriminating analysis, and sometimes only trivial or conventional wisdom. If we are to understand the mass of data that we can observe, record, and infer about social action, we must first of all devise taxonomies that break the data into many smaller groupings, increasingly amenable to the

---

society without concern for the sequence of introducing them. On this point see Dankwart A. Rustow, "Transitions to Democracy: Toward a Dynamic Model," *Comparative Politics*, 2 (April, 1970), 337-66.

limits of human rationality and intellect.[32] This is not to suggest that we engage, lemming-like, in reductionism until we race into a sea of empirical data, having cast away all conceptual vessels enroute. Instead we must look for appropriate stopping points for choosing deductive axioms. That is the cogent substance of Merton's case for "middle range" theory.[33] Middle-level models and concepts allow us to leave the panoramic views of grand theory and to descend to a more discriminating level of perception of social behavior.

The idea of "modernization" in political science has, to be sure, led to some grand models and theories.[34] But it has also encouraged criticism of the macro-models and a resort to lower level generalizations. Perhaps the most important advantage in adopting the modernization point of view is that it sensitizes us to the historical and dynamic dimensions of politics. Not only are we forced to think of the unique historical experience of a polity but also of its reaction to the developments in other polities, especially the technologically advanced ones.

"Organization" as a concept for analysis has a number of advantages. First, as we have seen, there are a significant number of middle-range generalizations that can be used for ordering and making sense of what we observe in organizational life. Second, complex hierarchical organization is widespread in the world. It is common to all

[32] For those who believe that descriptive classification and devising taxonomies in political science are an inferior kind of intellectual endeavor, Giovanni Sartori offers some sobering observations in "Concept Misinformation in Comparative Politics," *The American Political Science Review*, 64 (December, 1970), 1033-53. There are those, on the other hand, who view the study of politics primarily as a matter of clearing up category mistakes. See T. D. Weldon, *The Vocabulary of Politics* (Baltimore: Penguin, 1953), for an example of a linguistic philosopher at work.

[33] *Social Theory and Social Structure*, pp. 36-72.

[34] For a recent critique of modernization theories, see Huntington, "The Change to Change: Modernization, Development and Politics."

contemporary states. Thus we have a concept that allows us to generalize across the boundary that has developed between Soviet area studies and political science in general.

Third, hierarchical organizations have common properties regardless of the political system in which they exist. The key properties to emphasize for comparative purposes are those that affect the distribution of power.[35] It is clear from the case of Osoaviakhim and from organization theory that the absence of "one best way" to execute organizational tasks ensures that power can never be completely centralized in an organization. On the other side of this coin, hierarchy ensures that decision-making can never be wholly democratic. Several decades ago Mosca and Michels called our attention to the inescapable reality of oligarchy.[36] If doubt remains after their observations, Kenneth Arrow's formal proof, demonstrating that it is logically impossible to define and give expression to the collective wishes of a community using values of all individual members as the basis for social choices, should put to rest any doubt that there must inevitably be a dictatorial element in organizational policy.[37] Although hierarchical organizations differ widely in their distribution of power, none has total centralization and none has a genuine democratic diffusion of power. Arguments about the *sui generis* nature of totalitarian regimes, theories of democracy, and any other issues often framed on the monism-pluralism dichotomy do not detain us. Reality is more accurately seen as a continuum between the ideals of the dichotomy. Moreover, by moving across the boundary between Soviet area studies and political science at

[35] Etzioni, *A Comparative Analysis of Complex Organizations*, shows how this can be done. By using the term "compliance" instead of power, he is taking the viewpoint of the top of the organization, but he is sensitive to the power of subordinates.

[36] See W. G. Runciman, *Social Science and Political Theory*, pp. 109-34, for a critique of the views of Mosca and Michels.

[37] *Social Choice and Individual Value*.

the middle level, we eschew such arguments. Our attention can be devoted to the study of variations in distribution of power, how the oligarchic leadership exercises its power, how the participants at all other levels exercise their power, and how structural and cultural factors affect both the distribution of power and its exercise.

Fourth, this common characteristic of hierarchical organization is an excellent assumption for comparative analysis because it has been empirically and formally established. It is not like the assumptions in functionalism and systems theory that can neither be verified nor disproven.[38]

Finally, a caveat is necessary. The common properties of hierarchical organization do not compel every society to face them in the same fashion. To argue that they must, of course, is to advance one more version of the "convergence theory," which presumably has been put to rest.[39] The diversity of possible responses is unlimited. Nonetheless, the inherent nature of hierarchy provides a convenient conceptual isomorph against which different responses by different societies may be effectively compared.

For this study it was necessary to take an additional step and specify a subclassification of organization to which Osoaviakhim might properly belong. The classification would have two important implications. First, it would influence the perspectives of the study, sensitizing us to some relationships at the expense of others. Second, the defining attributes would help us find our way more quickly to relevant generalizations about organizational behavior. Rigorous taxonomies, however, are not uniform

[38] See Runciman, *op. cit.*, for a discussion of the assumptions in functionalism. See also Robert E. Dowse, "A Functionalist's Logic," *World Politics*, 18 (July, 1966), 607-23.

[39] Brzezinski and Huntington, in *Political Powers: USA/USSR*, removed all cogent reasoning for taking it seriously but it has a way of furtively reappearing. Jean Meynaud, *Technocracy* (London: Faber and Faber, 1968), more recently has restated the case against the convergence theory.

in the literature.[40] Therefore, it became necessary to work out a typology by specifying attributes as we did in the introduction.[41]

The most important aspect of our typology of a public mass voluntary society is the focus on the inherent value conflict between the ruling oligarchy and the membership. That focus sensitized us to the political character of life in an organization. It encouraged us to see the task of organizational management as a matter of government. In a Soviet mass voluntary organization, one should expect conflict to be intense, perhaps bordering on pathological, but there is no reason for such organizational life in Western societies to be generically different. To discover that it is not, one only need look at Mayer Zald's study, *Organizational Change: The Political Economy of the YMCA*.[42] Zald focuses on the "interplay of power" as he develops the concept of "political economy." As he elucidates the politics of the salaried staff of the YMCA, we begin to see comparisons with behavior in the Osoaviakhim apparatus. For example, voluntarism of a truly spontaneous sort is not always relied upon for expanding the organization into

[40] See Caplow, *Principles of Organization*, pp. 36-39, for a survey of available taxonomies. See also Etzioni, *A Comparative Analysis of Complex Organizations*, pp. 3-70. For a Soviet typology, see Iampol'skaia, *op. cit.*

[41] Sartori, *op. cit.*, pp. 1036 and 1039, remarks that "taxonomical requisites of comparability are currently neglected, if not disowned. . . . A taxonomical unfolding represents a requisite condition for comparability." And furthermore, "what establishes . . . the discriminating power of a category is the taxonomical infolding," i.e. addition of attributes.

[42] Chicago: The University of Chicago Press, 1970. Although the YMCA is not a public organization in the sense that Osoaviakhim was, its concern with the public interest makes its goals compatible with the government's interest in citizenship education. Selznick, of course, would probably contend that the YMCA is actually a public organization as are many other large institutions and business corporations. See his *Leadership in Administration*, pp. 58-59.

new neighborhoods. On occasions, outspoken opposition was successfully subverted by YMCA organizers. Zald also identifies what he calls the "operator syndrome," which turns out to be a series of gambits in the use of local discretion by certain staff members. Just as in Osoaviakhim, only more so, financial accounting was used for control of local organs.

It is Zald's choice of the "political economy" concept that facilitates comparison. It leads him to consider both the mechanistic character of rules and departmentalization and the latitude of choice open to individual staff members for pursuing their own ends as well as organizational goals. By way of contrast, it is instructive to look at Sills's study of the National Foundation for Infantile Paralysis, *The Volunteers*. Because "goal displacement," the central concept in the analysis, is treated as a mechanistic quality of bureaucracy, the inherent paradox of bureaucracy, political life is only vaguely apparent in the study. Comparison is difficult although one suspects that interesting analogies and contrasts could be found if Zald's analytical approach were used to interpret Sills's observations.

Our point is not that Zald's study is superior to Sills's work. Significant reasons can be found for choosing sociological and administrative science approaches in preference to those that take politics as the main concern in organization. Moreover, in a society where a consensus about basic political values prevails, politics in organization is more easily sublimated in categories of sociology, psychology, and management. Our point is that categories, if they are to have the taxonomical requisites for comparability of organizations in societies in different stages of modernization and with different approaches to modernity, must be made sensitive to the political nature of organizational life.

Bibliography

I. Soviet Periodicals and Newspapers

Aviatsiia i khimiia. Published by Osoaviakhim. Monthly, 1929-1931. Merged with *Khimiia i oborona* in 1932.
Available issues: 1929: December.
                         1930: January, May.
                         1931: January through July, and December.
Khimiia i oborona. Published by Osoaviakhim. Biweekly its first year, 1932, monthly thereafter.
Available issues: 1932: No. 1-7, 9, 10, 13, 15-20, 23-24.
                         1933: No. 1, 2, 5-11.
                         1934: No. 1, 4, 6, 7, 12.
                         1936: No. 8, 9, 10.
                         1937: No. 1-4.
Krasnaia zvezda. The Red Army daily newspaper.
Available issues: 1925: Complete.
                         1929: September 1 through December 31.
                         1930: July 12.
                         1932-1940: Complete through June 1940.
Krasnoarmeets. Published by the Military Political Administration and Osoaviakhim. Biweekly.
Available issues: 1927-1935: No. 94-95, 97-151.
Osoaviakhim. Published by Osoaviakhim. Biweekly.
Available issues: 1929-1939: Complete.

Pravda. Official organ of the CPSU. Daily.
> The Serial is complete for the period of this study, 1923-1940.

Samolet. Published by Osoaviakhim. Monthly.
> Available issues: 1932: Complete.
> 1936: Complete.
> 1938: Complete.

Voina i revoliutsiia. Official journal of the Military Scientific Society, 1925-1927; thereafter published by Osoaviakhim.
> Available issues: 1925: May-December.
> 1926: January, June, August-December.
> 1927: January-September, December.
> 1928-1935: Complete.

Voina i tekhnika. Published jointly by the Red Army and Osoaviakhim. Monthly.
> Available issues: January 1925 through September 1926, complete.
> 1928: Complete.
> 1929: 1-2, 4-6.

II. Records of Congresses, Conferences, and Plenums

Desiatyi s"ezd RKP(b). March 1921. Stenographic Record. Moscow: 1963.

Deviatyi s"ezd RKP(b). March 29-April 4, 1920. Stenographic Record. Moscow: 1920.

Moskovskoe obshchestvo druzei oborony i aviatsionno-khimicheskogo stroitel'stva. Gubernskii s"ezd. Rezoliutsii i postanovleniia. Moscow: 1929.

Osoaviakhim na novom etape. (II Plenum). Moscow: 1931.

Osoaviakhim na putiakh perestroiki. Itogi IV Plenuma TsS Osoaviakhima. Moscow: 1933.

Pervyi oblastnoi s"ezd Obshchestva druzei vozdushnogo flota Tatrespubliki, 15-17 Oktiabria 1924 g. Kazan: 1924.

Pervoe vsesoiuznoe soveshchanie revizionnykh kommissii Soiuza Osoaviakhima SSSR—1931 g. Moscow: 1931.
Rabotu Osoaviakhima—na rel'sy bol'shevistskoi organizovannosti. Itogi VI Plenuma TsS Osoaviakhim SSSR i RSFSR. Moscow: 1935.
Sbornik reshenii I(III) s"ezda Osoaviakhim Zapadnoi Sibiri, 25-29 Aprelia 1931 g. Novosibirsk: 1931.
Sed'moi s"ezd Rossiiskoi Kommunisticheskoi Partii. Stenographic Record. March 6-8, 1918. Moscow, Petrograd: 1923.
Trinadtsatyi s"ezd RKP(b). Stenographic Record. May 1924. Moscow: 1963.
Vos'maia konferentsiia RKP(b). Dekabria 1919. Protokoly. Moscow: 1961.
Vos'moi s"ezd RKP(b). 18-23 Marta 1919 g. Stenographic Record. Moscow: 1933.
Zamoskvoretskii raionnyi sovet. *Otchet o dokhodakh i raskhodakh Zamraisoveta Osoaviakhima za vremia s 1 oktiabria 1927 g. po 1 oktiabria 1928 g.* Moscow: 1929.

III. Osoaviakhim Texts, Brochures, and Documents

Baerskii, V. *Pekhota.* Moscow: 1938.
Belitskii, S. M. (ed.). *Besedy o voennom dele i Krasnoi Armii.* Sbornik dliia kruzhkov voennykh znanii. Moscow: 1928.
Borisenko, P., and V. Klevtsov. *K protivokhimicheskoi oborone bud' gotov.* Posobie dliia norm PVKhO. Kiev: 1936.
Burche, E. F. *Kak raspoznavat' vozdushnogo vraga.* Posobie. Moscow: 1939.
Dvadtsatiletie Krasnoi Armii i zadachi Osoaviakhima. Moscow: 1938.
Glagolev, A. *Avia agitatsiia i propaganda.* Metody i formy raboty. Moscow: 1925.
Iushkov, S. *Takticheskie ucheniia Osoaviakhima.* Moscow: 1937.
Kolesnikov, B. *Osoaviakhim v derevne.* Moscow: 1933.

Leont'ev, Boris. *Osoaviakhim—boevoi rezerv Krasnoi Armii.* Moscow: 1933.

―――. *Vooruzhennyi narod.* Moscow: 1936.

Levin, P. N., and D. E. Lipelis (eds.). *Spravochnik aktivista Osoaviakhim.* Moscow: 1931.

Markovin, Nikolai E. *Osoaviakhim—moguchii rezerv Krasnoi Armii i Flota.* Moscow: 1939.

Nizhegorodskii Gubernskii Sovet Osoaviakhima. *Osnovnye tekushchie zadachi po voennoi podgotovke trudiashchikhsia v Nizhegorodskoi Gubernii.* Novgorod: 1929.

Osoaviakhim v kolkhoze. Moscow: 1934.

Plan raboty presidiumov Soiuza Osoaviakhim SSSR i RSFSR. Moscow: 1928.

Popov, N. V. (ed.). *Osoaviakhim Ukrainy na boevom postu.* Sbornik. Kiev: 1936.

Posobie po degazatsii v punktakh i na ob"ektakh protivovozdushnoi oborony. Moscow: 1935.

Primernaia programma kruzhka voennykh znanii nachal'nogo tipa. 2d ed. Moscow: 1928.

Spravochnik po podgotovke trudiashchikhsia zhenshchin k oborone. Moscow: 1930.

Sputnik Osoaviakhima. Moscow: 1936.

Strutsa, V. N. (ed.). *Krepite oboronu SSSR.* Materialy po voennoi propagande dliia raboty voennykh kruzhkov. Kiev: 1927.

Ustavnoi sbornik Soiuza Osoaviakhima SSSR. Moscow: 1929.

IV. *Soviet Books, Pamphlets, and Collected Papers*

Baratov, Boris I. *Vozdushnyi flot SSSR i zadachi trudiashchikhsia.* Moscow: 1925.

Berkhin, I. B. *Voennaia reforma v SSSR (1924-1925).* Moscow: 1958.

Bubnov, A. S., S. S. Kamenev, R. P. Eideman, and M. N. Tukhachevskii (eds.). *Grazhdanskaia voina 1918-1921.* 3 vols. Moscow: 1928.

Bubnov, A. S. *O Krasnoi Armii*. Moscow: 1958.

———. *Vseobuch i politekhnizatsiia massovoi shkoly*. Moscow: 1931.

Entsiklopedicheskii slovar' Russkogo bibliograficheskogo instituta Granat. *Diateli Soiuza Sovetskikh Sotsialisticheskikh Respublik i oktiabr'skoi revoliutsii; avtobiografii i biografii*. Moscow: 1929. (Reprint, Cleveland: 1963.)

Frunze, M. V. *Edinaia voennaia doktrina i Krasnaia Armiia*. Moscow: 1921.

———. *Izbrannye proizvedeniia*. Moscow: 1950 (1934).

———. *O molodezhi*. Moscow: 1937.

Kalashnik, M. Kh. (ed.). *Narod i armiia—ediny*. Moscow: 1959.

Komsomol—boevoi drug DOSAAF. Moscow: 1958.

Kosiukov, A. A. *Voenno-pedagogicheskie vzgliady M. V. Frunze*. Moscow: 1960.

KPSS o vooruzhennykh silakh Sovetskogo Soiuza; Sbornik dokumentov, 1917-1958. Moscow: 1958.

Kuz'min, N. F. *Na strazhe mirnogo truda (1921-1940 gg.)*. Moscow: 1959.

Metodicheskie ukazaniia dliia postupaiushchikh v vysshie voenno-uchebnye zavedeniia RKKA. Moscow: 1928.

Movchin, N. *Komplektovanie Krasnoi Armii v 1918-1921 gg*. Moscow: 1926.

Ozerov, Georgii A. *Desiatiletie TsAGI*. Moscow: 1928.

5 let Krasnoi Armii (1918-1923); sbornik statei. Moscow: 1923.

Shatagin, N. I. *Sovetskaia Armiia—armiia novogo tipa*. Moscow: 1957.

Trotsky, Lev. *Kak vooruzhilas' revoliutsiia*. 3 vols. Moscow: 1923-1925.

Vlasov, I. I. *Lenin i stroitel'stvo Sovetskoi Armii*. Moscow: 1958.

Voroshilov, Kliment E. *Stat'i i rechi*. Moscow: 1937.

———. *The Red Army Today*. Moscow: Foreign Language Publishing House, 1939.

Zelenev, Nikolai A. *Voprosy fiziologii voennogo truda i professional'nogo otbora*. Sbornik statei. Moscow: 1928.

V. Selected Soviet Journal Articles

Aleksinskii, M. "Zadachi Osoaviakhim," *Voina i revoliutsiia*, 2 (February, 1927), 17-25.

Artemenko. "Rabota VNK v normal'nykh voennykh shkolakh," *Voina i revoliutsiia*, 8 (November-December, 1925), 237-52.

Belitskii, S. M. "Boevaia podgotovka Osoaviakhima," *Voina i revoliutsiia*, 8-9 (1932), 194-198.

————. "K itogam vsesoiuznogo s"ezda VNO," *Voina i revoliutsiia*, 3 (March, 1926), 3-9.

————. "Nauchno-issledovatel'skaia rabota v stroevykh chastiakh," *Voina i revoliutsiia*, 6 (October, 1925), 101-105.

Borisov, L. "Oboronno-massovaia rabota Osoaviakhima (1927-41 gg.)," *Voenno-istoricheskii zhurnal*, 8 (1967), 40-51.

Bukin, B. "Zadachi OSO v grazhdanskykh narkomakh," *Voina i revoliutsiia*, 8 (August, 1926), 120-29.

Dimanshtein, S. "Krasnaia Armiia na poroge vtoroi piatiletki," *Revoliutsiia i natsional'nosti*, 2 (1933), 8-16.

Eideman, R. P. "K III s"ezdu," *Samolet*, 9 (1936), 1-4.

————. "Po-boevomu perestroit' vsiu rabotu obshchestva," *Osoaviakhim*, 7-8 (1932), 5-12.

G. G. "Zadachi nauchno-issledovatel'skoi deiatel'nosti tsentral'nykh sektsii VNO i metody ee organizatsii," *Voina i revoliutsiia*, 3 (May, 1925), 103-09.

Gorshenin, P. S. "Ocherednye zadachi voennoi podgotovki komsomola," *Osoaviakhim*, 26 (1931), 5-6.

————. "Za vypolnenie plana 1938 g.," *Samolet*, 2 (1938). 18-19.

Kalnin, K. "Voennaia rabota sredi naseleniia," *Voina i revoliutsiia*, 4 (April, 1926), 120-30.

Konokotin, V. "K itogam chetyrekhmesiachnoi vnevoiskovoi podgotovki," *Voina i revoliutsiia*, 1 (January, 1928), 74-85.

Lebedev, V. "Rabota VNO v derevne," *Voina i revoliutsiia*, 6 (October, 1925), 106-10.

Levichev, V. "K postanovke voprosa o militsionno-territorial'nom stroitel'stve na s"ezde VNO," *Voina i revoliutsiia*, 1-2 (January-February, 1926), 11-20.

Levin, P. "O raionnom zvene," *Osoaviakhim*, 21 (1930), 9-10.

Malinovskii, L. P. "K itogam plenuma TsS Soiuza Osoaviakhima," *Samolet*, 4 (1932), 3-5.

——. "Partiia i Osoaviakhim," *Osoaviakhim*, 17-18 (June, 1930), 7-10.

——. "Zadachi Osoaviakhima po voennoi podgotovke v letnii period," *Voina i revoliutsiia*, 6 (June 1928), 3-17.

N. Sh. [sic] "VNO v derevne," *Voina i revoliutsiia*, 5 (August-September, 1925), 154-57.

Podgoretskii, K. "Novaia bolezn' rosta ili 'voiskovoi konservatizm'," *Voina i revoliutsiia*, 1-2 (January-February, 1926), 29-35.

Podshivalov, I. M. "Litsom k soiuzu," *Voina i revoliutsiia*, 3 (May, 1925), 123-28.

Raskin, L. "Kooperirovannoe proizvodstvo," *Samolet*, 7 (1932), 9-11.

Semashko, N. A. "Osoaviakhim i partrukovodstvo," *Osoaviakhim*, 17-18 (June, 1930), 6-7.

Sidev, "Prizyv natsional'nostei," *Voina i revoliutsiia*, 5 (May, 1927), 113-24; 6 (June, 1927), 66-82. Published in two parts.

VI. Books and Articles on Soviet Affairs

Adamheit, Theodor. *Rote Armee, Rote Weltrevolution, Rote Imperialismus.* Berlin: Nibelungen-verlag, 1935.

——. *Sowjet und Weltrevolution.* Berlin: Nibelungen-verlag, 1942.

Basseches, Nikolaus. *The Unknown Army.* Translated by Marion Saerchinger. New York: The Viking Press, 1943.

Berchin, Michel, and Eliahn Ben-Horin. *The Red Army.* New York: W. W. Norton, 1942.

Berliner, Joseph S. *Factory and Manager in the USSR.* Cambridge: Harvard University Press, 1957.

Brzezinski, Zbigniew K. *Ideology and Power in Soviet Politics.* New York: Frederick A. Praeger, 1962.

Daniels, Robert V. *The Conscience of the Revolution: Communist Opposition in Soviet Russia.* Cambridge: Harvard University Press, 1960.

Davies, Robert W. *The Development of the Soviet Budgetary System.* Cambridge: At the University Press, 1958.

Dobb, Maurice. *Soviet Economic Development Since 1917.* Revised enlarged ed. New York: International Publishers, 1966.

Dvoring, Folke. "Soviet Farm Mechanization in Perspective," *Slavic Review*, 25 (June, 1966), 287-302.

Erickson, John. *The Soviet High Command: A Military-Political History 1918-1941.* London: Macmillan, 1962.

Erlich, Alexander. *The Soviet Industrialization Debate, 1924-1928.* Cambridge: Harvard University Press, 1960.

Fainsod, Merle. *How Russia is Ruled.* Cambridge: Harvard University Press, 1956.

Fedotoff White, Dmitri. *The Growth of the Red Army.* Princeton, N.J.: Princeton University Press, 1944.

Fischer, Louis. *The Soviets in World Affairs.* 2 vols. Princeton, N.J.: Princeton University Press, 1951.

Fisher, Ralph T., Jr. *Pattern for Soviet Youth: A Study of the Congresses of the Komsomol, 1918-1954.* New York: Columbia University Press, 1959.

Fleron, Frederic J., Jr. (ed.). *Communist Studies and the Social Sciences: Essays on Methodology and Empirical Theory.* Chicago: Rand McNally, 1969.

Friedrich, Carl J., and Z. K. Brzezinski. *Totalitarian Dictatorship and Autocracy.* New York: Frederick A. Praeger, 1961.

Garder, Michel. *A History of the Soviet Army.* New York: Frederick A. Praeger, 1966.

Garthoff, Raymond L. *Soviet Military Policy: A Historical Analysis*. New York: Frederick A. Praeger, 1966.

Gatzke, Hans W. "Russo-German Military Collaboration During the Weimar Republic," *The American Historical Review*, 63 (1958), 565-97.

Gilison, Jerome M. "New Factors of Stability in Soviet Collective Leadership," *World Politics*, 19 (July, 1967), 563-81.

Granick, David. *Management of the Industrial Firm in the USSR: A Study in Soviet Economic Planning*. New York: Columbia University Press, 1954.

————. *The Red Executive*. Garden City, N.Y.: Doubleday, 1960.

————. *Soviet Metal-Fabricating and Economic Development: Practice versus Policy*. Madison, Wis.: The University of Wisconsin Press, 1967.

Guillaume, Augustin. *Soviet Arms and Soviet Power*. Washington: Infantry Journal Press, 1949.

Harper, Samuel N. *Civic Training in Soviet Russia*. Chicago: The University of Chicago Press, 1929.

Haudan, Erwin. "Das Motorisierungspotential der Sowjetunion." Thesis, Friedrich-Wilhelms Universitaet, Berlin, 1937.

Hazard, John N. *The Soviet Government*. 3d ed. Chicago: The University of Chicago Press, 1964.

Holzman, Franklyn D. *Soviet Taxation: The Fiscal and Monetary Problems of a Planned Economy*. Cambridge: Harvard University Press, 1955.

Hough, Jerry F. *The Soviet Prefects: The Local Party Organs in Industrial Decision-making*. Cambridge: Harvard University Press, 1969.

Ionescu, Ghita. *The Politics of the European Communist States*. New York: Frederick A. Praeger, 1967.

Just, Artur W. *Die Sowjetunion, Staat, Wirtschaft, Heer*. Berlin: Junker und Duennhaupt, 1940.

Kassof, Allen. *The Soviet Youth Program: Regimentation and Rebellion*. Cambridge: Harvard University Press, 1965.

Kolkowicz, Roman. *The Soviet Military and the Communist Party.* Princeton, N.J.: Princeton University Press, 1967.

Mackintosh, Malcolm. *Juggernaut: A History of the Soviet Armed Forces.* New York: The Macmillan Company, 1967.

Meyer, Alfred G. *The Soviet Political System: An Interpretation.* New York: Random House, 1965.

Miller, Robert F. "The Politotdel: A Lesson from the Past," *Slavic Review*, 25 (September, 1966), 475-96.

Morton, Henry W. *Soviet Sport: Mirror of Soviet Society.* New York: Collier Books, 1963.

Nove, Alec. *Economic Rationality and Soviet Politics.* New York: Frederick A. Praeger, 1964.

O'Ballance, Edgar. *The Red Army.* London: Faber and Faber, 1964.

Rigby, T. H. "Traditional, Market, and Organizational Societies and the USSR," *World Politics*, 16 (July, 1964), 539-57.

————. "Crypto-Politics," *Survey*, No. 50 (January, 1964), 183-94.

Ryavec, Karl W. "Soviet Industrial Managers, Their Superiors and the Economic Reform: A Study of an Attempt at Planned Behavioral Change," *Soviet Studies*, 21 (October, 1969), 208-29.

Skilling, H. Gordon, and Franklyn Griffiths (eds.). *Interest Groups in Soviet Politics.* Princeton, N.J.: Princeton University Press, 1971.

Stewart, Philip D. "Soviet Interest Groups and the Policy Process: The Repeal of Production Education," *World Politics*, 22 (October, 1969), 29-50.

Swearer, Howard R. "Decentralization in Recent Soviet Administrative Practice," *Slavic Review*, 21 (September, 1962), 456-70.

Trotsky, Leon. *The Revolution Betrayed.* Translated by Max Eastman. Garden City, N.Y.: Doubleday, Doran and Co., 1937.

Ulam, Adam. *The Unfinished Revolution.* New York: Vintage Books, 1964.

Wallace, Sir Donald MacKenzie. *Russia: On the Eve of War and Revolution.* Edited and introduced by Cyril E. Black. New York: Vintage Books, 1961.
Wollenberg, Eric. *The Red Army.* Translated by C. W. Sykes. London: Secker and Warburg, 1938.

VII. *Selected Books and Articles on Theory and Method*

Allison, Graham T. "Conceptual Models and the Cuban Missile Crisis," *The American Political Science Review*, 63 (September, 1969), 689-718.
Arrow, Kenneth J. *Social Choice and Individual Value.* New York: John Wiley and Sons, 1951.
Banfield, Edward C. *Political Influence.* Glencoe, Ill.: The Free Press, 1961.
Bentley, Arthur F. *The Process of Government: A Study of Social Pressures.* Chicago: The University of Chicago, 1908. John Harvard Library edition, off-set reprint, 1967.
Dahl, Robert A., and Charles E. Lindblom. *Politics, Economics, and Welfare.* New York: Harper and Row, 1953.
Deutsch, Karl W. *National and Social Communication.* New York: Published Jointly by Technology Press of MIT and John Wiley and Sons, 1953.
Easton, David. *Varieties of Political Theory.* Englewood Cliffs, N.J.: Prentice-Hall, 1966.
Kirchheimer, Otto. "Private Man and Society," *Political Science Quarterly*, 81 (March, 1966), pp. 1-25.
Lasswell, Harold D. *Politics: Who Gets What, When, How?* New York: Meridian Books, 1958 (1936).
Mannheim, Karl. *Freedom, Power and Democratic Planning.* New York: Oxford University Press, 1950.
Merelman, Richard M. "Learning and Legitimacy," *The American Political Science Review*, 60 (September, 1966), 548-61.
Pool, Ithiel de Sola (ed.). *Contemporary Political Science: Toward an Empirical Theory.* New York: McGraw-Hill, 1967.

Runciman, W. G. *Social Science and Political Theory*. 2d ed. Cambridge: At the University Press, 1969.

Sartori, Giovanni. "Concept Misinformation in Comparative Politics," *The American Political Science Review*, 64 (December, 1970), 1033-1053.

Verba, Sidney. *Small Groups and Political Behavior: A Study of Leadership*. Princeton, N.J.: Princeton University Press, 1961.

Wildavsky, Aaron. *The Politics of the Budgetary Process*. Boston: Little, Brown and Co., 1964.

Wolf, Robert Paul. *The Poverty of Liberalism*. Boston: Beacon Press, 1968.

Wolin, Sheldon. *Politics and Vision*. Boston: Little, Brown and Company, 1960.

VIII. *Books and Articles on Modernization and Political Development*

Almond, Gabriel A., and James S. Coleman (eds.). *The Politics of Developing Areas*. Princeton, N.J.: Princeton University Press, 1960.

Almond, Gabriel A., and G. Bingham Powell, Jr. *Comparative Politics: A Developmental Approach*. Boston: Little, Brown and Co., 1966.

Almond, Gabriel A., and Sidney Verba. *The Civic Culture*. Princeton, N.J.: Princeton University Press, 1963.

Apter, David E. *The Politics of Modernization*. Chicago: The University of Chicago Press, 1965.

Bienen, Henry (ed.). *The Military Intervenes: Case Studies in Political Development*. New York: Russell Sage Foundation, 1968.

deSchweinitz, Karl, Jr. "Growth, Development and Political Modernization," *World Politics*, 22 (July, 1970), 518-40.

Eckstein, Alexander. "Economic Development and Political Change in Communist Systems," *World Politics*, 22 (July, 1970), 475-95.

Eisenstadt, S. N. "Political Struggle in Bureaucratic Societies," *World Politics*, 9 (October, 1956), 15-36.

Esman, Milton J., and John D. Montgomery. "System Approaches to Technical Cooperation: The Role of Development Administration," *Public Administration Review*, 29 (September, 1969), 507-539.

Emerson, Rupert. *From Empire to Nation*. Boston: Beacon Press, 1960.

Finer, Samuel E. *The Man on Horseback: The Role of the Military in Politics*. New York: Frederick A. Praeger, 1962.

Finkle, Jason L., and Richard W. Gable (eds.). *Political Development and Social Change*. New York: John Wiley and Sons, 1966.

Gutteridge, William. *Military Institutions and Power in the New States*. New York: Frederick A. Praeger, 1965.

Hanning, Hugh. *The Peaceful Uses of Military Forces*. New York: Frederick A. Praeger, 1967.

Hirschman, Albert O. *The Strategy of Economic Development*. New Haven: Yale University Press, 1958.

Huntington, Samuel P. *Political Order in Changing Societies*. New Haven: Yale University Press, 1968.

Huntington, Samuel P. "The Change to Change: Modernization, Development and Politics," *Comparative Politics*, 3 (April, 1971), 283-322.

Huntington, Samuel P. (ed.). *Changing Patterns of Military Politics*. Glencoe, Ill.: The Free Press of Glencoe, 1962.

Janowitz, Morris. *The Military in the Political Development of New Nations*. Chicago: The University of Chicago Press, 1964.

Johnson, John J. (ed.). *The Role of the Military in Underdeveloped Countries*. Princeton, N.J.: Princeton University Press, 1962.

Jordan, Amos A., Jr. *Foreign Aid and the Defense of Southeast Asia*. New York: Frederick A. Praeger, 1962.

Kesselman, Mark. "Overinstitutionalization and Political Constraint: The Case of France," *Comparative Politics*, 3 (October, 1970), 21-44.

Kindelberger, Charles P. *Economic Development*. New York: McGraw-Hill Book Co., 1965.

LaPalombara, Joseph, and Myron Weiner (eds.). *Political Parties and Political Development*. Princeton, N.J.: Princeton University Press, 1966.

LaPalombara, Joseph (ed.). *Bureaucracy and Political Development*. Princeton, N.J.: Princeton University Press, 1963.

Levy, Marion J., Jr. *Modernization and the Structure of Societies: A Setting for International Affairs*. 2 vols. Princeton, N.J.: Princeton University Press, 1966.

Nordlinger, Eric A. "Soldiers in Mufti: The Impact of Military Rule Upon Non-Western States," *The American Political Science Review*, 64 (December, 1970), 1131-1148.

Parsons, Talcott, *Structure and Process in Modern Societies*. Glencoe, Ill.: The Free Press, 1960.

Perlmutter, Amos. "The Praetorian State and the Praetorian Army: Toward a Taxonomy of Civil-Military Relations in Developing Polities," *Comparative Politics*, 1 (April, 1969), 382-404.

Price, Robert M. "Military Officers and Political Leadership," *Comparative Politics*, 3 (April, 1971), 361-79.

Pye, Lucian (ed.). *Communications and Political Development*. Princeton, N.J.: Princeton University Press, 1963.

Pye, Lucian W. *Politics, Personality, and Nation Building: Burma's Search for Identity*. New Haven: Yale University Press, 1962.

Pye, Lucian W., and Sidney Verba (eds.). *Political Culture and Political Development*. Princeton, N.J.: Princeton University Press, 1965.

Rapoport, David C. "The Political Dimensions of Military Usurpation," *Political Science Quarterly*, 83 (December, 1968), 551-72.

Riggs, Fred W. *Thailand: The Modernization of a Bureaucratic Polity*. Honolulu: East-West Center Press, 1966.

Rustow, Dankwart A. *A World of Nations: Problems of*

Political Modernization. Washington, D.C.: The Brookings Institution, 1967.

Shils, Edward. *Political Development in the New States.* The Hague: Mouton and Co., 1966.

Sigmund, Paul E., Jr. (ed.). *The Ideologies of Developing Nations.* New York: Frederick A. Praeger, 1963.

Weidner, Edward (ed.). *Development Administration in Asia.* Durham, N.C.: Duke University Press, 1970.

Wolf, Charles, Jr. *United States Policy and the Third World: Problems and Analysis.* Boston: Little, Brown and Co., 1967.

IX. *Books and Articles on Organization Theory and Bureaucracy*

Albrow, Martin C. *Bureaucracy.* New York: Praeger Publishers, 1970.

Altshuler, Alan A. (ed.). *The Politics of the Federal Bureaucracy.* New York: Dodd, Mead and Co., 1968.

Andreskii, Stanislav. *Military Organization and Society.* 2d ed. London: Routledge and Kegan Paul, 1968.

Babchuk, Nicolas, and C. Wayne Gordon. *The Voluntary Organization in the Slum.* New Series No. 27. University of Nebraska, October, 1962.

Barker, Ernest. *The Development of Public Services in Western Europe 1660-1930.* Hamden, Conn.: Archon Books, 1966.

Blau, Peter M. *Bureaucracy in Modern Society.* New York: Random House, 1956.

Bor, Mikhail. *Aims and Methods of Soviet Planning.* New York: International Publishers, 1967.

Boulding, Kenneth E. *Conflict and Defense: A General Theory.* New York: Harper Torchbooks, 1962.

Caplow, Theodore. *Principles of Organization.* New York: Harcourt, Brace and World, 1964.

Coser, Lewis. *The Functions of Social Conflict.* New York: The Free Press, 1956.

Crozier, Michel. *The Bureaucratic Phenomenon.* Chicago: The University of Chicago Press, 1964.

Downs, Anthony. *Inside Bureaucracy.* Boston: Little, Brown and Co., 1967.

Etzioni, Amitai. *A Comparative Analysis of Complex Organizations.* New York: The Free Press of Glencoe, 1961.

————. *Complex Organizations: A Sociological Reader.* New York: Holt, Reinhart, and Winston, 1961.

Fox, Sherwood D. "Voluntary Associations and Social Structure." Unpublished Ph.D. Dissertation, Harvard University, 1952.

Georgopoulos, Basil S., and Arnold S. Tannenbaum. "A Study of Organizational Effectiveness," *American Sociological Review,* 22 (1957), 534-40.

Gouldner, Alvin. *Patterns of Industrial Bureaucracy.* Glencoe, Ill.: The Free Press, 1954.

Grusky, Oscar, and George A. Miller (eds.). *The Sociology of Organizations: Basic Studies.* New York: The Free Press, 1970.

Hammond, Paul Y. "A Functional Analysis of Defense Department Decision-Making in the McNamara Administration," *The American Political Science Review,* 62 (March, 1968), 57-69.

Hitch, Charles J., and Roland N. McKean. *The Economics of Defense in the Nuclear Age.* Cambridge: Harvard University Press, 1960.

Homans, George C. *The Human Group.* New York: Harcourt, Brace and World, 1950.

Heady, Ferrel, and Sybil L. Stokes (eds.) *Papers in Comparative Public Administration.* Ann Arbor, Mich.: Institute of Public Administration, The University of Michigan, 1962.

Huntington, Samuel P. *The Common Defense: Strategic Programs in National Politics.* New York: Columbia University Press, 1961.

Hyneman, C. S. *Bureaucracy in a Democracy.* New York: Harper, 1950.

Iampol'skaia, Ts. A. *Obshchestvennye organizatsii v SSSR.* Moscow: 1972.

Kahn, Robert L., and Elise Boulding (eds.). *Power and Conflict in Organizations.* New York: Basic Books, 1964.

Lawrence, Paul R., and John A. Seiler, *et al. Organizational Behavior and Administration: Cases, Concepts, and Research Findings.* Revised ed. Homewood, Ill.: Richard D. Irwin and the Dorsey Press, 1965.

March, James G. (ed.). *Handbook of Organizations.* Chicago: Rand McNally, 1965.

March, James G., and Herbert A. Simon. *Organizations.* New York: John Wiley and Sons, 1958.

Marx, Morstein F. *The Administrative State.* Chicago: The University of Chicago Press, 1957.

Merton, Robert K. *et al.* (eds.). *Reader in Bureaucracy.* New York: The Free Press, 1952.

Merton, Robert K. *Social Theory and Social Structure.* Enlarged ed. New York: The Free Press, 1968.

Meynaud, Jean. *Technocracy.* Translated by Paul Barnes. London: Faber and Faber, 1968.

Michels, Robert. *Political Parties.* Translated by Eden and Cedar Paul with an introduction by S. M. Lipset. 2d ed. New York: The Free Press, 1968.

Miller, Walter B. "Two Concepts of Authority," *American Anthropologist,* 57 (April, 1955), pp. 271-89.

Olson, Mancur, Jr. *The Logic of Collective Action: Public Goods and the Theory of Groups.* New York: Schocken Books, 1968.

Presthus, Robert. *The Organizational Society: An Analysis and a Theory.* New York: Alfred A. Knopf, 1962.

Rourke, Francis E. *Bureaucracy, Politics, and Public Policy.* Boston: Little, Brown and Co., 1969.

Selznick, Philip. *Leadership in Administration.* New York: Harper and Row, 1957.

————. *The Organizational Weapon: A Study of Bolshevik Strategy and Tactics.* Glencoe, Ill.: The Free Press, 1960.

Selznick, Philip. *TVA and the Grass Roots*. Berkeley: The University of California Press, 1953.

Sills, David L. *The Volunteers: Means and Ends in a National Organization*. Glencoe, Ill.: The Free Press, 1957.

Simon, Herbert A. *Administrative Behavior*. 2d ed. New York: The Macmillan Co., 1957.

Swerdlow, Irving (ed.). *Development Administration: Concepts and Problems*. Syracuse: Syracuse University Press, 1963.

Thompson, Victor A. *Modern Organization*. New York: Alfred A. Knopf, 1961.

Weber, Max. *Basic Concepts in Sociology*. Translated and introduced by H. P. Secher. New York: The Citadel Press, 1962.

——————. *From Max Weber: Essays in Sociology*. Translated, edited, and introduced by H. H. Gerth and C. Wright Mills. New York: Oxford University Press, 1958.

Weidner, Edward W. (ed.). *Development Administration in Asia*. Durham, N.C.: Duke University Press, 1970.

Wilson, James Q. "The Bureaucracy Problem," *The Public Interest*, 6 (Winter, 1967), 3-9.

Zald, Mayer N. *Organizational Change: The Political Economy of the YMCA*. Chicago: The University of Chicago Press, 1970.

X. *Archives*

"Records of All-Union (Russian) Communist Party, Smolensk District, Record Group 1056," National Archives Microfilm publication No. T87. See especially files: WKP-135; WKP-150; WKP-166; WKP-186; WKP-189; WKP-225; WKP-232; WKP-237; WKP-512.

Microfilm T88, Serial 1, Party Archive. Reel 57. Item No. RS 921-924, p. 63. Located at Columbia University.

Index